ebenefits.va.gov

D0832462

Federal Benefits for Veterans, Dependents and Survivors

2014 Edition

Department of Veterans Affairs

810 Vermont Ave., N.W.
Washington, DC 20420

Cover: Uncle Sam, arguably the most popular personification of the United States, was created by James Flagg in 1917 based on his own appearance. For more information visit the Library of Congress at http://www.loc.gov/exhibits/treasures/trm015.html.

U.S. GOVERNMENT OFFICIAL EDITION NOTICE

Use of ISBN

This is the official U.S. government edition of this publication and is herein identified to certify its authenticity. Use of the 0-16 ISBN prefix is for U.S. Government Printing Office Official Editions only. The Superintendent of Documents of the U.S. Government Printing Office requests that any reprinted edition clearly be labeled as a copy of the authentic work with a new ISBN.

Legal Status and Use of Seals and Logos

The seal of the Department of Veterans Affairs authenticates the 2014 edition of Federal Benefits for Veterans, Dependents and Survivors as the official summary of benefits that have been separately promulgated under Federal regulations established under Register Act. Under the provisions of 38 Code of Federal Regulations 1.9(f), it is prohibited to use the official seal, replicas, reproductions, or embossed seals of the Department of Veterans Affairs on any republication of this material without the express, written permission of the Secretary or Deputy Secretary of Veterans Affairs. Any person using official seals and logos of the Department of Veterans Affairs in a manner inconsistent with the provisions of 38 Code of Federal Regulations 1.9 may be subject to the penalties specified in 18 United States Code 506, 701, or 1017 as applicable.

For sale by the Superintendent of Documents, U.S. Government Printing Office
Internet: bookstore.gpo.gov Phone: toll free (866) 512-1800; DC area (202) 512-1800
Fax: (202) 512-2104 Mail: Stop IDCC, Washington, DC 20401

978-0-16-092508-5

Contents

Introduction

Veterans of the United States armed forces may be eligible for a broad range of benefits and services provided by the U.S. Department of Veterans Affairs (VA). Some of these benefits may be utilized while on active duty. These benefits are codified in Title 38 of the United States Code. This booklet contains a summary of these benefits effective Jan. 1, 2014. For additional information, visit www.va.gov/.

La versión en español de este folleto se encuentra disponible en formato Adobe Acrobat a través de el link: http://www.va.gov/opa/publications/benefits_book/federal_benefits_spanish.pdf

General Eligibility: Eligibility for most VA benefits is based upon discharge from active military service under other than dishonorable conditions. Active service means full-time service, other than active duty for training, as a member of the Army, Navy, Air Force, Marine Corps, Coast Guard, or as a commissioned officer of the Public Health Service, Environmental Science Services Administration or National Oceanic and Atmospheric Administration, or its predecessor, the Coast and Geodetic Survey.

Dishonorable and bad conduct discharges issued by general courts-martial may bar VA benefits. Veterans in prison must contact VA to determine eligibility. VA benefits will not be provided to any Veteran or dependent wanted for an outstanding felony warrant.

Certain VA Benefits Require Wartime Service: under the law, VA recognizes these periods of war:

Mexican Border Period: May 9, 1916, through April 5, 1917, for Veterans who served in Mexico, on its borders or in adjacent waters.

World War I: April 6, 1917, through Nov. 11, 1918; for Veterans who served in Russia, April 6, 1917, through April 1, 1920; extended through July 1, 1921, for Veterans who had at least one day of service between April 6, 1917, and Nov. 11, 1918.

World War II: Dec. 7, 1941, through Dec. 31, 1946.

Korean War: June 27, 1950, through Jan. 31, 1955.

Vietnam War: Aug. 5, 1964 (Feb. 28, 1961, for Veterans who served "in country" before Aug. 5, 1964), through May 7, 1975.

Gulf War: Aug. 2, 1990, through a date to be set.

Important Documents

In order to expedite benefits delivery, Veterans seeking a VA benefit for the first time must submit a copy of their service discharge form (DD-214, DD-215, or for World War II Veterans, a WD form), which documents service dates and type of discharge, or provides full name, military service number, and branch and dates of service.

The Veteran's service discharge form should be kept in a safe location accessible to the Veteran and next of kin or designated representative.

The following documents will be needed for claims processing related to a Veteran's death:

1. Veteran's marriage certificate for claims of a surviving spouse or children.
2. Veteran's death certificate if the Veteran did not die in a VA health care facility.
3. Children's birth certificates or adoption papers to determine children's benefits.
4. Veteran's birth certificate to determine parents' benefits.

eBenefits

eBenefits is a joint VA/Department of Defense (DoD) Web portal that provides resources and self-service capabilities to Servicemembers, Veterans, and their families to apply, research, access, and manage their VA and military benefits and personal information through a secure Internet connection.

Through eBenefits Veterans can: apply for benefits, view their disability compensation claim status, access official military personnel documents (e.g., DD Form 214, Certificate of Release or Discharge from Active Duty), transfer entitlement of Post-9/11 GI Bill to eligible dependents (Servicemembers only), obtain a VA-guaranteed home loan Certificate of Eligibility, and register for and update direct deposit information for certain benefits. New features are added regularly.

Accessing eBenefits: The portal is located at www.ebenefits. va.gov. Servicemembers or Veterans must register for an eBenefits account at one of two levels: Basic or Premium. A Premium account allows the user to access personal data in VA and DoD systems, as well as apply for benefits online, check the status of claims, update address records, and more. The Basic account allows access to information entered into eBenefits by the Servicemember or Veteran only. Basic accounts limit the self-service features that can be accessed in eBenefits.

In order to register for an eBenefits account, Veterans must be listed in the Defense Enrollment Eligibility Reporting System (DEERS) and first obtain a DoD Self Service (DS) Logon. Servicemembers can access eBenefits with a DS Logon or Common Access Card (CAC). They can choose from two levels of registration: DS Logon Level 1 (Basic) and DS Logon Level 2 (Premium). Note: If Veterans attempt to register and they are informed they have no DEERS record, VA will first need to verify their military service and add them to DEERS. All VA regional offices have staff familiar with the procedures for adding a Veteran to DEERS.

A DS Logon is an identity (user name and password) that is used by various DoD and VA Websites, including eBenefits. Those registered in DEERS are eligible for a DS Logon. A DS Logon is valid for the rest of your life.

Identity verification: Many people will be able to verify their identity online by answering a few security questions. A few may need to visit a VA regional office or TRICARE Service Center to have their identities verified. Servicemembers may verify their identity online by using their CAC.

Military retirees may verify their identity online using their Defense Finance and Accounting Service (DFAS) Logon. Veterans in receipt of VA benefits via direct deposit may have their identity verified by calling 1-800-827-1000 and selecting option 7. Others may need to visit a VA regional office or TRICARE Service Center to have their identities verified in person.

Abbreviations

ALS – Amyotrophic Lateral Sclerosis
CHAMPVA – Civilian Health and Medical Program of VA
CLC – Community Living Center
C&P – Compensation and Pension
COE – Certificate of Eligibility
CRDP – Concurrent Retirement and Disability Payments
CRSC – Combat-Related Special Compensation
CWT – Compensated Work Therapy
CZTE – Combat Zone Tax Exclusion
DIC – Dependency and Indemnity Compensation
DoD -- Department of Defense
FHA – Federal Housing Administration
FSGLI – Family Servicemembers' Group Life Insurance
HUD – Department of Housing and Urban Development
IRR – Individual Ready Reserve
MGIB – Montgomery GI Bill
MIA – Missing in Action
NPRC – National Personnel Records Center
NSLI – National Service Life Insurance
OEF – Operation Enduring Freedom
OIF – Operation Iraqi Freedom
OND – Operation New Dawn
OPM – Office of Personnel Management
POW -- Prisoner of War
PTSD – Post-Traumatic Stress Disorder
SAH – Specially Adapted Housing
SBA – Small Business Administration
S-DVI – Service-Disabled Veterans' Insurance
SGLI – Servicemembers' Group Life Insurance
SSB – Special Separation Benefits
TAP – Transition Assistance Program
TSGLI – Servicemembers' Group Life Insurance Traumatic Injury Protection
USCIS – U.S. Citizenship and Immigration Services
USDA – U.S. Department of Agriculture
VA – Department of Veterans Affairs
VEAP – Veterans Educational Assistance Program
VEOA – Veterans' Employment Opportunities Act
VGLI – Veterans' Group Life Insurance
VHA – Veterans Health Administration
VMET – Verification of Military Experience and Training
VMLI – Veterans' Mortgage Life Insurance
VR&E – Vocational Rehabilitation and Employment
VSI – Voluntary Separation Incentive
WAAC – Women's Army Auxiliary Corps
WASPs – Women Air Force Service Pilots

Chapter 1

Health Care Benefits

VA operates the nation's largest integrated health care system with more than 1,700 sites of care, including hospitals, community clinics, community living centers, domiciliaries, Vet Centers, and various other facilities. For additional information on VA health care, visit: www.va.gov/health.

Basic Eligibility

A person who served in the active military, naval, or air service and who was discharged or released under conditions other than dishonorable may qualify for VA health care benefits. Reservists and National Guard members may also qualify for VA health care benefits if they were called to active duty (other than for training only) by a Federal order and completed the full period for which they were called or ordered to active duty.

Minimum Duty Requirements: Veterans who enlisted after Sept. 7, 1980, or who entered active duty after Oct. 16, 1981, must have served 24 continuous months or the full period for which they were called to active duty in order to be eligible. This minimum duty requirement may not apply to Veterans discharged for hardship, early out or a disability incurred or aggravated in the line of duty.

Enrollment

For most Veterans, entry into VA health care system begins by applying for enrollment. Veterans can now apply and submit their application for enrollment (VA Form 1010EZ), online at www.1010ez.med. va.gov/sec/vha/1010ez/. If assistance is needed while completing the on-line enrollment form, an online chat representative is available to answer questions Monday - Friday between 8 a.m. and 8 pm EST. Veterans can also enroll by calling 1-877-222-VETS (8387) Monday through Friday, 8 a.m. to 8 p.m. ESTS, or at any VA health care facility or VA regional office. Once enrolled, Veterans can receive health care at VA health care facilities anywhere in the country.
Veterans enrolled in VA health care system are afforded privacy

rights under federal law. VA's Notice of Privacy Practices, which describes how VA may use and disclose Veterans' medical information, is also available on line at www.va.gov/vhapublications/viewpublication.asp?pub_ID=1089

The following four categories of Veterans are not required to enroll, but are urged to do so to permit better planning of health resources:
1. Veterans with a service-connected disability of 50 percent or more.
2. Veterans seeking care for a disability the military determined was incurred or aggravated in the line of duty, but which VA has not yet rated, within 12 months of discharge.
3. Veterans seeking care for a service-connected disability only.
4. Veterans seeking registry examinations (Ionizing Radiation, Agent Orange, Gulf War/Operation Enduring Freedom/ Operation Iraqi Freedom/ Operation New Dawn (OEF/OIFOND) depleted uranium, airborne hazards and Airborne Hazards and Open Burn Pit Registry)..

Priority Groups

During enrollment, each Veteran is assigned to a priority group. VA uses priority groups to balance demand for VA health care enrollment with resources. Changes in available resources may reduce the number of priority groups VA can enroll. If this occurs, VA will publicize the changes and notify affected enrollees. A description of priority groups follows:

Group 1: Veterans with service-connected disabilities rated 50 percent or more and/or Veterans determined by VA to be unemployable due to service-connected conditions.

Group 2: Veterans with service-connected disabilities rated 30 or 40 percent.

Group 3:
Veterans who are former prisoners of war (POWs).
Veterans awarded the Purple Heart medal.
Veterans awarded the Medal of Honor.
Veterans whose discharge was for a disability incurred or aggravated in the line of duty.
Veterans with VA service-connected disabilities rated 10 percent or 20 percent.

Veterans awarded special eligibility classification under Title 38, U.S.C., § 1151, "benefits for individuals disabled by treatment or vocational rehabilitation."

Group 4:

Veterans receiving increased compensation or pension based on their need for regular aid and attendance or by reason of being permanently housebound.

Veterans determined by VA to be catastrophically disabled.

Group 5:

Nonservice-connected Veterans and noncompensable service-connected Veterans rated 0 percent, whose annual income and/or net worth are not greater than VA financial thresholds.

Veterans receiving VA Pension benefits.

Veterans eligible for Medicaid benefits.

Group 6:

Compensable 0 percent service-connected Veterans.

Veterans exposed to ionizing radiation during atmospheric testing or during the occupation of Hiroshima and Nagasaki.

Project 112/SHAD participants.

Veterans who served in the Republic of Vietnam between Jan. 9, 1962 and May 7, 1975.

Veterans who served in the Southwest Asia theater of operations from Aug. 2, 1990, through Nov. 11, 1998.

Veterans who served in a theater of combat operations after Nov.11, 1998, as follows:

Veterans discharged from active duty on or after Jan. 28, 2003, for five years post discharge;

Veterans who served on active duty at Camp Lejeune, N.C., for no fewer than 30 days beginning Jan. 1, 1957 and ending Dec. 31, 1987.

Group 7:

Veterans with incomes below the geographic means test income thresholds and who agree to pay the applicable copayment.

Group 8:

Veterans with gross household incomes above VA national income threshold and the geographically-adjusted income threshold for their resident location and who agrees to pay copayments. Veterans eligible for enrollment: Noncompensable 0-percent service-connected:

Subpriority a: Enrolled as of Jan. 16, 2003, and who have remained enrolled since that date and/ or placed in this subpriority due to changed eligibility status.

Subpriority b: Enrolled on or after June 15, 2009 whose income exceeds the current VA national income thresholds or VA national geographic income thresholds by 10 percent or less

Veterans eligible for enrollment: nonservice-connected and

Subpriority c: Enrolled as of Jan. 16, 2003, and who remained enrolled since that date and/ or placed in this subpriority due to changed eligibility status

Subpriority d: Enrolled on or after June 15, 2009 whose income exceeds the current VA national income thresholds or VA national geographic income thresholds by 10 percent or less

Veterans NOT eligible for enrollment: Veterans not meeting the criteria above:

Subpriority e: Noncompensable 0 percent service-connected

Subpriority f: Nonservice-connected

VA's income thresholds change annually and current levels can be located at: http://www.va.gov/healthbenefits/cost/income_thresholds. asp.

Recently Discharged Combat Veterans

Veterans, including activated reservists and members of the National Guard, are eligible for the enhanced combat Veteran benefits if they served on active duty in a theater of combat operations after Nov. 11, 1998, and have been discharged under other than dishonorable conditions.

Combat Veterans discharged from active duty on or after Jan. 28, 2003, are eligible for enhanced enrollment placement into Priority Group 6 (unless eligible for higher enrollment Priority Group placement) for five years post discharge and are eligible to receive VA health care and medication at no cost for any condition that may be related to their combat service.

Veterans who enroll with VA under this combat Veteran authority will remain enrolled even after their five-year post discharge period ends. At the end of their post discharge period, VA will reassess the Veteran's information (including all applicable eligibility factors) and make a new enrollment decision. For additional information, call 1-877-222-VETS (8387), Monday through Friday between 8:00 a.m. and 8:00 p.m. Eastern time.

Special Access to Care

Service-disabled Veterans: who are rated by VA as 50 percent or more disabled from service-connected conditions, unemployable due to service-connected conditions, or receiving care for a service-connected disability receive priority in scheduling of hospital or outpatient medical appointments.

Women Veterans

Women Veterans are eligible for the same VA benefits as male Veterans. Comprehensive health services are available to women Veterans including primary care, specialty care, mental health care, residential treatment and reproductive health care services

VA provides management of acute and chronic illnesses, preventive care, contraceptive and gynecology services, menopause management, and cancer screenings, including pap smears and mammograms. Maternity care is covered in the Medical Benefits package. Women Veterans can receive maternity care from an OB/GYN, family practitioner, or certified nurse midwife who provides pregnancy care.

VA covers the costs of care for newborn children of women Veterans for seven days after birth. Infertility evaluation and limited treatments are also available. Women Veterans Program Managers are available at all VA facilities to assist women Veterans in their health care and benefits. For more information, visit http://www.womenshealth. va.gov/.

Lesbian Gay Bisexual and Transgender (LGBT) Veterans

LGBT Veterans are eligible for the same VA benefits as any other Veteran and will be treated in a welcoming environment. Comprehensive health services are available to LGBT Veterans including primary care, specialty care, mental health care, residential treatment and reproductive health care services. VA provides management of acute and chronic illnesses, preventive care, contraceptive and gynecology services, menopause management, and cancer screenings.

Transgender Veterans will be treated based upon their self-iden-
tified gender, including room assignments in residential and inpatient settings. Eligible transgender Veterans can receive cross-sex
hormone therapy, gender dysphoria counseling, preoperative evaluations, as well as post-operative and long-term care following sex
reassignment surgeries.

Same-Sex Couples:VA launched a new website to inform Veterans
and beneficiaries of the recent changes in the law and procedures
involving same-sex marriages. The new website provides important
information to help Veterans and beneficiaries understand the eligibility requirements under federal law and VA regulations, and answers
frequently asked questions. Veterans can learn more about VA's
guidance regarding same-sex marriages at http://www.va.gov/opa/
marriage/ or by reaching out to VA call centers at 1-800-827-1000.

Military Sexual Trauma
Military sexual trauma (MST) is the term that the Department of Veterans Affairs uses to refer to sexual assault or repeated, threatening
sexual harassment that occurred while a Veteran was serving on active duty (or active duty for training if the service was in the National
Guard or Reserves). VA health care professionals provide counseling
and treatment to help Veterans overcome health issues related to
MST. Veterans who are not otherwise eligible for VA health care may
still receive these services. Appropriate services are provided for any
injury, illness or psychological condition related to such trauma. For
additional information visit: http://www.mentalhealth.va.gov/msthome.
asp

Presumptive Eligibility for Psychosis and Other Mental Illness
Certain Veterans who experienced psychosis within a specified time-
frame are to have their psychosis presumed to be service-connected
for purposes of VA medical benefits. In addition, VA will presume
that Persian Gulf War Veterans are service-connected for purposes
of VA medical benefits if such Veterans develop mental illness other
than psychosis within two years after discharge or release from
service and before the end of the 2-year period beginning on the last
day of the Persian Gulf War. Under this authority Veterans who are
not otherwise eligible for VA health care and meet the description
stated can receive treatment only for psychosis or mental illness and

other conditions directly related to psychosis or mental illness at no cost.

Psychosis: Eligibility for treatment of psychosis, and such condition is exempted from copayments for any Veteran who served in the United States active duty military, naval, or air service and developed such psychosis within two years after discharge or release from the active military duty, naval or air service; and before the following date associated with the war or conflict in which the Veteran served:

Veteran Served During	Date:
World War II	July 26, 1949
Korean Conflict	February 1, 1957
Vietnam Era	May 8, 1977
Persian Gulf War	Date to be determined

Mental Illness (other than Psychosis). Eligibility for benefits is established for treatment of an active mental illness (other than psychosis), and such condition is exempted from copayments for any Veteran of the Persian Gulf War who developed such mental illness:
   a. Within two years after discharge or release from the active duty military, naval, or air service; and
   b. Before the end of the two-year period beginning on the last day of the Persian Gulf War (end date not yet determined).

Veterans with Spinal Cord Injury/Disorders

There are 24 VA-operated Spinal Cord Injury Centers (SCI) that provide services for Veterans with spinal cord injuries and disorders (SCI/D). Comprehensive rehabilitation, SCI/D specialty care, medical, surgical, primary, preventive, psychological, respite, and home care are provided at these centers by interdisciplinary teams which include physicians, nurses, therapists (physical, occupational, kinesiotherapists, therapeutic recreation), psychologists, social workers, vocational counselors, dieticians, respiratory therapy, and other specialists as needed.

There are five SCI centers that provide long-term care for Veterans with SCI/D. In VA facilities that do not have SCI centers, there is a designated team that consists of a physician, nurse, and social worker to address primary care needs for Veterans with SCI/D and to make referrals to SCI Centers. These SCI Centers and the teams in facilities that do not have centers, comprise VA SCI System of Care.

Some of the services provided in this system of care include rehabilitation, prosthetics and durable medical equipment, orthotics, sensory aids, assistive technology, environmental modifications, telehealth, ventilator weaning and care, chronic pain management, mental health treatment, drivers training, peer counseling, substance abuse treatment, vocational counseling, and caregiver training and support.

There is a long-standing memorandum of agreement between VA and the Department of Defense (DoD) to provide specialized care at VA medical facilities for Active Duty Servicemembers who have sustained a spinal cord injury. Ongoing collaboration and education between VA and DoD ensures continuity of care and services. For more information about SCI/D care and the eligibility requirements for the above benefits and services, contact your local VA SCI/D Center and/or visit http://www.sci.va.gov.

OEF/OIF/OND Care Management

Each VA medical center has an Operation Enduring Freedom/Operation Iraqi Freedom/Operation New Dawn (OEF/OIF/OND) Care Management team in place to coordinate patient care activities and ensure that Servicemembers and Veterans are receiving patient-centered, integrated care and benefits. All OEF/OIF/OND era Veterans are screened for the need for case management services to identify Veterans who may be at risk so VA can intervene early and provide assistance. More information for connecting with OEF/OIF/OND Care Management teams can be found at www.oefoif.va.gov

Health Care Law

The Affordable Care Act, also known as the health care law, was created to expand access to affordable health care coverage, lower costs, and improve quality and care coordination. Under the law, people will:

*   have health coverage that meets a minimum standard (called minimum essential coverage) by Jan.1, qualify for an exemption; or pay a fee when filing their taxes if they have affordable options but remain uninsured.

Key Information for Veterans about the Health Care Law

*   VA wants all Veterans to get health care that improves their health and well-being.
*   Veterans who are enrolled in VA health care don't need to take additional steps to meet the health care law coverage

standards.
- The health care law does not change VA health benefits or Veterans' out-of-pocket costs.
- Veterans who are not enrolled in VA health care can apply at any time.

For additional information about the VA and the health care law, visit www.va.gov/aca call 1-877-222-VETS (8387).

Financial Assessment
Most Veterans not receiving VA disability compensation or pension payments must provide a financial assessment, also known as a means test, upon initial application to determine whether they are below VA income thresholds. VA is currently not enrolling new applicants who decline to provide financial information unless they have a special eligibility factor exempting them from disclosure. VA's income thresholds are located at: www.va.gov/healtheligibility/Library/AnnualThresholds.asp

The financial assessment includes all household income and net worth, including Social Security, retirement pay, unemployment insurance, interest and dividends, workers' compensation, black lung benefits and any other income. Also considered are assets such as the market value of property that is not the primary residence, stocks, bonds, notes, individual retirement accounts, bank deposits, savings accounts and cash.

Beginning in 2014, VA will no longer require enrolled non-service connected and 0 percent noncompensable service connected Veterans to provide their financial information annually. A means test will continue to be collected from Veterans at the time of application for enrollment. In lieu of the annual financial reporting, VA will confirm the Veteran's financial information using information obtained from the Internal Revenue Service and Social Security Administration.

Medical Services and Medication Copayments
Some Veterans are required to make copayments (copays) to receive VA health care and/or medications.

Inpatient Care: Priority Group 7 and certain other Veterans are responsible for paying 20 percent of VA's inpatient copay, which totals $243.20 for the first 90 days of inpatient hospital care during any 365-day period. For each additional 90-day period, the charge is $121.60. In addition, there is a $2 per diem charge. Copay amounts may change on an annual basis.

Priority Group 8 and certain other Veterans are responsible for VA's inpatient copay , which totals $1,216 for the first 90 days of care during any 365-day period. For each additional 90-day period, the charge is $ 608. In addition, there is a $10 per diem charge. Copay amounts may change on an annual basis.

Extended Care Services: Veterans may be subject to a copay for extended care services. The copay amount is based on the Veteran's available resources and is determined by a calculation using the financial information from VA Form 10-10EC, Application for Extended Care Services. The copay can range from $0 to a maximum copay amount of $97 a day.

Note: VA social workers or case managers will counsel Veterans or their family representatives on the potential copay amounts for extended care services. Veterans determined to be catastrophically disabled are exempt from copays applicable to the receipt of non-institutional respite care, non-institutional geriatric evaluation, non-institutional adult day health care, homemaker/home health aide, purchase skilled home care, home-based primary care, hospice services and any other non-institutional alternative extended care services. Copayments for other extended care services not mentioned (e.g. Nursing Home Care) may be subject to copays.

Outpatient Care: While many Veterans qualify for free health care services based on a VA compensable service-connected condition or other qualifying factor, most Veterans are asked to provide a financial assessment, to determine if they qualify for free services. Veterans whose income exceeds the established VA Income Thresholds as well as those who choose not to complete the financial assessment must agree to pay required copays to become eligible for VA health care services.
  Primary Care Services: $15
  Specialty Care Services: $50

NOTE: The copay amount is limited to a single charge per visit regardless of the number of health care providers seen in a single day. The copay amount is based on the highest level of clinical service received.

Outpatient Visits Not Requiring Copays: Certain services are not charged a copay. Copays do not apply to publicly announced VA health fairs or outpatient visits solely for preventive screening and/ or vaccinations, such as vaccinations for influenza and pneumococcal, or screening for hypertension, hepatitis B, tobacco, alcohol, hyperlipidemia, breast cancer, cervical cancer, Human papillomavirus (HPV), colorectal cancer by fecal occult blood testing, education about the risks and benefits of prostate cancer screening, HIV testing and prevention counseling (including the distribution of condoms), and weight reduction or smoking cessation counseling (individual and group). Laboratory, flat plain film radiology, electrocardiograms, and hospice care and in-home video telehealth are also exempt from copays. While hepatitis C screening and HIV testing and counseling are exempt, medical care for HIV and hepatitis C are NOT exempt from copays.

Medication Copays: While many Veterans are exempt for medication copays, nonservice-connected Veterans in Priority Groups 7 and 8 are charged $9 for each 30-day or less supply of medication provided on an outpatient basis for the treatment of a nonservice-connected condition. Veterans enrolled in Priority Groups 2 through 6 are charged $8 for each 30-day or less supply of medication; the maximum copay for medications that will be charged in calendar year 2013 is $960 for nonservice-connected medications.

NOTE: Copays apply to prescription and over-the-counter medications, such as aspirin, cough syrup or vitamins, dispensed by a VA pharmacy. Copays are not charged for medical supplies, such as syringes or alcohol wipes. Copays do not apply to condoms.

Health Savings Accounts (HSA) can be utilized to make VA copayments. HSAs are usually linked to High Deductible Health Plans (HDHPs).

Private Health Insurance Billing

VA is required to bill private health insurance providers for medical care, supplies and medications provided for treatment of Veterans' nonservice-connected conditions. Generally, VA cannot bill Medicare, but can bill Medicare supplemental health insurance and/or TRICARE for Life (TFL) for covered services. VA is authorized to bill and accept reimbursement from High Deductible Health Plans (HDHPs) for care provided for nonservice-connected conditions.VA may also accept reimbursement from Health Reimbursement Arrangements (HRAs) for care provided for nonservice-connected conditions.

Release of Information (ROI) for Sensitive Diagnosis
An ROI authorization form VAF 10-5345 is a VA standard form used to obtain authorization to release sensitive (protected) health information to an insurance company for purposes of reimbursement.. Veterans/patients who were treated or offered treatment for a sensitive condition of drug abuse, alcohol abuse or alcoholism, HIV testing or treatment, and sickle cell anemia or trait must provide written authorization to allow VA to release their sensitive information to a third party (insurance company).

NOTE: Any non-service connected care provided by the VA that has a sensitive diagnosis cannot be billed to the Veteran's third party health insurance without a signed release of information (ROI) by the Veteran. The Veteran is either co-pay exempt or co-pay required based upon their means test and/or eligibility. If the Veteran does not sign the ROI form permitting VA to bill his/her insurance and is also in a required co-pay status, then the Veteran will be responsible for their entire co-pay amount because VA is not able to offset the Veteran's account dollar for dollar based on what the insurance company would have reimbursed.

Reimbursement of Travel Costs
Eligible Veterans and non-veterans may be provided mileage reimbursement or, when medically indicated, special mode transport (e.g. wheelchair van, ambulance) when travel is in relation to VA medical care.

Mileage reimbursement is 41.5 cents per mile and is subject to a deductible of $3 for each one-way trip and $6 for a round trip; with a maximum deductible of $18 or the amount after six one-way trips (whichever occurs first) per calendar month.

The deductible may be waived when travel is; in relation to a VA compensation or pension examination; by a special mode of transportation; by an eligible non-Veteran; will cause a severe financial hardship, as defined by current regulatory guidelines.

Eligibility: The following are eligible for VA travel benefits:
   Veterans rated 30 percent or more service-connected.
   Veterans traveling for treatment of service-connected.
   conditions.
   Veterans who receive a VA pension.
   Veterans traveling for scheduled compensation or pension.
   examinations.
   Veterans whose income does not exceed the maximum.
   annual VA pension rate.
   Veterans in certain emergency situations.
   Veterans whose medical condition requires a special mode of
   transportation and travel is pre-authorized. (Advanced
   authorization is not required in an emergency and a delay
   would be hazardous to life or health).
   Certain non-Veterans when related to care of a Veteran
   (caregivers, attendants, donors and other claimants subject to
   current regulatory guidelines)

Beneficiary travel fraud can take money out of the pockets of de-
serving Veterans. Inappropriate uses of beneficiary travel benefits
include: incorrect addresses provided resulting in increased mileage; driving/riding together and making separate claims; and taking
no cost transportation, such as DAV, and making claims. Veterans
making false statements for beneficiary travel reimbursement may be
prosecuted under applicable laws.
Reporting Fraud: Help VA's Secretary ensure integrity by reporting
suspected fraud, waste or abuse in VA programs or operations.

Report fraud to:
VA Inspector General Hotline
P.O. Box 50410
Washington, DC 20091-0410
E-mail: vaoighotline@va.gov
VAOIG hotline 1-800-488-8244
Fax: (202) 565-7936

VA Medical Programs

Veteran Health Registries
Certain Veterans can participate in a VA health registry and receive
free evaluations. These evaluations include a medical history, physical exam, and if deemed necessary by the clinician, laboratory tests

or other studies.   VA maintains health registries to provide special health evaluations and health-related information. To participate, contact the Environmental Health Coordinator at the nearest VA health care facility or visit www.publichealth.va.gov/exposures to see a directory which lists Environmental Health Coordinators by state and U.S. territory. Veterans should be aware that a health registry evaluation is not a disability compensation exam. A registry evaluation does not start a claim for compensation and is not required for any VA benefits.

Gulf War Registry: For Veterans who served on active military duty in Southwest Asia during the Gulf War, which began in 1990 and continues to the present, and includes Operation Iraqi Freedom (OIF) and Operation New Dawn (OND). The Gulf War registry was designed to identify possible health effects resulting from U.S. military personnel service in certain areas of Southwest Asia. Potential exposures include endemic infectious diseases and hazardous occupational or environmental exposures, including heavy metals, air pollutants (particulate matter and gases such as nitrogen oxides, carbon monoxide sulfur oxides, and hydrocarbons).

Depleted Uranium Registries: Depleted uranium (DU) is uranium left over after most of the more radioactive U-235 isotope has been removed. DU possesses about 60 percent of the radioactivity of naturally occurring uranium; it is a radiation hazard only in very large exposures for prolonged time. DU has some chemical toxicity related to being a heavy metal (similar to lead) which occurs at lower doses and is the main concern for Veterans with embedded DU fragments.

Veterans who are identified by the DoD or have concerns about possible depleted uranium (DU) exposure are eligible for a DU evaluation at their local facility.

Embedded Fragment Registry: OEF, OIF, and OND Veterans who have or likely have an embedded fragment as the result of an injury they received while serving in an area of conflict are eligible for inclusion into the Embedded Fragment Registry. This registry was designed to identify track and conduct long-term medical surveillance of Veterans who potentially have embedded fragments. Clinical data captured in the Embedded Fragment Registy will be used to help develop medical and surgical guidelines to allow VA clinicians to deliver appropriate medical care to these Veterans

Agent Orange Registry: Agent Orange is an herbicide the U.S. military used between 1962 and 1971 during the Vietnam War to remove jungle that provided enemy cover. Veterans serving in Vietnam were possibly exposed to Agent Orange or its dioxin contaminant. Veterans eligible for this registry evaluation are those who served on the ground in Vietnam between Jan. 9,1962, and May 7,1975, regardless of the length of service; this includes Veterans who served aboard boats that operated on inland waterways ("Brown Water Navy") or who made brief visits ashore.

Other Veterans with possible exposure who are eligible include those who served: along the demilitarized zone in Korea (between Apr. 1, 1968 and Aug. 31, 1971), on certain bases or in certain units in Thailand (between Feb. 28, 1961 and May 7, 1975), or on certain U.S. bases or locations in other countries where Agent Orange or other herbicides were tested or stored.

VA maintains a DoD-provided list of locations and dates where Agent Orange or other herbicides were tested or stored at military bases in the U.S. or locations in other countries at www.publichealth.va.gov/exposures. For sites not listed, the Veteran should provide some proof of exposure to obtain a registry evaluation. Information is also available through VA's Special Issues Helpline at 1-800-749-8387.

Ionizing Radiation Registry: For Veterans who have received nasopharyngeal (nose and throat) radium irradiation treatments while on active duty and Veterans possibly exposed to radiation during the following "radiation-risk activities:"

On-site participation in:
- An atmospheric detonation of a nuclear device, whether or not the testing nation was the United States;
- Occupation of Hiroshima or Nagasaki from Aug. 6, 1945, through July 1, 1946; or
- Internment as a POW in Japan during World War II, which VA determines resulted in an opportunity for exposure to ionizing radiation comparable to that of Veterans involved in the occupation of Hiroshima or Nagasaki, or service at
- Department of Energy gaseous diffusion plants at Paducah, Ky.; Portsmouth, Ohio; or the K-25 area at Oak Ridge, Tenn., for

at least 250 days before Feb. 1, 1992, if the Veteran was
monitored for each of the 250 days using dosimetry badges to
monitor radiation to external body parts; or
• Amchitka Island, Alaska, before Jan. 1, 1974, if the Veteran
served for at least 250 days in a position that had exposures
comparable to a job that was monitored using dosimetry badges
in proximity to Longshot, Milrow, or Cannikin underground
nuclear tests.

Airborne Hazards and Open Burn Pit Registry:
Participation in the Airborne Hazards and Open Burn Pit Registry
is voluntary and open to any Veteran or active-duty Servicemember who served in one or more of the following locations during
eligible timeframes: OEF/OIF/ON: Djibouti, Africa after Sept.11,
2001;, Operations Desert Shield or Desert Storm;, or the Southwest
Asia theater of operations after Aug. 2, 1990. The Southwest Asia
theater of operations includes Iraq, Saudi Arabia, Bahrain, Gulf of
Aden, Gulf of Oman, Oman, Qatar, United Arab Emirates, waters of
the Persian Gulf, Arabian Sea, and the Red Sea. Eligible Servicemembers and Veterans can enroll in the registry by completing a
web-based self-assessment questionnaire. Veterans will be asked
about deployments, environmental and work-related exposures,
health care usage, and current health. Unlike other registries, when
Veterans complete the Airborne Hazards and Open Burn Pit Registry self-assessment questionnaire via the internet, they are in the
registry. No in-person medical evaluation is required to become
registered. However, Veteran participants are eligible for an optional
no-cost medical evaluation from VA. Participants already enrolled in
VA health care should contact their primary care provider or Patient
Aligned Care Team (PACT) to schedule an evaluation. Veterans not
already enrolled in VA health care should contact an Environmental
Health Coordinator at a nearby VA facility by visiting the following
link: (http://www.publichealth.va.gov/exposures/coordinators.asp) or
calling 1-877-222-8387.

Vet Center Readjustment Counseling Services
VA provides readjustment counseling services, to include direct
counseling, outreach, and referral, through 300 community-based
Vet Centers located in all 50 states, the District of Columbia, Guam,
Puerto Rico, and American Samoa.

Eligibility: Veterans and active-duty Servicemembers, to include federally-activated members of the National Guard and Reserve components, are eligible to receive readjustment counseling services at a Vet Center if they:

- Have served on active military duty in any combat theater or area of hostility such as World War II, the Korean War, the Vietnam War, the Gulf War, or the campaigns in Lebanon, Grenada, Panama, Somalia, Bosnia, Kosovo, Afghanistan, and Iraq;
- Experienced a military sexual trauma while serving on active military duty;
- Provided direct emergent medical care or mortuary services, while serving on active military duty, to the casualties of war;
- Served as a member of an unmanned aerial vehicle crew that provided direct support to operations in a combat zone or area of hostility; or
- Are Veterans who served in the active military during the Vietnam-era, but not in the Republic of Vietnam, and have requested services at a Vet Center before January 1, 2004.

Vet Center readjustment counseling services are free to the eligible Veterans and their family without time limitations. Servicemembers and Veterans are not required to enroll in the VA health care system or have received a service connection for conditions caused by military service. These services are also provided regardless of the nature of the Veteran's discharge. This includes service provision to those individuals with problematic discharges.

Services Offered: Vet Center counselors provide individual, group, marriage, and family readjustment counseling to those individuals that have served in combat zones or areas of hostilities to assist them in making a successful transition from military to civilian life; to include treatment for posttraumatic stress disorder (PTSD) and help with any other military related problems that affect functioning within the family, work, school or other areas of everyday life. Other psycho-social services include outreach, education, medical referral, homeless Veteran services, employment, VA benefit referral, and the brokering of non-VA services.

The Vet Centers also provide counseling to individuals who have experienced military sexual trauma of both genders and of any era of military service.

Bereavement Counseling related to Servicemembers: Bereavement counseling is available through VA's Vet Centers to all immediate family members (including spouses, children, parents, and siblings) of Servicemembers who die while serving on active service. This includes federally-activated members of the National Guard and reserve components. Vet Center bereavement services for surviving family members of Servicemembers may be accessed by calling (202) 461-6530. For additional information, contact the nearest Vet Center, listed in the back of this book, or visit www.vetcenter.va.gov/.

Vet Center Combat Call Center: (1-877-WAR-VETS) is an around the clock confidential call center where combat Veterans and their families can call to talk about their military experience or any other issue they are facing in their readjustment to civilian life. The staff is comprised of combat Veterans from several eras as well as family members of combat Veterans.

Prosthetic and Sensory Aids

Veterans receiving VA care for any condition may receive VA prosthetic appliances, equipment and services, such as home respiratory therapy, artificial limbs, orthopedic braces and therapeutic shoes, wheelchairs, powered mobility, crutches, canes, walkers, special aids, appliances, optical and electronic devices for visual impairment and other durable medical equipment and supplies. Veterans who are approved for a guide or service dog may also receive service dog benefits including veterinary care and equipment.

VA medical services include diagnostic audiology and diagnostic and preventive eye care services. VA will provide hearing aids and eyeglasses to the following Veterans:

(a) Those with any compensable service-connected disability.

(b) Those who are former Prisoners of War (POWs).

(c) Those who were awarded a Purple Heart.

(d) Those in receipt of benefits under Title 38 United States Code (U.S.C.) 1151.

(e) Those in receipt of an increased pension based on being rated permanently housebound or in need of regular aid and attendance.

(f) Those with vision or hearing impairment resulting from diseases or the existence of another medical condition for which the Veteran is receiving care or services from VHA, or which resulted from treatment of that medical condition, e.g., stroke, polytrauma, traumatic brain injury, diabetes, multiple sclerosis, vascular disease, geriatric chronic illnesses, toxicity from drugs, ocular photosensitivity from drugs, cataract surgery, and/or other surgeries performed on the eye, ear, or brain resulting in vision or hearing impairment.

(g) Those with significant functional or cognitive impairment evidenced by deficiencies in the ability to perform activities of daily living. but not including normally occurring visual or hearing impairments. Note: Veterans with normally occurring visual and/or hearing impairments that interfere with their medical care are eligible for eyeglasses and hearing aids.

(h) Those who have vision or hearing impairment or combined visual and hearing impairments severe enough that it interferes with their ability to participate actively in their own medical treatment. Note: The term "severe" is to be interpreted as a vision and/or hearing loss that interferes with or restricts access to, involvement in, or active participation in health care services (e.g., communication or reading medication labels). The term is not to be interpreted to mean that a severe hearing or vision loss must exist to be eligible for hearing aids or eyeglasses.

(i) Veterans who have a service-connected hearing disabilitiy that contributes to a loss of communication ability. However, hearing aids are to be provided only as needed for the service-connected hearing disability.

Nonservice-connected (NSC) Veterans are eligible for hearing aids or eyeglasses on the basis of medical need. All such Veterans (including Medal of Honor recipients who do not have entitling conditions or circumstances and catastrophically disabled Veterans) must receive a hearing evaluation by a state-licensed audiologist prior to determining eligibility for hearing aids or an appropriate evaluation by an optometrist or ophthalmologist prior to determining eligibility for eyeglasses to establish medical justification for provision of these devices. These Veterans must meet the following criteria for eligibility based on medical need:

(a) Be enrolled at VA medical facility where they receive their health care; and

(b) Have hearing or vision loss that interferes with or restricts communication to the extent that it affects their active participation in the provision of health care services as determined by an audiologist or an eye care practitioner or provider.

For additional information, contact the prosthetic chief or representative at the nearest VA medical center or go to www.prosthetics.

va.gov.

Home Improvements and Structural Alterations
VA provides up to $6,800 lifetime benefits for service-connected Veterans/Servicemembers and up to $2,000 lifetime benefits for nonservice-connected Veterans to make home improvements and/or structural changes necessary for the continuation of treatment or for disability access to the Veterans/Servicemembers home and essential lavatory and sanitary facilities.

Modifications can include but are not limited to: Ramps allowing entrance to, or exit from, the Veterans/Servicemembers primary residence; Widening of doorways to allow access to essential lavatory and sanitary facilities; Raising or lowering kitchen or bathroom sinks and/or counters; Improving entrance paths or driveways in immediate area of the home to facilitate access to the home by the Veteran/Servicemember; Improving plumbing or electrical systems made necessary due to installation of dialysis equipment or other medically sustaining equipment in the home.

For application information, contact the Prosthetic Representative at the nearest VA medical center.

Special Eligibility Programs
Special Eligibility for Children with Spina Bifida: VA provides comprehensive health care benefits, including outpatient, inpatient, pharmacy, prosthetics, medical equipment, and supplies for certain Korea and Vietnam Veterans' birth children diagnosed with spina bifida (except spina bifida occulta).

Special Eligibility for Veterans Participating in Vocational Rehabilitation: Veterans participating in VA's vocational rehabilitation program may receive VA health care benefits including prosthetics, medical equipment, and supplies.

Limitations on Benefits Available to Veterans outside the U.S.: Veterans outside the U.S. are eligible for prosthetics, medical equipment, and supplies only for a service-connected disability or any disability associated with, or found to be aggravating, a service-connected disability.

Services for Blind and Visually Impaired Veterans
Severely disabled blind Veterans may be eligible for case management services at a VA medical center and for admission to an inpatient or outpatient VA blind or vision rehabilitation program. In addi-

tion, blind Veterans enrolled in VA health care system may receive:
1. A total health and benefits review as well as counseling on obtaining benefits that may be due to the Veteran but have not been received.
2. Adjustment to blindness training and counseling.
3. Home improvements and structural alterations.
4. Specially adapted housing and adaptations.
5. Automobile grant.
6. Rehabilitation assessment and training to improve independence and quality of life.
7. Low-vision devices and training in their use.
8. Electronic and mechanical aids for the blind, including adaptive computers and computer-assisted devices such as reading machines and electronic travel aids.
9. Facilitation and recommendation for guide dogs and support in the use of guide dogs.
10. Costs for veterinary care and equipment for guide dogs.
11. Talking books, tapes and Braille literature.
12. Family education and support.

Eligible visually impaired Veterans (who are not severely visually disabled) enrolled in VA health care system may be eligible for services at a VA medical center or for admission to an outpatient VA blind rehabilitation program and may also receive:
1. A total health and benefits review.
2. Adjustment to vision loss counseling.
3. Rehabilitation assessment and training to improve independence and quality of life.
4. Low-vision devices and training in their use.
5. Electronic and mechanical aids for the visually impaired, including adaptive computers and computer-assisted devices, such as reading machines and electronic travel aids, and training in their use.
6. Family education and support.

Mental Health Care Treatment

Veterans eligible for VA medical care may receive general and specialty mental health treatment as needed. Mental health services are available in primary care clinics (including Home Based Primary Care), general and specialty mental health outpatient clinics, inpatient mental health units, residential rehabilitation and treatment programs, specialty medical clinics, and Community Living Centers.

Mental Health services are also available in medical settings in which patients are receiving treatment, such as inpatient medicine and out-patient specialty medical clinics. In addition to general mental health care, this may include specialized PTSD services, treatment for Veterans with psychological conditions related to a history of military sexual trauma, psychosocial rehabilitation and recovery services, treatment for substance use disorders, suicide prevention programs, geriatric mental health problems, violence prevention, evidence-based psycho-therapy programs, treatment with psychiatric medications consistent with the VA National Formulary, integrated care services, and mental health disaster response/post deployment activities. Extended hours care is available for Veterans at VA medical centers. Veterans should contact their local facility mental health service for more information.

Specialized programs, such as mental health intensive case management, psychosocial rehabilitation and recovery centers, and work programs are provided for Veterans with serious mental health problems. VA's Program of Comprehensive Assistance for Family Caregivers entitles the designated primary and secondary family caregiver(s) access to mental health. These services may be offered at VA and/or contracted agencies. General caregivers (of all era Veterans) can receive counseling and other services when necessary if the treatment supports the Veteran's treatment plan. For more information on VA mental health services visit http://www.mentalhealth.va.gov/VAMental-HealthGroup.asp

Veterans Crisis Line: Veterans experiencing an emotional distress/crisis or who need to talk to a trained mental health professional may call the Veterans Crisis Line 1-800-273-TALK (8255). The hotline is available 24 hours a day, seven days a week. When callers press "1", they are immediately connected with a qualified and caring provider who can help.

Chat feature: Veterans Chat is located at the Veterans Crisis Line and enables Veterans, their families and friends to go online where they can anonymously chat with a trained VA counselor. Veterans chat can be accessed through the suicide prevention website www.Veterancrisisline.net by clicking on the Veterans chat tab on the right side of the webpage.

Text feature: Those in crisis may text 83-8255 free of charge to receive confidential, personal and immediate support.

European access: Veterans and members of the military community in Europe may now receive free, confidential support from the European Military Crisis Line, a new initiative recently launched by VA. Callers in Europe may dial 0800-1273-8255 or DSN 118 to receive confidential support from responders at the Veterans Crisis Line in the U.S. For more information about VA's suicide prevention program, visit: http://www.mentalhealth.va.gov/suicide_prevention/ or www.veteranscrisisline.net.

Make the Connection Resources help Veterans and their family members connect with information and services to improve their lives. Visitors to MakeTheConnection.net will find a one-stop resource where Veterans and their family and friends can privately explore information, watch stories similar to their own, research content on mental health issues and treatment, and easily access support and information that will help them live more fulfilling lives.

At the heart of Make the Connection are powerful personal testimonials, which illustrate true stories of Veterans who faced life events, physical injuries or psychological symptoms; then reached out for support; and found ways to overcome their challenges. Veterans and their families are encouraged to "make the connection" - with strength and resilience of Veterans like themselves, with other people who care, and with information and available resources for getting their lives on a better track. For more information, go to www.MakeTheConnection.net

Coaching Into Care: works with family members or friends who become aware of the Veteran's post-deployment difficulties, and supports their efforts to find help for the Veteran. This national clinical service provides information and help to Veterans and the loved ones who are concerned about them. More information about the service can be found at http://www.mirecc.va.gov/coaching/contact.asp

VA's **National Center for PTSD** serves as a resource for health care professionals, Veterans and families. Information, self-help resources, and other helpful information can be found at www.ptsd.va.gov.

The **PTSD Coach** is a mobile application that provides information about PTSD, self-assessment and symptom management tools and information tabout how to connect with resources that are available for those who might be dealing with post trauma effects. The PTSD Coach is available as a free download for iPhone or Android devices.

Mental Health Residential Rehabilitation
Mental Health Residential Rehabilitation Treatment Programs (MH RRTP) including domiciliaries, provide residential rehabilitative and clinical care to Veterans who have a wide range of problems, illnesses, or rehabilitative care needs, which can be medical, psychiatric, substance use, homelessness, vocational, educational, or social. The MH RRTP provides a 24-hour therapeutic setting utilizing a peer and professional support environment. The programs provide a strong emphasis on psychosocial rehabilitation and recovery services that instill personal responsibility to achieve optimal levels of independence upon discharge to independent or supportive community living. The MH RRTP also provides rehabilitative care for homeless Veterans.

Eligibility: VA may provide domiciliary care to Veterans whose annual gross household income does not exceed the maximum annual rate of VA pension or to Veterans whom the Secretary of Veterans Affairs determines have no adequate means of support. The copays for extended care services apply to domiciliary care. Call the nearest benefits or health care facility to obtain the latest information.

Outpatient Dental Treatment
Dental benefits are provided by VA according to law. In some instances, VA is authorized to provide extensive dental care, while in other cases treatment may be limited by law. This Fact Sheet table describes dental eligibility criteria and contains information to assist Veterans in understanding their eligibility for VA dental care.

By law, the eligibility for outpatient dental care is not the same as for most other VA medical benefits. It is categorized in classes. Those eligible for VA dental care under Class I, IIA, IIC, or IV are eligible for any necessary dental care to maintain or restore oral health and masticatory function, including repeat care. Other classes have time and/or service limitations.

*Note: Public Law 83 enacted June 16, 1955, amended Veterans' eligibility for outpatient dental services. As a result, any Veteran who received a dental award letter from VBA dated before 1955 in which VBA determined the dental conditions to be non-compensable are no longer eligible for Class II outpatient dental treatment.
Veterans receiving hospital, nursing home, or domiciliary care will be provided dental services that are professionally determined by a VA dentist, in consultation with the referring physician, to be essential to the management of the patient's medical condition under active

treatment. For more information about eligibility for VA medical and dental benefits, contact VA at 1-877-222-8387, Monday through Friday between 8 am and 8 pm EST or www.va.gov/healthbenefits.   (See chart on page 26)

VA Dental Insurance Program (VADIP)

Veterans enrolled in VA health care and CHAMPVA beneficiaries have the opportunity to purchase dental insurance coverage at a reduced cost through Delta Dental and MetLife.
Delta Dental and MetLife offer multiple plans to choose from. Coverage, available throughout the United States and its territories, includes diagnostic, preventative, surgical, emergency, and endodontic/restorative treatment and services.

Enrolled Veterans and CHAMPVA beneficiaries may sign up to participate in VADIP by completing an application with Delta Dental or MetLife – online, over the phone, or by mail – for the plan that best meets their dental needs and budget. Each participant will pay fixed monthly premiums for coverage and copayments identified in the plan they select. The program is voluntary and there are no eligibility limitations based on service-connected disability or other factors. Participation in the program does not affect eligibility for VA-provided dental services and treatment.

Vocational and Work Assistance Programs

VHA Therapeutic & Supported Employment Services (TSES) Programs: VHA provides vocational assistance and therapeutic work opportunities through three primary TSES programs for Veterans enrolled in the VAhealth care system. These programs are designed to assist Veterans to live and work as independently as possible in their respective communities. Participation in TSES vocational services cannot be used to deny or discontinue VA disability benefits. Payments received from Compensated Work Therapy Sheltered Workshop and Transitional Work and Incentive Therapy cannot be used to deny or discontinue SSI and/or SSDI payments and they are not subject to IRS taxes.

Compensated Work Therapy/Transitional Work (CWT/TW) is a vocational assessment program that operates in VA medical centers and/or local community business and industry. CWT/TW participants are matched to real life work assignments for a time-limited basis. Veterans are supervised by personnel of the sponsoring site, under the same job expectations experienced by non-CWT workers. Veter-

Dental Eligibility Chart

If you:	You are eligible for:	Through
Have a service-connected compensable dental disability or condition.	Any needed dental care.	Class I
Are a former prisoner of war.	Any needed dental care.	Class IIC
Have service-connected disabilities rated 100 percent disabling, or are unemployable and paid at the 100 percent rate due to service-connected conditions.	Any needed dental care. [note: Veterans paid at the 100 percent rate based on a temporary rating, are not eligible for comprehensive outpatient dental services.	Class IV
Apply for dental care within 180 days of discharge or release from of active duty (under conditions other than dishonorable) of 90 days or more during the Gulf War era.	One-time dental care if a DD214 certificate of discharge does not indicate that a complete dental examination and all appropriate dental treatment had been rendered prior to discharge.(**NOTE**)	Class II
Have a service-connected noncompensable dental condition or disability resulting from combat wounds or service trauma.	Any dental care necessary to provide and maintain a functioning dentition. A Dental Trauma Rating (VA Form 10-564-D) or VA RO Decision letter (VA Form 10-7131) identifies the tooth/teeth/condition(s) that are trauma rated.	Class IIA
Have a dental condition clinically determined by VA to be associated with and aggravating a service-connected medical condition.	Dental care to treat the oral conditions that are determined by a VA dental professional to have a direct and material detrimental effect to a service-connected medical condition.	Class III
Are actively engaged in a 38 USC Chapter 31 vocational rehabilitation program.	Dental care to the extent necessary to: to enter, achieve goals, and prevent interruption of a rehab program; hasten the return to a rehab program because of a dental condition; or to secure and adjust to employment during employment assistance, or enable to achieve maximum independence in daily living.	Class V
Are receiving VA care or are scheduled for inpatient care and require dental care for a condition complicating a current medical condition	Dental care to treat the oral conditions that are determined by a VA dental professional to complicate a medical condition currently under treatment.	Class VI
Are an enrolled Veteran who may be homeless and receiving care under VHA Directive 2007-039.	A one-time course of dental care that is determined medically necessary to relieve pain, assist in gaining employment, or treat moderate to severe gingival and periodontal conditions.	Class IIB

ans participating in the CWT/TW program are not employees of either the Federal government or a host company and, as such, receive no traditional employee benefits. CWT/TW participants receive, at a minimum, the greater of Federal or state minimum wage for all hours worked. Approximately 40 percent of participants secure competitive employment at the time of discharge.

CWT/Supported Employment (CWT/SE) is a recovery-based intervention provided through an integrated partnership with the primary Mental Health treatment team. The employment is intended to be an extension of treatment to manage symptoms and advance recovery. CWT/SE consists of full- or part-time competitive employment with extensive clinical supports to Veterans, and accommodations/supervision guidance to employers.

Other Initiatives include the adaption of SE evidence-based principles for specialty TSES programs for Veterans diagnosed with spinal cord injury, polytrauma, traumatic brain injury, and/or posttraumatic stress disorder. A list of CWT program sites can be found on the Location Page at http://www.cwt.va.gov.

Vocational Assistance is a set of assessment, guidance, counseling, or other related services that may be offered to groups or individuals. These services are designed to enable Veterans to realize skills, resources, attitudes and expectations needed to prepare for searching for employment, succeeding in the employment interview process, and succeeding in employment.

CWT/Sheltered Workshop (CWT/SW) operates sheltered workshops at approximately 25 VA medical centers. CWT/SW is a pre-employment vocational activity that provides an opportunity for work hardening and assessment in a simulated work environment. Participating Veterans are paid the greater of Federal or state minimum wage on a piece rate basis.

Incentive Therapy (IT) is a pre-employment program that provides a limited work experience at VA medical centers for Veterans who are not actively seeking competitive employment and exhibit severe mental illness and/or physical impairments. IT services may consist of full- or part-time work with nominal remuneration limited to the maximum of one half of the Federal minimum wage.

Long-term Services

VA provides institution based services (nursing home level of care) to Veterans through three national programs: VA owned and operated Community Living Centers (CLC), State Veterans' Homes owned and operated by the states, and the community nursing home program. Each program has admission and eligibility criteria specific to the program. VA is obligated to pay the full cost of nursing home services for enrolled Veterans who need nursing home care for a service-connected disability, or Veterans or who have a 70 percent or greater service-connected disability and Veterans with a rating of total disability based on individual un-employability. VA provided nursing home care for all other Veterans is based on available resources. Institution based nursing home care is expected to be person centered and serves Veterans of all ages.

VA Community Community Living Centers (CLC) provide a dynamic array of short stay (less than 90 days) and long stay (91 days or more) services. Short stay services include but are not limited to skilled nursing, respite care, rehabilitation, hospice, and continuing care for Veterans awaiting placement in the community. Long stay services include but are not limited to dementia care and continuing care to maintain the Veteran's level of functioning. Short stay and long stay services are available for Veterans who are enrolled in VA health care and require CLC services.

State Veterans' Home Program: State Veterans homes are owned and operated by the states. The states petition VA for grant dollars for a portion of the construction costs followed by a request for recognition as a state home. Once recognized, VA pays a portion of the per diem if the state meets VA standards. States establish eligibility criteria and determine services offered for short and long-term care. Specialized services offered are dependent upon the capability of the home to render them.

Community Nursing Home Program: VA health care facilities establish contracts with community nursing homes. The purpose of this program is to meet the nursing home needs of Veterans who require long-term nursing home care in their own community close to their families, and who meet the enrollment and eligibility requirements.

Admission Criteria: The general criteria for nursing home placement in each of the three programs requires that a resident must be medically stable, i.e. not acutely ill, have sufficient functional deficits to require inpatient nursing home care, and be determined by an appropriate medical provider to need institutional nursing home care. Furthermore, the Veteran must meet the specific eligibility criteria for community living center care or the contract nursing home program and the eligibility criteria for the specific state Veterans home.

Home and Community Based Services: IVA offers a variety of community-based non-institutional long-term services and supports these services either directly or by contract with community-based agencies. Home and community based services are expected to be person centered and serve Veterans of all ages. Veterans receiving these services may be subject to a copay.

In-Home and Community Based Care: Skilled home health care, homemaker/home health aide services, community adult day health care; Hhospice and Ppalliative Ccare, Veteran Ddirected Ccare.

Respite Care: Designed to relieve the fFamily Caregiver from the constant burden of caring for a chronically ill or disabled Veteran at home. Services can include in-home care, a short stay in an institutional setting or adult day health care.

Primary Care: Geri Patient Aligned Care Teams (PACT) provide geriatric focused primary care in an outpatient setting; Home Based Primary Care PACT provides primary care in the home; Geriatric Evaluation and Management (GEM) provides inpatient or outpatient short- term comprehensive geriatric evaluation and management.

Emergency Medical Care in U.S. Non-VA Facilities

In the case of medical emergencies, VA may reimburse or pay for emergency non-VA medical care not previously authorized that is provided to certain eligible Veterans when VA or other federal facilities are not feasibly available. This benefit may be dependent upon other conditions, such as notification to VA, the nature of treatment sought, the status of the Veteran, the presence of other health care insurance, and third party liability.

Because there are different regulatory requirements that may affect VA payment and Veteran liability for the cost of care, it is very important that the nearest VA medical facility to where emergency services are furnished be notified as soon as possible after emergency treatment is sought. If emergency inpatient services are required, VA will assist in transferring the Veteran to a Department facility, if available. Timely filing claim limitations apply. For additional information, contact the nearest VA medical facility. Please note that reimbursement criteria for Veterans living or traveling outside the United States fall under VA's Foreign Medical Program (FMP), and differ from the criteria for payment of emergency treatment received in the United States.

Foreign Medical Program

VA may authorize reimbursement for medical services for service-connected disabilities or any disability associated with and found to be aggravating a service-connected disability for those Veterans living or traveling outside the United States. This program may also reimburse for the treatment of foreign medical services needed as part of an approved VA vocational rehabilitation program. Veterans receiving health care services in the Philippines should register with the U.S. Veterans Affairs office in Pasay City. Veterans calling from within the Philippines may contact the VA office in Pasay City at 1-800-1888-8782. If calling from outside of the Philippines, the number is 011-632-318-8387. Veterans may also register by email at IRIS.va.gov. All other Veterans living or planning to travel outside the U.S. should register with the Foreign Medical Program, P.O. Box 469061, Denver, CO 80246-9061, USA; telephone 303-331-7590. For information visit: http://www.va.gov/hac/forbeneficiaries/fmp/fmp.asp.

Some Veterans traveling or living overseas can telephone the Foreign Medical Program toll free from these countries: Germany 0800-1800-011; Australia 1800-354-965; Italy 800-782-655; United Kingdom (England and Scotland) 0800-032-7425; Mexico 001-877-345-8179; Japan 00531-13-0871; Costa Rica 0800-013-0759; and Spain 900-981-776. (Note: Veterans in Mexico or Costa Rica must first dial the United States country code.)

On occasion Veterans will ask to have prescriptions mailed outside the United States and its territories. VA Pharmacy Service is not authorized to ship medications or medical/surgical supply items outside of the United States or US Territories (Virgin Islands, Guam, American Samoa, and the Commonwealth of the Northern Mariana Islands). For Veterans registered with the Foreign Medical Program, prescription reimbursement is approved only for United States Food and Drug Administration (FDA) approved medications.

Within the United States and prior to travel abroad, VA facilities may opt to fill outpatient medications prior to the normal dispensing date in the event that a Veteran will be traveling and unable to obtain medications while abroad. This may be done on a limited basis and requires prior consultation with the Veteran's VA provider prior to dispensing.

Online Health Services

VA offers Veterans, Servicemembers, their dependents and caregivers their own personal health record through My HealtheVet, found at www.myhealth.va.gov.

My HealtheVet 's free, online Personal Health Record is available 24 hours a dya, seven days a week with Internet access. Those with an upgraded account (obtained by completing the one-time in-person authentication* process) can:

- Participate in secure messaging with VA health care team members
- View key portions of DoD military service information
- Get VA wellness reminders
- View VA appointments
- View VA lab results
- View VA allergies, adverse reactions and other key portions of their VA electronic health record
- View their VA Comprehensive Care Document (CCD)

With My HealtheVet, Veterans can access trusted health information to better manage personal health care and learn about other VA benefits and services.

My HealtheVet helps Veterans partner with VA health care teams by providing tools to make shared, informed decisions. Simply follow the directions on the website to register. VA patients registered on My HealtheVet can begin to refill VA medications online. Veterans can also use VA Blue Button to view, print, or download the health data currently in their My HealtheVet account. Veterans can share this information with family, caregivers or others such as non-VA health care providers. It puts the Veteran in control of their information stored in My HealtheVet. VA Blue Button also provides Veterans who were discharged from military service after 1979 access to DoD Military Service Information. This information may include Military Occupational Specialty (MOS) codes, pay details, service dates, deployment, and retirement periods.

*To access the advanced My HealtheVet features, Veterans will need to get an upgraded account by completing a one-time process at their VA facility. Visit My HealtheVet at www.myhealth.va.gov, register and learn more about in-person authentication plus the many features and tools available with Internet access. Veterans with questions should contact the My HealtheVet Coordinator at their VA facility.

Caregiver Programs and Services

VA has long supported family caregivers as vital partners in providing care worthy of the sacrifices by America's Veterans and Service-members. Each VA medical center has a Caregiver Support Program coordinated by a Caregiver Support Coordinator (CSC). The CSC coordinates caregiver activities and serves as a resource expert for Veterans, their families and VA providers. Several programs are available for all Veteran caregivers including:

In-Home and Community Based Care: Skilled home health care, homemaker/home health aide services, community adult day health care and Home Based Primary Care.

Respite Care: Designed to relieve the family caregiver from the constant burden of caring for a chronically ill or disabled Veteran at home. Services can include in-home care, a short stay in an institutional setting or adult day health care.

Post-9/11 Caregiver Program: The Caregivers and Veterans Omnibus Health Services Act of 2010 allows VA to provide unprecedented benefits to eligible Caregivers (a parent, spouse, child, step-family member, extended family member, or an individual who lives with the Veteran, but is not a family member) of eligible Veterans who incurred or aggravated a serious injury in the line of duty on or after Sept. 11, 2001 (post-9/11 Veterans) under the Program of Comprehensive Assistance for Family Caregivers.
Services include:
- Monthly stipend based on the personal care needs of the Veteran
- Travel expenses, including lodging and per diem while accompanying Veterans undergoing care
- Access to health care insurance through the Civilian Health and Medical Program of the Department of Veterans Affairs (CHAMPVA) if the Caregiver is not already entitled to care or services under a health plan

- Mental Health services and counseling
- Comprehensive VA Caregiver training
- Respite care
- Appropriate caregiving instruction and training

VA currently provides multiple training opportunities, which include pre-discharge care instruction and specialized caregiver programs in multiple severe traumas such as traumatic brain injury (TBI), spinal cord injury/disorders, and blind rehabilitation. VA has a caregiver website, www.caregiver.va.gov, which provides tools, resources, and information to Family Caregivers.

Family Support Services: These support groups can be face-to-face or on the telephone. They include family counseling, spiritual and pastoral care, family leisure and recreational activities and temporary lodging in Fisher Houses.

Travel: VA's Comprehensive Assistance for family caregivers Program entitles the designated family caregiver to beneficiary travel benefits. These benefits include:
- Transport, lodging, and subsistence for period of caregiver training
- Transport, lodging, and subsistence while traveling as Veteran's attendant to and from VA Health care as well as duration of care at VA or VA authorized facility.
- Mileage or common carrier transport.
- Lodging and/or subsistence at 50 percent of local federal employee rates

Other Benefits: VA provides durable medical equipment and prosthetic and sensory aides to improve function, financial assistance with home modification to improve access and mobility, and transportation assistance for some Veterans to and from medical appointments.

Veterans Canteen Service

Established in 1946, the Veterans Canteen Service (VCS) was created to provide merchandise and services at reasonable prices to Veterans enrolled in the VA health care system, caregivers, and visitors. The VCS PatriotStoreDirect 1-800-664-8258 provides services to those who cannot visist a VA facility. For more information, visit VCS online at www.vacanteen.va.gov for more information

Chapter 2

Service-connected Disabilities

Disability Compensation

Disability compensation is a monetary benefit paid to Veterans who are determined by VA to be disabled by an injury or illness that was incurred or aggravated during active military service. These disabilities are considered to be service connected. To be eligible for compensation, the Veteran must have been separated or discharged under conditions other than dishonorable.

Monthly disability compensation varies with the degree of disability and the number of eligible dependents. Veterans with certain severe disabilities may be eligible for additional special monthly compensation (SMC). Disability compensation benefits are not subject to federal or state income tax.

The payment of military retirement pay, disability severance pay and separation incentive payments, known as Special Separation Benefit (SSB) and Voluntary Separation Incentive (VSI), may affect the amount of VA compensation paid to disabled Veterans. For additional details on types of disability claims and how to apply, go to http://benefits.va.gov/benefits/ or apply online at https://www.ebenefits.va.gov/.

* Veterans with disability ratings of at least 30 percent are eligible for additional allowances for dependents, including spouses, minor children, children between the ages of 18 and 23 who are attending school, children who are permanently incapable of self-support because of a disability arising before age 18, and dependent parents. The additional amount depends on the disability rating and the number of dependents.

Additional Benefits for Eligible Military Retirees

Concurrent Retirement and Disability Pay (CRDP) is a DoD program that allows some individuals to receive both military retired pay and VA disability compensation. Normally, such concurrent receipt is prohibited.

Veterans do not need to apply for this benefit, as payment is coordinated between VA and the military pay center.

To qualify for CRDP, Veterans must have a VA service-connected rating of 50 percent or greater, be eligible to receive retired pay, and:

- Be retired from military service based on longevity, including Temporary Early Retirement Authority (TERA) retirees; or
- Be retired due to disability with 20 or more qualifying years of service*; or
- Be retired from National Guard or Reserve service with 20 or more qualifying years.

* For Veterans who retired due to disability with 20 or more qualifying years, CRDP is subject to an offset for the difference between retired pay based on disability and retired pay based on longevity.

Combat-Related Special Compensation (CRSC) is a DoD program that provides a tax-free monthly payment to eligible retired Veterans with combat-related disabilities. CRSC, in effect, restores retired pay lost due to VA disability compensation offset. Veterans must apply for CRSC through their branch of service.

To qualify for CRSC, Veterans must be eligible to receive retired pay, and:

- Be retired from military service based on longevity, including Temporary Early Retirement Authority (TERA) retirees; or

2014 VA Disability Compensation

Disability Rating	Monthly Rate
10 percent	$130.94
20 percent	$258.83
30 percent*	$400.93
40 percent*	$577.54
50 percent*	$822.15
60 percent*	$1,041.39
70 percent*	$1,312.40
80 percent*	$1,525.55
90 percent*	$1,714.34
100 percent*	$2,858.24

- Be retired due to disability, including Veterans with less than 20 years of service*; or
- Be retired from National Guard or Reserve service with 20 or more qualifying years, and
- Have waived retired pay to receive VA compensation, and
- Have a compensable service-connected disability

*For Veterans who retired due to disability, CRSC is subject to an offset for the difference between retired pay based on disability and retired pay based on years of service.

Disabilities related to in-service exposure to hazards (e.g., Agent Orange, Gulf War illnesses, radiation exposure) for which VA awards compensation are considered combat-related for CRSC purposes. However, Veterans still must apply to their branch of service for a combat-related determination.

For more information, visit www.defense.gov, or call the toll-free phone number for the Veteran's branch of service:

Army 1-866-281-3254, https://www.hrc.army.mil/TAGD/CRSC or e-mail at usarmy.knox.hrc.mbx.tagd-crsc-claims@mail.mil

Air Force 1-800-525-0102, http://www.afpc.af.mil/library/combat.asp or email at AFPC.DPPDC.AFCRSC@RANDOLPH.AF.MIL

Navy/Marine Corps 1-877-366-2772, http://www.public.navy.mil/as-nmra/corb/CRSCB/Pages/CRSCB%20main%20page.aspx or email at crsc@navy.mil

Coast Guard 1-703-872-6626, http://www.uscg.mil/adm1/crsc.asp

Disability Compensation for Presumptive Conditions
Certain chronic and tropical diseases (for example, multiple sclerosis, diabetes mellitus, and arthritis) may be service connected if the disease becomes at least 10 percent disabling within the applicable time limit following service. For a comprehensive list of these chronic diseases, see 38 CFR 3.309; for applicable time limits, see 38 CFR 3.307.

All Veterans who develop Amyotrophic Lateral Sclerosis (ALS), also known as Lou Gehrig's Disease, at any time after separation from service may be eligible for compensation for that disability. To be eligible, the Veteran must have served a minimum of 90 consecutive days of active service.

Prisoners of War: For former prisoners of war (POWs) who were imprisoned for any length of time, VA presumes the following dis-abilities to be service connected if they become at least 10 percent disabling any time after military service: psychosis, any of the anxiety states, dysthymic disorder, organic residuals of frostbite, post-trau-matic osteoarthritis, atherosclerotic heart disease or hypertensive vascular disease and their complications, stroke and its complica-tions, and, effective Oct.10, 2008, osteoporosis if the Veteran has post-traumatic stress disorder (PTSD).

For former POWs who were imprisoned for at least 30 days, the following conditions are also presumed to be service connected: avitaminosis, beriberi, chronic dysentery, helminthiasis, malnutrition (including optic atrophy associated with malnutrition), pellagra and/or other nutritional deficiencies, irritable bowel syndrome, peptic ulcer disease, peripheral neuropathy except where related to infectious causes, cirrhosis of the liver, and, effective Sept. 28, 2009, osteopo-rosis.

Veterans Exposed to Agent Orange and Other Herbicides: A Veteran who served in the Republic of Vietnam between Jan. 9, 1962, and May 7, 1975, is presumed to have been exposed to Agent Orange and other herbicides used in support of military operations.

VA presumes the following diseases to be service-connected for such exposed Veterans: AL amyloidosis, chloracne or other acne-form disease similar to chloracne, porphyria cutanea tarda, soft-tis-sue sarcoma (other than osteosarcoma, chondrosarcoma, Kaposi's sarcoma or mesothelioma), Hodgkin's disease, multiple myeloma, respiratory cancers (lung, bronchus, larynx, trachea), non-Hodgkin's lymphoma, prostate cancer, acute and sub-acute peripheral neurop-athy, diabetes mellitus (Type 2), all chronic B-cell leukemias (includ-ing, but not limited to, hairy-cell leukemia and chronic lymphocytic leukemia), Parkinson's disease, and ischemic heart disease.

Veterans Exposed to Radiation: For Veterans who participated in radiation risk activities as defined in VA regulations while on active duty, active duty for training, or inactive duty training, the following conditions are presumed to be service connected: all forms of leukemia (except for chronic lymphocytic leukemia); cancer of the thyroid, breast, pharynx, esophagus, stomach, small intestine, pancreas, bile ducts, gall bladder, salivary gland, urinary tract (renal pelvis, ureter, urinary bladder and urethra), brain, bone, lung, colon, and ovary; bronchiolo-alveolar carcinoma; multiple myeloma; lymphomas (other than Hodgkin's disease), and primary liver cancer (except if cirrhosis or hepatitis B is indicated).

To determine service connection for other conditions or exposures not eligible for presumptive service connection, VA considers factors such as the amount of radiation exposure, duration of exposure, elapsed time between exposure and onset of the disease, gender and family history, age at time of exposure, the extent to which a nonservice exposure could contribute to disease, and the relative sensitivity of exposed tissue.

Gulf War Veterans with Chronic Disabilities: Some Veterans may receive disability compensation for chronic disabilities resulting from undiagnosed illnesses and/or medically unexplained chronic multi-symptom illnesses defined by a cluster of signs or symptoms. A disability is considered chronic if it has existed for at least six months.

The undiagnosed illness must have appeared either during active service in the Southwest Asia theater of operations during the Gulf War period of Aug. 2, 1990, to July 31, 1991, or to a degree of at least 10 percent at any time since then through Dec.31, 2016. This theater of operations includes Iraq, Kuwait, Saudi Arabia, the neutral zone between Iraq and Saudi Arabia, Bahrain, Qatar, the United Arab Emirates, Oman, the Gulf of Aden, the Gulf of Oman, the Persian Gulf, the Arabian Sea, the Red Sea, and the airspace above these locations.

Examples of symptoms of an undiagnosed illness and medically unexplained chronic multi-symptom illness defined by a cluster of signs and symptoms include: chronic fatigue syndrome, fibromyalgia, functional gastrointestinal disorders, fatigue, signs or symptoms involving the skin, headache, muscle pain, joint pain, neurological signs or symptoms, neuropsychological signs or symptoms, signs or symptoms involving the respiratory system (upper or lower), sleep disturbances, gastrointestinal signs or symptoms, cardiovascular signs or symptoms, abnormal weight loss, and menstrual disorders.

Presumptive service connection may be granted for the following infectious diseases if found compensable within a specific time period: Brucellosis, Campylobacter jejuni, Coxiella burnetti (Q fever), Malaria, Mycobacterium tuberculosis, non-typhoid Salmonella, Shigella, Visceral leishmaniasis, and West Nile virus. Qualifying periods of service for these infectious diseases include active military, naval, or air service in the above stated Southwest Asia theater of operations during the Gulf War period of Aug. 2, 1990, until such time as the Gulf War is ended by Congressional action or Presidential proclamation; and active military, naval, or air service on or after Sept. 19, 2001, in Afghanistan.

Housing Grants for Disabled Veterans

Certain Servicemembers and Veterans with service-connected disabilities may be entitled to a housing grant from VA to help build a new specially adapted house, to adapt a home they already own, or buy a house and modify it to meet their disability-related requirements. Eligible Veterans or Servicemembers may now receive up to three grants, with the total dollar amount of the grants not to exceed the maximum allowable. Previous grant recipients who had received assistance of less than the current maximum allowable may be eligible for an additional grant.

Specially Adapted Housing (SAH) Grant: VA may approve a grant of not more than 50 percent of the cost of building, buying, or adapting existing homes or paying to reduce indebtedness on a currently owned home that is being adapted, up to a maximum of $67,555. In certain instances, the full grant amount may be applied toward remodeling costs. Veterans and Servicemembers must be determined eligible to receive compensation for permanent and total service-connected disability due to one of the following:

1. Loss or loss of use of both lower extremities, which so affects the functions of balance or propulsion to preclude ambulating without the aid of braces, crutches, canes or a wheelchair.
2. Loss or loss of use of both upper extremities at or above the elbow.
3. Blindness in both eyes, having only light perception, plus loss or loss of use of one lower extremity.
4. Loss or loss of use of one lower extremity together with (a) residuals of organic disease or injury, or (b) the loss or loss of use of one upper extremity which so affects the functions of balance or propulsion as to preclude locomotion without the

use of braces, canes, crutches or a wheelchair.

5. Severe burn injuries, which are defined as full thickness or subdermal burns that have resulted in contractures with limitation of motion of two or more extremities or of at least one extremity and the trunk.

6. The loss, or loss of use of one or more lower extremities due to service on or after Sept. 11, 2001, which so affects the functions of balance or propulsion as to preclude ambulating without the aid of braces, crutches, canes, or a wheelchair.

Special Home Adaption (SHA) Grant: VA may approve a benefit amount up to a maximum of $13,511 for the cost of necessary adaptations to a Servicemember's or Veteran's residence or to help him/her acquire a residence already adapted with special features for his/her disability, to purchase and adapt a home, or for adaptations to a family member's home in which they will reside.

To be eligible for this grant, Servicemembers and Veterans must be entitled to compensation for permanent and total service-connected disability due to one of the following:

1. Blindness in both eyes with 20/200 visual acuity or less.
2. Anatomical loss or loss of use of both hands.
3. Severe burn injuries (see above).

Temporary Residence Adaptation (TRA): Eligible Veterans and Servicemembers who are temporarily residing in a home owned by a family member may also receive a TRA grant to help the Veteran or Servicemember adapt the family member's home to meet his or her special needs. Those eligible for a $67,555 grant would be permitted to use up to $29,657 and those eligible for a $13,511 grant would be permitted to use up to $5,295. Grant amounts are adjusted Oct.1 every year based on a cost-of-construction index. These adjustments will increase the grant amounts or leave them unchanged; grant amounts will not decrease. Under the Honoring America's Veterans and Caring for Camp Lejeune Families Act of 2012, TRA grant amounts do not count against SAH grant maximum amounts starting Aug. 6, 2013.

The property may be located outside the United States, in a country or political subdivision which allows individuals to have or acquire a beneficial property interest, and in which the Secretary of Veterans Affairs, in his or her discretion, has determined that it is reasonably practicable for the Secretary to provide assistance in acquiring specially adapted housing. For more information on SAH, visit http://www.benefits.va.gov/homeloans/sah.asp.

Supplemental Financing: Veterans and Servicemembers with available loan guaranty entitlement may also obtain a guaranteed loan or a direct loan from VA to supplement the grant to acquire a specially adapted home. Amounts with a guaranteed loan from a private lender will vary, but the maximum direct loan from VA is $33,000. Additional information about the Specially Adapted Housing Program is available at http://www.benefits.va.gov/homeloans/sah.asp.

Automobile Allowance: As of Oct. 1, 2013, Veterans and Servicemembers may be eligible for a one-time payment of not more than $19,817 toward the purchase of an automobile or other conveyance if they have service-connected loss or permanent loss of use of one or both hands or feet, or permanent impairment of vision of both eyes to a certain degree.

They may also be eligible for adaptive equipment, and for repair, replacement, or reinstallation required because of disability or for the safe operation of a vehicle purchased with VA assistance. To apply, contact a VA regional office at 1-800-827-1000 or the nearest VA health care facility.

Clothing Allowance: Any Veteran who has service-connected disabilities that require a prosthetic or orthopedic appliances may receive clothing allowances. This allowance is also available to any Veteran whose service-connected skin condition requires prescribed medication that irreparably damages outer garments. To apply, contact the prosthetic representative at the nearest VA medical center.

Allowance for Aid and Attendance or Housebound Veterans
A Veteran who is determined by VA to be in need of the regular aid and attendance of another person, or a Veteran who is permanently housebound, may be entitled to additional disability compensation or pension payments. A Veteran evaluated at 30 percent or more disabled is entitled to receive an additional payment for a spouse who is in need of the aid and attendance of another person.

Chapter 3

Vocational Rehabilitation and Employment

Vocational Rehabilitation and Employment (VR&E), sometimes referred to as the Chapter 31 program, provides services to eligible Servicemembers and Veterans with service-connected disabilities to help them prepare for, obtain, and maintain suitable employment or achieve independence in daily living.

Eligibility for Veterans
A Veteran must have a VA service-connected disability rating of at least 20 percent with an employment handicap, or rated 10 percent with a serious employment handicap, and be discharged or released from military service under other than dishonorable conditions.

Eligibility for Servicemembers
Servicemembers are eligible to apply if they expect to receive an honorable discharge upon separation from active duty, obtain a rating of 20 percent or more from VA, obtain a proposed Disability Evaluation System (DES) rating of 20 percent or more from VA, or obtain a referral to a Physical Evaluation Board (PEB) through the Integrated Disability Evaluation System (IDES).

Entitlement
A Vocational Rehabilitation Counselor (VRC) works with the Veteran to determine if an employment handicap exists. An employment handicap exists if a Veteran's service-connected disability impairs his/her ability to prepare for, obtain, and maintain suitable career employment. After an entitlement decision is made, the Veteran and VRC work together to develop a rehabilitation plan. The rehabilitation plan outlines the rehabilitation services to be provided.

Services
Based on their individualized needs, Veterans work with a VRC to

select one of five tracks to employment. The Five Tracks to Employment provide greater emphasis on exploring employment options early in the rehabilitation planning process, greater informed choice for the Veteran regarding occupational and employment options, faster access to employment for Veterans who have identifiable and transferable skills for direct placement into suitable employment, and an option for Veterans who are not able to work, but need assistance to lead a more independent life. If a program of training is selected, VA pays the cost of the approved training and services (except those coordinated through other providers) that are included in an individual's rehabilitation plan, including subsistence allowance.

The Five Tracks to Employment are:

Reemployment with Previous Employer
This track is for Veterans who served on active military service or in the National Guard or Reserves, and are now returning to employers for whom they worked prior to going on active duty.

Rapid Access to Employment
This track is for Veterans who express a desire to obtain employment as soon as possible and already have the necessary skills to qualify for competitive employment in a suitable career.

Self-Employment
This track is targeted to Veterans who have limited access to traditional employment, need flexible work schedules, or need a more accommodating work environment due to their disabling conditions or other life circumstances.

Employment through Long-Term Services
This track is targeted to Veterans who need long-term services, such as remedial or refresher courses, specialized training, and/or post-secondary education, to obtain and maintain suitable employment.

Independent Living Services
This track is for Veterans who are not currently able to work due to the effects of their disability, and services are needed to improve their independence in daily living.

Length of a Rehabilitation Program

The basic period of eligibility in which VR&E benefits may be used is 12 years from the later of the following: 1) A Veteran's date of separation from active military service, or 2) The date VA first notified a Veteran that he/she has a compensable service-connected disability. Depending on the length of program needed, Veterans may be provided up to 48 months of full-time services or the part-time equivalent. Rehabilitation plans that only provide services to improve independence in daily living are limited to 30 months. These limitations may be extended in certain circumstances.

Subsistence Allowance

In some cases, a Veteran may require additional education or training to become employable. A subsistence allowance is paid each month during training and is based on the rate of attendance (full-time or part-time), the number of dependents, and the type of training. (See Chart on Page 46)

Veterans who are eligible for both VR&E services and Post-9/11 GI Bill benefits may elect a special subsistence allowance that is based on the monthly basic allowance for housing paid to active duty military. The monthly amount varies depending on the ZIP code of the training facility and is usually greater than the following regular subsistence allowance rates that are available to Veterans with no Post-9/11 GI Bill eligibility who are using VR&E benefits. Active-duty Servicemembers are not eligible for subsistence allowance until after release from active duty.

Employment Services

VR&E staff assists Veterans and Servicemembers with achieving their employment goals by providing job development and placement services, which include: on-the-job training, job-seeking skills, resume development, interviewing skills and direct placement. VR&E has partnerships with federal, state and private agencies to provide direct placement of Veterans or Servicemembers. VR&E can assist with placement using the following resources:

On the Job Training (OJT) Program

Employers hire Veterans at an apprentice wage, and VR&E supplements the salary up the journeyman wage (up to maximum allowable under OJT). As the Veterans progress through training, the employers begin to pay more of the salary until the Veterans reach journeyman level and the employers are paying the entire salary. VR&E will also pay for any necessary tools. Employers are also eligible for a federal tax credit for hiring an individual who participated in a vocational rehabilitation program.

Non-Paid Work Experience (NPWE)
The NPWE program provides eligible Veterans the opportunity to obtain training and practical job experience concurrently. This program is ideal for Veterans or Servicemembers who have a clearly established career goal, and who learn easily in a hands-on environment. This program is also well suited for Veterans who are having difficulties obtaining employment due to lack of work experience. The NPWE program may be established in a federal, state, or local (i.e. city, town, school district) government agencies only. The employer may hire the Veteran at any point during the NPWE.

Special Employer Incentive (SEI)
The SEI program is for eligible Veterans who face challenges in obtaining employment. Veterans approved to participate in the SEI program are hired by participating employers and employment is expected to continue following successful completion of the program. Employers may be provided this incentive to hire Veterans. If approved, the employer will receive reimbursement for up to 50 percent of the Veteran's salary during the SEI program, which can last up to six months.

The Veterans Employment Center (www.ebenefits.va.gov/ebenefits/jobs) is the federal government's single authoritative online source for connecting transitioning Servicemembers, Veterans, and military families with meaningful career opportunities with both public and private-sector employers.

Job seekers can use the site to translate their military skills into civilian skills that employers can understand, post a public resume that is searchable by employers, and conduct a job search for both public and private-sector positions. Employers can use the site to post job opportunities, search verified resumes, make public commitments to hire Veterans, and obtain additional hiring and employment resources. All referral links direct job seekers to the employer's website and their unique job application system.

VR&E Subsistence Allowance Rates

Training	Time	No dependents	One dependent	Two dependents	Each Additional dependent
Institutional*	Full-Time	$594.47	$737.39	$868.96	$63.34
	3/4-Time	$446.67	$553.85	$649.68	$48.71
	1/2-Time	$298.88	$370.30	$435.27	$32.50
Farm Co-op Apprentice OJT**	Full-Time	$519.77	$628.55	$724.41	$47.12
Extended Evaluation Services in Rehab Facility	Full-Time	$594.47	$737.39	$868.96	$63.34
	3/4-Time	$446.67	$553.85	$649.68	$48.71
	1/2-Time	$298.88	$370.30	$435.27	$32.50
	1/4-Time	$149.41	$185.17	$217.64	$16.21
Independ. Living	Full-Time	$594.47	$737.39	$868.96	$63.34
	3/4-Time	$446.67	$553.85	$649.68	$48.71
	1/2-Time	$298.88	$370.30	$435.27	$32.50

VetSuccess On Campus (VSOC)

The VSOC program is designed to assist Veterans as they make the transition to college life. Through the VSOC program, VR&E is strengthening partnerships with institutions of higher learning and creating opportunities to help Veterans achieve success by providing outreach and transition services to the general Veteran population during their transition from military to college life.

The VSOC program provides:a VA Vocational Rehabilitation Counselor assigned to each VSOC school to provide vocational testing and career, academic, and readjustment counseling services, and a VA Vet Center Outreach Coordinator, co-located on many campuses, to provide peer-to-peer counseling and referral services.

VSOC counselors ensure that Veterans receive the support and assistance needed to pursue their educational and employment goals.

Because the VSOC counselors are easily accessible on campuses, they help resolve any problems that could potentially interfere with a Veteran's educational program, to include assisting with disability requirements. If needed, they can also provide referrals for health services through VA Medical Centers, Community-Based Outpatient Clinics, or Vet Centers.

Current VSOC locations include: American River College, Arizona State University, Austin Community College, Austin Peay State University – Clarksville, Bellevue University, Bluegrass Community College, Boise State University, California State University – LA, California State University-Long Beach, Central New Mexico Community College, Central Texas College, Citrus College, Cleveland State University, Community College of Rhode Island, East Carolina University, Eastern Kentucky University, Eastern Michigan University, Ecpi University, Florida International University, Florida State College at Jacksonville, Florida State University, George Mason University, George Washington University, Harrisburg Area Community College, Hawaii Pacific University, Houston Community College, Irvine Valley College, Johnson County Community College, Kalamazoo Valley Community College, Kellogg Community College, LA City College, Leeward Community College, Liberty University, Lone Star College System-University Park, Long Beach City College, Middle Tennessee State University, Middlesex Community College, Midlands Technical College, Mira Costa College, Mt. San Antonio College, Norfolk State University, Northern Virginia Community College – Alexandria, Northern Virginia Community College – Annandale, Northwest Arkansas College, Northwest Florida State College, Old Dominion University, Pasadena City College, Portland Community College, Portland State University, Rhode Island College, Rutgers University, Saddleback College, Salt Lake Community College, Sam Houston State University, San Antonio College, San Diego State University, Santa Fe Community College, Southwestern Illinois College, St. Leo University - South Hampton, Syracuse University, Tallahassee Community College, Tarrant County College District-NorthEast, Tarrant County College District-South, Texas A&M University - College Station, Texas A&M University-Central Texas, The Ohio State University, Tidewater Community College - Virginia Beach, Tidewater Community College –Chesapeake, Tidewater Community College –Portsmouth, Tidewater Community College-Norfolk, Troy University, University of Alabama, University of Alaska – Anchorage, University of Arkansas, University of Cincinnati, University of Florida, University of Hawaii-

Manoa, University of Houston, University of Illinois – Champaign, University of Kentucky, University of Maryland - University College, University of Michigan - Ann Arbor, University of Nebraska (Omaha), University of Nevada - Las Vegas, University of New Mexico, University of South Florida, University of Texas – Arlington, University of Texas-San Antonio, University of Utah, University of West Florida, University of Wisconsin – Milwaukee, Washtenaw Community College, Webster University-St. Louis, and Western Michigan University

Integrated Disability Evaluation System (IDES): VR&E is providing earlier access to VR&E benefits to wounded, ill or injured Servicemembers pending a medical separation from military service. VRCs are assigned to military installations hosting an IDES site and provide VR&E services to assist Servicemembers in the transition from active-duty to entering the labor market in viable careers. At these sites, Servicemembers will have a mandatory meeting with a VRC when referred to the Physical Evaluation Board (PEB). Servicemembers receive services ranging from a comprehensive rehabilitation evaluation to determine abilities, skills and interests for employment purposes; entry into training programs; and case management and support to become job ready and employed.

Current IDES locations include: Ft. Meade, Patuxent River NMC, Ft. Drum, New England NHC, West Point, McGuire AFB, Ft. Benning, Ft. Gordon, Ft. Stewart, Robins AFB, Beaufort NH, Ft. Jackson, Charleston NH, Shaw AFB, Fort Knox, Pensacola NH, Maxwell AFB, Fort Rucker, Redstone Arsenal, Ft. Campbell, Ft. Eustis, Portsmouth NMC, Ft. Lee, Langley JB, Jacksonville NH, MacDill AFB, Bethesda NNMC/WRAMC, Quantico NHC, Andrews AFB, Ft. Belvoir, Camp Lejeune, Ft. Bragg, Seymour Johnson AFB, Cherry Point NH, Fort Buchanan, Ft. Sam Houston, San Antonio JB (Lakeland), Little Rock AFB, Ft. Sill, Sheppard AFB, Tinker AFB, Ft. Polk, Ft. Leonard Wood, Ft. Bliss, Ft. Hood, Dyess AFB, Ft. Riley, Kirtland AFB, Richardson JB, Ft. Wainwright, Elmendorf AFB, Ft. Carson, F.E. Warren AFB, Peterson AFB, Schofield Barracks, Tripler AMC, Ft. Irwin, 29 Palms, Travis AFB, Lemoore NH, Ft. Huachuca, Davis-Monthan AFB, Luke AFB, Nellis AFB, Hill AFB, San Diego NMC, Camp Pendleton, Ft. Lewis, Bremerton NH, Oak Harbor NH, and Fairchild AFB

Additional information on VR&E benefits is available at www.benefits. va.gov/vocrehab

Chapter 4

VA Pensions

Eligibility for Veterans Pension

Low-income wartime Veterans may qualify for pension if they meet certain service, income and net worth limits set by law, are age 65 or older, or permanently and totally disabled, or a patient in a nursing home receiving skilled nursing care, or receiving Social Security Disability Insurance, or receiving Supplemental Security Income. Generally, a Veteran must have at least 90 days of active duty service, with at least one day during a VA recognized wartime period. The 90-day active service requirement does not apply to Veterans discharged from the military due to a service-connected disability.

Note: Veterans may have to meet longer minimum periods of active duty if they entered active duty on or after Sept. 8, 1980, or, if they were officers who entered active duty on or after Oct. 16,1981. The Veteran's discharge must have been under conditions other than dishonorable and the disability must be for reasons other than the Veteran's own willful misconduct.

Payments are made to bring the Veteran's total income, including other retirement or Social Security income, to a level set by Congress. Unreimbursed medical expenses may reduce countable income for VA purposes.

Protected Pension

Pension beneficiaries, who were receiving a VA pension on Dec. 31, 1978, and do not wish to elect the Improved Pension, will continue to receive the pension rate received on that date. This rate generally continues as long as the beneficiary's income remains within established limits, or net worth does not bar payment, and the beneficiary does not lose any dependents.

Beneficiaries must continue to meet basic eligibility factors, such as permanent and total disability for Veterans. VA must adjust rates for other reasons, such as a Veteran's hospitalization in a VA facility.

Medal of Honor Pension

VA administers a pension benefit to recipients of the Medal of Honor. This entitlement is not based on income level or need. Congress set the monthly pension at $1,277.89 for 2014.

Veterans Pension

Congress establishes the maximum annual Veterans Pension rates. Payments are reduced by the amount of countable income of the Veteran, spouse, and dependent children. When a Veteran without a spouse or a child is furnished nursing home or domiciliary care by VA, the pension is reduced to an amount not to exceed $90 per month after three calendar months of care. The reduction may be delayed if nursing-home care is being continued to provide the Veteran with rehabilitation services.

Aid and Attendance and Housebound Benefits
(Special Monthly Pension)

Veterans and surviving spouses who are eligible for VA pensions are eligible for higher maximum pension rates if they qualify for aid and attendance or housebound benefits. An eligible individual may qualify if he or she requires the regular aid of another person in order to perform personal functions required in everyday living, or is bedridden, a patient in a nursing home due to mental or physical incapacity, blind, or permanently and substantially confined to his/her immediate premises because of a disability.

Veterans and surviving spouses who are ineligible for basic pension based on excessive annual income may still be eligible for special monthly pension (SMP) if they require the aid and attendance of another in performing their daily functions, or if they are housebound due to a nonservice-connected condition as a higher income limit applies to SMP entitlement. In addition, unreimbursed medical expenses for nursing home or home-health care may be used to reduce countable annual income.

Claimants may apply for aid and attendance or housebound benefits by completing VA Form 21-2680 (available through www.va.gov). Claimants may also write to the nearest VA regional office and include copies of any evidence, preferably a report from an attending physician or a nursing home, validating the need for aid and attendance or housebound care. The report should be in sufficient detail to determine whether there is disease or injury producing physical or mental impairment, loss of coordination, or conditions affecting the ability to dress and undress, to feed oneself, to attend to sanitary needs, and to keep oneself ordinarily clean and presentable. In addition, VA may need to determine whether the claimant is confined to the home or immediate premises.

VA also pays a special $90 monthly rate to pension-eligible Veterans or surviving spouses with no dependents who receive Medicaid-covered nursing home care. These funds are available for the beneficiary's personal use and may not be used to offset the cost of his or her care.

2014 VA Improved Pension - Veterans Rates	
Status of Veteran's Family Situation and Caretaking Needs	**Maximum Annual Rate**
Veteran without dependents	$12,652
Veteran with one dependent	$16,569
Veteran permanently housebound, no dependents	$15,462
Veteran permanently housebound, one dependent	$19,380
Veteran needing regular aid and attendance, no dependents	$21,107
Veteran needing regular aid and attendance, one dependent	$25,022
Two Veterans married to one another	$16,569
Increase for each additional dependent child	$2,161

* Additional information can be found in the Pension Benefits section at www.benefits.va.gov/pension.

Chapter 5
Education and Training

This chapter provides a summary of VA educational and training benefits. Additional information can be found at www.benefits.va.gov/gibill/ or by calling 1-888-GI-BILL-1 (1-888-442-4551).

Post–9/11 GI Bill

Eligibility

The Post-9/11 GI Bill is an education benefit program for Service-members and Veterans who served on active duty after Sept.10, 2001. Benefits are payable for training pursued on or after Aug. 1, 2009. No payments can be made under this program for training pursued before that date.

To be eligible, the Servicemember or Veteran must serve at least 90 aggregate days on active duty after Sept. 10, 2001, and remain on active duty or be honorably discharged. Active duty includes active service performed by National Guard members under title 32 U.S.C. for the purposes of organizing, administering, recruiting, instructing, or training the National Guard; or under section 502(f) for the purpose of responding to a national emergency.   Veterans may also be eligible if they were honorably discharged from active duty for a service-connected disability after serving 30 continuous days after Sept. 10, 2001. Generally, Servicemembers or Veterans may receive up to 36 months of entitlement under the Post-9/11 GI Bill.

Eligibility for benefits expires 15 years from the last period of active duty of at least 90 consecutive days. If released for a service-connected disability after at least 30 days of continuous service, eligibility ends 15 years from when the member is released for the service-connected disability. If, on Aug. 1, 2009, the Servicemember or Veteran is eligible for the Montgomery GI Bill; the Montgomery GI Bill – Selected Reserve; or the Reserve Educational Assistance Program, and qualifies for the Post-9/11 GI Bill, an irrevocable election must be made to receive benefits under the Post-9/11 GI Bill.
In most instances, once the election to receive benefits under the Post-9/11 GI Bill is made, the individual will no longer be eligible to receive benefits under the relinquished program.

Based on the length of active duty service, eligible participants are entitled to receive a percentage of the following:
- Cost of in-state tuition and fees at public institutions and for the 2013-2014 academic year, up to $19,198.31 toward tuition and fee costs at private and foreign institutions (paid directly to the school),
- Monthly housing allowance* equal to the basic allowance for housing payable to a military E-5 with dependents, in the same ZIP code as the primary school (paid directly to the Servicemember, Veteran, or eligible dependents),
- Yearly books and supplies stipend of up to $1,000 per year (paid directly to the Servicemember, Veteran, or eligible dependents), and
- A one-time payment of $500 paid to certain individuals relocating from highly rural areas.

Housing allowance is not payable to individuals pursuing training at half time or less.

Approved training under the Post-9/11 GI Bill includes graduate and undergraduate degrees, vocational/technical training, on-the-job training, flight training, correspondence training, licensing and national testing programs, and tutorial assistance.

Individuals serving an aggregate period of active duty after Sept. 10, 2001, can receive the following percentages based on length of service:

Individuals serving an aggregate period of active duty after Sept. 10, 2001, can receive the percentages listed in the chart on page 54 based on length of service:
1. Includes service on active duty in entry level and skill training.
2. Excludes service on active duty in entry level and skill training.
3. If the individual would only qualify at the 70 percent level when service on active duty in entry level and skill training is excluded, then VA can only pay at the 70 percent level.

The Yellow Ribbon G.I. Bill Education Enhancement Program
This program may assist eligible individuals with payment of their tuition and fees in instances where costs exceed the in-state tuition charges at a public institution or the national maximum payable at private and foreign institutions. To be eligible, the student must be: a Veteran receiving benefits at the 100-percent benefit rate payable,

Active Duty Service	Maximum Benefit
At least 36 months	100 percent
At least 30 continuous days and discharged due to service-connected disability	100 percent
At least 30 months < 36 months (1)	90 percent
At least 24 months < 30 months (1)	80 percent
At least 18 months < 24 months (2)	70 percent
At least 12 months < 18 months (2)	60 percent
At least 6 months < 12 months (2)	50 percent
At least 90 days < 6 months (2)	40 Percent

(1) Includes service on active duty in entry level and skill training. (2) Excludes service on active duty in entry level and skill training. (3) If the individual would only qualify at the 70 percent level when service on active duty in entry level and skill training is excluded, then VA can only pay at the 70 percent level.

a transfer-of-entitlement-eligible dependent child, or a transfer-of-entitlement-eligible spouse of a Veteran.

The school of attendance must have accepted VA's invitation to participate in the program, state how much student tuition will be waived (up to 50 percent) and how many participants will be accepted into the program during the current academic year. VA will match the school's percentage (up to 50 percent) to reduce or eliminate out-of-pocket costs for eligible participants.

Transfer of Entitlement
DoD may offer members of the armed forces on or after Aug. 1, 2009, the opportunity to transfer benefits to a spouse or dependent children. DoD and the military services must approve all requests for this benefit. Members of the armed forces approved for transfer of entitlement may only transfer any unused portion of their Post-9/11 GI Bill benefits while a member of the armed forces, subject to their period of eligibility.

Marine Gunnery Sergeant John David Fry Scholarship
This scholarship entitles children of those who die in the line of duty on or after Sept. 11, 2001, to use Post-9/11 GI Bill benefits.

Eligible children:
 • Are entitled to 36 months of benefits at the 100 percent level,

- Have 15 years to use the benefit beginning on their 18th birthday,
- May use the benefit until their 33rd birthday, and
- Are not eligible for the Yellow Ribbon Program.

VetSuccess on Campus

This is designed to provide on-campus benefits assistance and readjustment counseling to assist Veterans in completing their college educations and entering the labor market in viable careers. Under this program, a full-time, experienced Vocational Rehabilitation Counselor and a part-time Vet Center Outreach Coordinator are assigned at each campus to provide VA benefits outreach, support, and assistance to ensure their health, educational, and benefit needs are met.

Montgomery GI Bill

Eligibility

VA educational benefits may be used while the Servicemember is on active duty or after the Servicemember's separation from active duty with a fully honorable military discharge. Discharges "under honorable conditions" and "general" discharges do not establish eligibility.

Eligibility generally expires 10 years after the Servicemember's discharge. However, there are exceptions for disability, re-entering active duty, and upgraded discharges. All participants must have a high school diploma, equivalency certificate, or have completed 12 hours toward a college degree before applying for benefits.

Previously, Servicemembers had to meet the high school requirement before they completed their initial active duty obligation. Those who did not may now meet the requirement and reapply for benefits. If eligible, they must use their benefits within 10 years from the date of last discharge from active duty.

Additionally, every Veteran must establish eligibility under one of four categories.

Category 1: Service after June 30, 1985
For Veterans who entered active duty for the first time after June 30, 1985, did not decline MGIB in writing, and had their military pay reduced by $100 a month for 12 months. Servicemembers can apply after completing two continuous years of service. Veterans

must have completed three continuous years of active duty, or two continuous years of active duty if they first signed up for less than three years or have an obligation to serve four years in the Selected Reserve (the 2x4 program) and enter the Selected Reserve within one year of discharge.

Servicemembers or Veterans who received a commission as a result of graduation from a service academy or completion of an ROTC scholarship are not eligible under Category 1 unless they received their commission:

• After becoming eligible for MGIB benefits (including completing the minimum service requirements for the initial period of active duty), or

• After Sept. 30, 1996, and received less than $3,400 during any one year under ROTC scholarship.

Servicemembers or Veterans who declined MGIB because they received repayment from the military for education loans are also ineligible under Category 1. If they did not decline MGIB and received loan repayments, the months served to repay the loans will be deducted from their entitlement.

Early Separation from Military Service: Servicemembers who did not complete the required period of military service may be eligible under Category 1 if discharged for one of the following:

1. Convenience of the government – with 30 continuous months of service for an obligation of three or more years, or 20 continuous months of service for an obligation of less than three years,
2. Service-connected disability,
3. Hardship,
4. A medical condition diagnosed prior to joining the military,
5. A condition that interfered with performance of duty and did not result from misconduct,
6. A reduction in force (in most cases)
7. Sole Survivorship (if discharged after 9/11/01).

Category 2: Vietnam Era GI Bill Conversion
For Veterans who had remaining entitlement under the Vietnam Era GI Bill on Dec. 31, 1989, and served on active duty for any number of days during the period Oct. 19, 1984, to June. 30, 1985, for at least three continuous years beginning on July 1, 1985; or at least

two continuous years of active duty beginning on July 1, 1985, followed by four years in the Selected Reserve beginning within one year of release from active duty. Veterans not on active duty on Oct. 19, 1984, may be eligible under Category 2 if they served three continuous years on active duty beginning on or after July 1, 1985, or two continuous years of active duty at any time followed by four continuous years in the Selected Reserve beginning within one year of release from active duty.

Veterans are barred from eligibility under Category 2 if they received a commission after Dec. 31, 1976, as a result of graduation from a service academy or completion of an ROTC scholarship.
However, such a commission is not disqualifying if they received the commission after becoming eligible for MGIB benefits, or received the commission after Sept. 30, 1996, and received less than $3,400 during any one year under ROTC scholarship.

Category 3: Involuntary Separation/Special Separation
For Veterans who meet one of the following requirements:

1. Elected MGIB before being involuntarily separated, or
2. Were voluntarily separated under the Voluntary Separation Incentive or the Special Separation Benefit program, elected MGIB benefits before being separated, and had military pay reduced by $1,200 before discharge.

Category 4: Veterans Educational Assistance Program
For Veterans who participated in the Veterans Educational Assistance Program (VEAP) and:

1. Served on active duty on Oct. 9, 1996.
2. Participated in VEAP and contributed money to an account.
3. Elected MGIB by Oct. 9, 1997, and paid $1,200.

Veterans who participated in VEAP on or before Oct. 9, 1996, may also be eligible even if they did not deposit money in a VEAP account if they served on active duty from Oct. 9, 1996, through April 1, 2000, elected MGIB by Oct. 31, 2001, and contributed $2,700 to MGIB.

Certain National Guard Servicemembers may also qualify under Category 4 if they:

1.　Served for the first time on full-time active duty in the National Guard between June 30, 1985, and Nov. 29, 1989, and had no previous active duty service.
2.　Elected MGIB during the nine-month window ending on July 9, 1997; and
3.　Paid $1,200.

Payments
Effective Oct. 1, 2013, the rate for full-time training in college, technical or vocational school is $1,648 a month for those who served three years or more or two years plus four years in the Selected Reserve. For those who served less than three years, the monthly rate is $1,339.

Benefits are reduced for part-time training. Payments for other types of training follow different rules. VA will pay an additional amount, called a "kicker" or "college fund," if directed by DoD. Visit www. benefits.va.gov/gibill for more information. The maximum number of months Veterans can receive payments is 36 months at the full-time rate or the part-time equivalent.

The following groups qualify for the maximum
Veterans who served the required length of active duty, Veterans with an obligation of three years or more who were separated early for the convenience of the government and served 30 continuous months, and Veterans with an obligation of less than three years who were separated early for the convenience of the government and served 20 continuous months.

Types of Training Available:
- Courses at colleges and universities leading to associate, bachelor or graduate degrees, including accredited independent study offered through distance education.
- Courses leading to a certificate or diploma from business, technical or vocational schools.
- Apprenticeship or on-the-job training for those not on active duty, including self-employment training begun on or after June 16, 2004, for ownership or operation of a franchise.
- Correspondence courses, under certain conditions.
- Flight training, if the Veteran holds a private pilot's license upon beginning the training and meets the medical requirements.
- State-approved teacher certification programs.

- Preparatory courses necessary for admission to a college or graduate school.
- License and certification tests approved for Veterans.
- Entrepreneurship training courses to create or expand small businesses.
- Tuition assistance using MGIB as "Top-Up" (active duty Servicemembers).

Accelerated payments for certain high-cost programs are authorized.

Work-Study Program

Participants who train at the three-quarter or full-time rate may be eligible for a work-study program in which they work for VA and receive hourly wages. Students under the work-study program must be supervised by a VA employee, and all duties performed must relate to VA. The types of work allowed include:

- The preparation and processing of necessary papers and other documents at educational institutions
- Any activity at a VA facility
- Any activity at Department of Defense, Coast Guard, or National Guard facilities relating to the administration of Chapters 1606 or 1607 of Title 10 U.S.C.
- Any activity of a State Veterans agency related to providing assistance to Veterans in obtaining any benefit under Title 38, U.S.C. or the laws of the State
- A position working in a Center for Excellence for Veteran Student Success, as established under 20 U.S.C. 1161t, which purpose is to support and coordinate academic, financial, physical, and social needs of Veteran students
- A position working in a cooperative program carried out jointly by VA and an Institution of Higher Learning
- Any Veterans-related position in an institution of higher learning, such as:
Assisting with dissemination of general information regarding Veteran benefits and/or services
    * providing assistance to Veteran students with general inquiries about Veteran benefits via phone, email, or in person; or
    * Maintaining and organizing Veteran-related files

Veterans' Educational Assistance Program

Eligibility
Active duty personnel could participate in the Veterans' Educational Assistance Program (VEAP) if they entered active duty for the first time after Dec. 31, 1976, and before July 1, 1985, and made a contribution prior to Apr. 1, 1987.

The maximum contribution is $2,700. Active duty participants may make a lump-sum contribution to their VEAP account. For more information, visit www. www.benefits.va.gov/gibill/.

Servicemembers who participated in VEAP are eligible to receive benefits while on active duty if:

1. At least three months of contributions are available, except for high school or elementary, in which only one month is needed.
2. And they enlisted for the first time after Sept. 7, 1980, and completed 24 months of their first period of active duty.

Servicemembers must receive a discharge under conditions other than dishonorable for the qualifying period of service. Servicemembers who enlisted for the first time after Sept. 7, 1980, or entered active duty as an officer or enlistee after Oct. 16, 1981, must have completed 24 continuous months of active duty, unless they meet a qualifying exception.

Eligibility generally expires 10 years from release from active duty, but can be extended under special circumstances.

Payments
DoD will match contributions at the rate of $2 for every $1 put into the fund and may make additional contributions, or "kickers," as necessary. For training in college, vocational or technical schools, the payment amount depends on the type and hours of training pursued. The maximum amount is $300 a month for full-time training.

Training, Work-Study, Counseling
VEAP participants may receive the same training, work-study benefits and counseling as provided under the MGIB with the exception of preparatory courses.

Chapter 6

Home Loan Guaranty

VA home loan guaranties are issued to help eligible Servicemembers, Veterans, Reservists, National Guard members, and certain surviving spouses obtain homes, condominiums, and manufactured homes, and to refinance loans. For additional information or to obtain VA loan guaranty forms, visit http://www.benefits.va.gov/homeloans/.

Loan Uses

A VA guaranty helps protect lenders from loss if the borrower fails to repay the loan. It can be used to obtain a loan to:

1. Buy or build a home.
2. Buy a residential condominium unit.
3. Repair, alter, or improve a residence owned by the Veteran and occupied as a home.
4. Refinance an existing home loan.
5. Buy a manufactured home and/or lot.
6. Install a solar heating or cooling system or other energy-efficient improvements.

Eligibility

In addition to the periods of eligibility and conditions of service requirements, applicants must have a good credit rating, sufficient income, a valid Certificate of Eligibility (COE), and agree to live in the property in order to be approved by a lender for a VA home loan. Lenders can apply for a COE online through the Veterans Information Portal (https://vip.vba.va.gov/portal/VBAH/Home).   Active duty Servicemembers and Veterans can also apply online at http://www.ebenefits.va.gov. Although it's preferable to apply electronically, it is possible to apply for a COE using VA Form 26-1880, Request for Certificate of Eligibility.

In applying for a hard-copy COE from VA Eligibility Center using VA Form 26-1880, it is typically necessary that the eligible Veteran present a copy of his/her report of discharge or DD Form 214, Certificate of Release or Discharge from Active Duty, or other adequate substitute evidence to VA. An eligible active duty Servicemember should obtain and submit a statement of service signed by an appropriate military official to the VA Eligibility Center. A completed VA Form 26-1880 and any associated documentation should be mailed to Atlanta Regional Loan Center, Attn: COE (262), P.O. Box 100034, Decatur, GA 30031.Please note that while VA's electronic applications can establish eligibility and issue an online COE in a matter of seconds, not all cases can be processed online. The system can only process those cases for which VA has sufficient data in its records. If a COE cannot be issued immediately, users have the option of submitting an electronic application.

Periods of Eligibility:

World War II
(1) Active duty service after Sept.15, 1940, and prior to July 26, 1947; (2) discharge under other than dishonorable conditions; and (3) at least 90 days total service unless discharged early for a service-connected disability.

Post-World War II period
(1) Active duty service after July 25, 1947, and prior to June 27, 1950; (2) discharge under other than dishonorable conditions; and (3) 181 days continuous active duty service unless discharged early for a service-connected disability.

Korean War
(1) Active duty after June 26, 1950, and prior to Feb. 1, 1955; (2) discharge under other than dishonorable conditions; and (3) at least 90 days total service, unless discharged early for a service-connected disability.

Post-Korean War period
(1) Active duty after Jan. 31, 1955, and prior to Aug. 5, 1964; (2) discharge under other than dishonorable conditions; (3) 181 days continuous service, unless discharged early for a service-connected disability.

Vietnam War
(1) Active duty after Aug. 4, 1964, and prior to May 8, 1975; (2) discharge under other than dishonorable conditions; and (3) 90 days to-

tal service, unless discharged early for a service-connected disability. For Veterans who served in the Republic of Vietnam, the beginning date is Feb. 28,1961.

Post-Vietnam period

(1) Active duty after May 7, 1975, and prior to Aug. 2, 1990; (2) active duty for 181 continuous days, all of which occurred after May 7, 1975; and (3) discharge under conditions other than dishonorable or early discharge for service-connected disability.
24-Month Rule

If service was between Sept. 8, 1980, (Oct. 16, 1981, for officers) and Aug. 1, 1990, Veterans must generally complete 24 months of continuous active duty service or the full period (at least 181 days) for which they were called or ordered to active duty, and be discharged under conditions other than dishonorable.

Exceptions are allowed if the Veteran completed at least 181 days of active duty service but was discharged earlier than 24 months for (1) hardship, (2) the convenience of the government, (3) reduction-in-force, (4) certain medical conditions, or (5) service-connected disability.

Gulf War

Veterans of the Gulf War era – Aug. 2, 1990, to a date to be determined – must generally complete 24 months of continuous active duty service or the full period (at least 90 days) for which they were called to active duty, and be discharged under other than dishonorable conditions.

Exceptions are allowed if the Veteran completed at least 90 days of active duty but was discharged earlier than 24 months for (1) hardship, (2) the convenience of the government, (3) reduction-in-force, (4) certain medical conditions, or (5) service-connected disability. Reservists and National Guard members are eligible if they were activated after Aug. 1, 1990, and completed the full period for which they were called to active duty, served at least 90 days, and were discharged under other than dishonorable conditions.

Active Duty Personnel

Until the Gulf War era is ended, persons on active duty are eligible after serving 90 continuous days.

Eligibility for Reserves and/or Guard (not activated)
Members of the Reserves and National Guard who are not otherwise eligible for loan guaranty benefits are eligible upon completing
6 years of service in the Reserves or Guard (unless released earlier
due to a service-connected disability). The applicant must have
received an honorable (a general or under honorable conditions is
not qualifying) discharge from such service unless he or she is either
in an inactive status awaiting final discharge, or still serving in the
Reserves or Guard.

Surviving Spouses: Some spouses of Veterans may have home
loan eligibility. They are:

- the unmarried surviving spouse of a Veteran who died as a result
  of service or service-connected causes,
- the surviving spouse of a Veteran who dies on active duty or
  from service-connected causes, who remarries on or after
  attaining age 57 and on or after Dec. 16, 2003, and
- the spouse of an active duty member who is listed as missing in
  action (MIA) or a prisoner of war (POW) for at least 90 days.

Eligibility under this MIA/POW provision is limited to one-time use
only.

Surviving spouses of Veterans who died from nonservice-connected
causes may also be eligible if any of the following conditions are met:
The Veteran was rated totally service-connected disabled for 10
years or more immediately preceding death, or was rated totally disabled for not less than five years from date of discharge or release
from active duty to date of death, or was a former prisoner of war
who died after Sept. 30, 1999, and was rated totally service-connected disabled for not less than one year immediately preceding death.

Under the Home Loan Guaranty Program, VA does not make loans
to Veterans and Servicemembers; VA guarantees loans made by
private-sector lenders. The guaranty amount is what VA could pay a
lender should the loan go to foreclosure.

It is important to note that VA does not impose a maximum loan
amount that a Veteran may borrow to purchase a home; instead, the
law directs the maximum amount that VA may guarantee on a home
loan. Because most VA loans are pooled in mortgage securities that

require a 25 percent guaranty, the effective no-downpayment loan limit on VA loans tends to be four times VA's maximum guaranty amount. Loans for more than the effective no-downpayment loan limit generally require downpayments. Then, VA's effective no-downpayment loan limits are established annually, and vary, depending on the size of the loan and the location of the property. are established annually, and vary, depending on the size of the loan and the location of the property.

An eligible borrower can use a VA-guaranteed Interest Rate Reduction Refinancing Loan to refinance an existing VA loan to lower the interest rate and payment. Typically, no credit underwriting is required for this type of loan. The loan may include the entire outstanding balance of the prior loan, the costs of energy-efficient improvements, as well as closing costs, including up to two discount points.

An eligible borrower who wishes to obtain a VA-guaranteed loan to purchase a manufactured home or lot can borrow up to 95 percent of the home's purchase price. The amount VA will guarantee on a manufactured home loan is 40 percent of the loan amount or the Veteran's available entitlement, up to a maximum amount of $20,000. These provisions apply only to a manufactured home that will not be placed on a permanent foundation.

VA Appraisals
No loan can be guaranteed by VA without first being appraised by a VA-assigned fee appraiser. A lender can request a VA appraisal through VA systems. The Veteran borrower typically pays for the appraisal upon completion, according to a fee schedule approved by VA. This VA appraisal estimates value of the property. It is not an inspection and does not guarantee the house is free of defects. VA guarantees the loan, not the condition of the property. A thorough inspection of the property by a reputable inspection firm may help minimize any problems that could arise after loan closing. In an existing home, particular attention should be given to plumbing, heating, electrical, and roofing components.

Closing Costs
For purchase home loans, payment in cash is required on all closing costs, including title search and recording fees, hazard insurance premiums and prepaid taxes. For refinancing loans, all such costs may be included in the loan, as long as the total loan does not

2014 VA Funding Fee Rates

Loan Category	Active Duty and Veterans	Reservists and National Guard
Loans for purchase or construction with downpayments of less than 5 percent, refinancing, and home improvement	2.15 percent	2.40 percent
Loans for purchase or construction with downpayments of at least 5 percent but less than 10 percent	1.50 percent	1.75 percent
Loans for purchase or construction with downpayments of 10 percent or more	1.25 percent	1.50 percent
Loans for manufactured homes	1 percent	1 percent
Interest rate reduction refinancing loans	.50 percent	.50 percent
Assumption of a VA-guaranteed loan	.50 percent	.50 percent
Second or subsequent use of entitlement with no downpayment	3.3 percent	3.3 percent

exceed the reasonable value of the property. Interest rate reduction loans may include closing costs, including a maximum of two discount points.

VA Funding Fees
A funding fee must be paid to VA unless the Veteran is exempt from such a fee. The fee may be paid in cash or included in the loan.

Closing costs such as VA appraisal, credit report, loan processing fee, title search, title insurance, recording fees, transfer taxes, survey charges, or hazard insurance may not be included for purchase home loans.

All Veterans, except those who are specified by law as exempt, are charged a VA funding fee (See chart above). Currently, exemptions from the funding fee are provided for those Veterans and Service-members receiving VA disability compensation, those who are rated by VA as eligible to receive compensation as a result of pre-discharge disability examination and rating, and those who would be in receipt of compensation, but who were recalled to active duty or reenlisted and are receiving active-duty pay in lieu of compensation. Additionally, unmarried surviving spouses in receipt of Dependency and Indemnity Compensation may be exempt from the funding fee. For all types of loans, the loan amount may include this funding fee.

VA funding fee and up to $6,000 of energy-efficient improvements can be included in VA loans. However, no other fees, charges, or discount points may be included in the loan amount for regular purchase or construction loans. For refinancing loans, most closing costs may be included in the loan amount.

Required Occupancy

To qualify for a VA home loan, a Veteran or the spouse of an active-duty Servicemember must certify that he or she intends to occupy the home. A dependent child of an active-duty Servicemember also satisfies the occupancy requirement. When refinancing a VA-guaranteed loan solely to reduce the interest rate, a Veteran need only certify to prior occupancy.

Financing, Interest Rates and Terms

Veterans obtain VA-guaranteed loans through the usual lending institutions, including banks, credit unions, and mortgage brokers. VA-guaranteed loans can have either a fixed interest rate or an adjustable rate, where the interest rate may adjust up to one percent annually and up to five percent over the life of the loan. VA does not set the interest rate. Interest rates are negotiable between the lender and borrower on all loan types.

Veterans may also choose a different type of adjustable rate mort-gage called a hybrid ARM, where the initial interest rate remains fixed for three to 10 years. If the rate remains fixed for less than five years, the rate adjustment cannot be more than one percent annually and five percent over the life of the loan. For a hybrid ARM with an initial fixed period of five years or more, the initial adjustment may be up to two percent. The Secretary has the authority to determine annual adjustments thereafter.

Currently annual adjustments may be up to two percentage points and six percent over the life of the loan. If the lender charges discount points on the loan, the Veteran may negotiate with the seller as to who will pay points or if they will be split between buyer and seller. Points paid by the Veteran may not be included in the loan (with the exception that up to two points may be included in interest rate reduction refinancing loans). The term of the loan may be for as long as 30 years and 32 days.

Loan Assumption Requirements and Liability
VA loans made on or after March 1, 1988, are not assumable without the prior approval of VA or its authorized agent (usually the lender collecting the monthly payments). To approve the assumption, the lender must ensure that the purchaser is a satisfactory credit risk and will assume all of the Veteran's liabilities on the loan. If approved, the purchaser will have to pay a funding fee that the lender sends to VA, and the Veteran will be released from liability to the federal government.

Loans made prior to Mar. 1, 1988, are generally freely assumable, but Veterans should still request the lender's approval in order to be released of liability. Veterans whose loans were closed after Dec. 31, 1989, usually have no liability to the government following a foreclosure, except in cases involving fraud, misrepresentation, or bad faith, such as allowing an unapproved assumption. However, for the entitlement to be restored, any loss suffered by VA must be paid in full.

A release of liability does not mean that a Veteran's guaranty entitlement is restored. That occurs only if the borrower is an eligible Veteran who agrees to substitute his or her entitlement for that of the seller. If a Veteran allows assumption of a loan without prior approval, then the lender may demand immediate and full payment of the loan, and the Veteran may be liable if the loan is foreclosed and VA has to pay a claim under the loan guaranty.

VA Assistance to Veterans in Default

VA urges all Veterans who are encountering problems making their mortgage payments to speak with their servicers as soon as possible to explore options to avoid foreclosure. Contrary to popular opinion, servicers do not want to foreclose because foreclosure costs money. Depending on a Veteran's specific situation, servicers may offer any of the following options to avoid foreclosure:

- Repayment Plan – The borrower makes a regular installment each month plus part of the missed installments.
- Special Forbearance – The servicer agrees not to initiate foreclosure to allow time for borrowers to repay the missed installments. An example of when this would be likely is when a borrower is waiting for a tax refund.
- Loan Modification– Provides the borrower a fresh start by adding the delinquency to the loan balance and establishing a new payment schedule.
- Additional time to arrange a private sale – The servicer agrees to delay foreclosure to allow a sale to close if the loan will be paid off.
- Short Sale – When the servicer agrees to allow a borrower to sell his/her home for a lesser amount than what is currently required to pay off the loan.
- Deed-in-Lieu of Foreclosure – The borrower voluntarily agrees to deed the property to the servicer instead of going through a lengthy foreclosure process.

Servicemembers Civil Relief Act

Veteran borrowers may be able to request relief pursuant to the Servicemembers Civil Relief Act (SCRA). In order to qualify for certain protections available under the Act, their obligation must have originated prior to their current period of active military service. SCRA may provide a lower interest rate during military service and for up to one year after service ends, provide forbearance, or prevent foreclosure or eviction up to nine months from period of military service.

Assistance to Veterans with VA-Guaranteed Home Loans

When a VA-guaranteed home loan becomes delinquent, VA may provide supplemental servicing assistance to help cure the default. The servicer has the primary responsibility of servicing the loan to resolve the default.

However, in cases where the servicer is unable to help the Veteran borrower, VA has loan technicians in eight Regional Loan Centers and a special servicing center in Hawaii who take an active role in interceding with the mortgage servicer to explore all options to avoid foreclosure. Veterans with VA-guaranteed home loans can call 1-877-827-3702 to reach the nearest VA office where loan specialists are prepared to discuss potential ways to help save the loan.

VA Acquired Property Sales

VA acquires properties as a result of foreclosures of VA-guaranteed and VA-owned loans. A private contractor is currently marketing the acquired properties through listing agents using local Multiple Listing Services. A listing of "VA Properties for Sale" may be found at http://listings.vrmco.com/. Contact a real estate agent for information on purchasing a VA-acquired property.

Preventing Veteran Homelessness

Veterans who feel they may be facing homelessness as a result of losing their home can call 1-877-4AID VET (877-424-3838) or go to http://www.va.gov/HOMELESS/index.asp to receive assistance from VA.

Assistance to Veterans with Non-VA Guaranteed Home Loans

For Veterans or Servicemembers who have a non-VA-guaranteed or sub-prime loan, VA has a network of eight Regional Loan Centers and a special servicing centers in Hawaii that can offer advice and guidance. Borrowers may visit www.benefits.va.gov/homeloans/, or call toll free -1-877-827-3702 to speak with a VA loan technician. However, unlike when a Veteran has a VA-guaranteed home loan, VA does not have the authority to intervene on the borrower's behalf. It is imperative that a borrower contact his/her servicer as quickly as possible.

VA Refinancing of a Non-VA Guaranteed Home Loan

Veterans with non-VA guaranteed home loans now have new options for refinancing to a VA-guaranteed home loan. These new options are available as a result of the Veterans' Benefits Improvement Act of 2008. Veterans who wish to refinance their subprime or conventional mortgage may now do so for up to 100 percent of value of the property.

Additionally, Congress raised VA's maximum loan guaranty for these types of refinancing loans. Loan limits were effectively raised from

$144,000 to $417,000. High-cost counties have even higher maximum loan limits. VA county loan limits can be found at http://www.benefits.va.gov/homeloans/. These changes will allow more qualified Veterans to refinance through VA, allowing for savings on interest costs and avoiding foreclosure.

Other Assistance for Delinquent Veteran Borrowers

If VA is not able to help a Veteran borrower retain his/her home (whether a VA-guaranteed loan or not), the Department of Housing and Urban Development (HUD) offers assistance to homeowners by sponsoring local housing counseling agencies. To find an approved agency in your area, please search online at http://www.hud.gov/offices/hsg/sfh/hcc/hcs.cfm, or call HUD's interactive voice system at (800) 569-4287.

Loans for Native American Veterans

Eligible Native American Veterans can obtain a loan from VA to purchase, construct, or improve a home on federal Trust Land, or to reduce the interest rate on such a VA loan. Native American Direct Loans are only available if a memorandum of understanding exists between the tribal organization and VA.

Veterans who are not Native American, but who are married to Native American non-Veterans, may be eligible for a direct loan under this program. To be eligible for such a loan, the qualified non-Native American Veteran and the Native American spouse must reside on federal Trust Land, both the Veteran and spouse must have a meaningful interest in the dwelling or lot, and the tribal authority which has jurisdiction over the Trust Land must recognize the non-Native American Veteran as subject to its authority.

Safeguards

The following safeguards have been established to protect Veterans:
1. VA may suspend from the loan program those who take unfair advantage of Veterans or discriminate because of race, color, religion, sex, disability, family status, or national origin.
2. The builder of a new home (or new manufactured home) is required to give the purchasing Veteran either a one-year warranty or a 10-year insurance-backed protection plan.
3. The Veteran obtaining a loan may only be charged closing costs allowed by VA.

4.   The Veteran can prepay without penalty the entire loan or any part not less than one installment or $100.
5.   VA encourages holders to extend forbearance if a Veteran becomes temporarily unable to meet the terms of the loan.

Chapter 7

VA Life Insurance

For complete details on government life insurance, visit www. benefits.va.gov/insurance/ or call VA's Insurance Center toll-free at 1-800-669-8477. Specialists are available between the hours of 8:30 a.m. and 6 p.m., Eastern Time, to discuss premium payments, insurance dividends, address changes, policy loans, naming beneficiaries, reporting the death of the insured, and other insurance issues.

If the insurance policy number is not known, provide whatever information is available, such as the Veteran's VA file number, date of birth, Social Security number, military serial number or military service branch and dates of service. To provide the information by mail, send it to:

Department of Veterans Affairs
Insurance Center
PO Box 42954
Philadelphia, PA 19101

For information about Servicemembers' Group Life Insurance, Veterans' Group Life Insurance, Servicemembers' Group Life Insurance Traumatic Injury Protection, or Servicemembers' Group Life Insurance Family Coverage, visit the Website above or call the Office of Servicemembers' Group Life Insurance directly at 1-800-419-1473.

Servicemembers' Group Life Insurance (SGLI)
The following are automatically insured for $400,000 under SGLI:

1. Active duty members of the Army, Navy, Air Force, Marines and Coast Guard.
2. Commissioned members of the National Oceanic and Atmospheric Administration (NOAA) and the Public Health Service (PHS).
3. Cadets or midshipmen of the U.S. military academies.
4. Members, cadets and midshipmen of the ROTC while

engaged in authorized training and practice cruises.

5. Members of the Ready Reserves/National Guard who are scheduled to perform at least 12 periods of inactive training per year.
6. Members who volunteer for a mobilization category in the Individual Ready Reserve.

Individuals may elect in writing to be covered for a lesser amount or to decline coverage. SGLI coverage is available in $50,000 increments up to the maximum of $400,000.

Full-time Servicemembers on active duty are covered 24/7, 365 days of the year. Coverage is in effect during the period of active duty or inactive duty training and for 120 days following separation or release from duty. Reservists or National Guard members who have been assigned to a unit in which they are scheduled to perform at least 12 periods of inactive duty that is creditable for retirement purposes are also covered 24/7, 365 days of the year and for 120 days following separation or release from duty.

Part-time coverage is provided for Reservists or National Guard members who do not qualify for the full-time coverage described above. Part-time coverage generally applies to Reservists/National Guard members who drill only a few days in a year. These individuals are covered only while on active duty or active duty for training, or traveling to and from such duty. Members covered part-time do not receive 120 days of free coverage after separation unless they incur or aggravate a disability during a period of duty

SGLI Traumatic Injury Protection (TSGLI)
Members of the armed services serve our nation heroically during times of great need, but what happens when they experience great needs of their own because they have sustained a traumatic injury? TSGLI provides for payment traumatically injured Servicemembers who have suffered certain physical losses. The TSGLI benefit ranges between $25,000 and $100,000 depending on the loss,. TSGLI helps Servicemembers by allowing their families to be with them during their recovery or by helping with other expenses incurred during their recovery period.

TSGLI is attached to SGLI. An additional $1.00 is added to the Servicemember's SGLI premium to cover TSGLI. After Dec. 1, 2005, all Servicemembers who are covered by SGLI are automatically also covered by TSGLI. TSGLI cannot be declined unless the Service-member also declines basic SGLI. TSGLI claims are adjudicated by the individual military branches of service.

In addition, there is retroactive TSGLI coverage for Servicemembers who sustained a qualifying loss between Oct. 7, 2001, and Nov. 30, 2005, regardless of where it occurred TSGLI coverage is payable to these Servicemembers regardless of whether they had SGLI cover-age in force at the time of their injury.

For more information and branch of service contact information, visit http://benefits.va.gov/insurance/tsgli.asp, or call 1-800-237-1336 (Army); 1-800-368-3202 (Navy); 1-877-216-0825 (Marine Corps); 1-800-433-0048 (Active Duty Air Force); 1-800-525-0102 (Air Force Reserves); 1-240-612-9140 (Air National Guard); 1-703-872-6647 (U.S. Coast Guard); 1-301-427-3280 (PHS); or 1-301-713-3444 (NOAA).

Servicemembers' Group Life Insurance Family Coverage (FS-GLI): coverage consists of spousal coverage and dependent child coverage. FSGLI provides up to $100,000 of life insurance coverage for spouses of Servicemembers with full-time SGLI coverage, not to exceed the amount of SGLI the member has in force. Premiums for spouse coverage are based on the age of the spouse and the amount of FSGLI coverage. FSGLI is a Servicemembers' benefit; the member pays the premium and is the only person allowed to be the beneficiary of the coverage. FSGLI spousal coverage ends 120 days after any of the following events: 1) the Servicemember elects in writing to terminate coverage on the spouse; 2) the Servicemember elects to terminate his or her own SGLI coverage; 3) the Service-member dies; 4) the Servicemember separates from service; or 5) the Servicemember is divorced from the spouse. The insured spouse may convert his or her FSGLI coverage to a permanent policy of-fered by participating private insurers within 120 days of the date of any of the termination events noted above. FSGLI dependent cover-age of $10,000 is also automatically provided for dependent children of Servicemembers insured under SGLI, with no premium required.

Veterans' Group Life Insurance (VGLI)
SGLI may be converted to VGLI, which provides renewable term coverage to:

1.   Veterans who had full-time SGLI coverage upon separation from active duty or the Reserves.
2.   Members of the Ready Reserves/National Guard with part-time SGLI coverage who incur a disability or aggravate a pre-existing disability during a period of active duty or a period of inactive duty for less than 31 days that renders them uninsurable at standard premium rates.
3.   Members of the Individual Ready Reserve and Inactive National Guard.

Servicemembers must apply for VGLI within one year and 120 days from separation. Servicemembers discharged on or after November 1, 2012, who apply for VGLI within 240 days of separation do not need to submit evidence of good health, while Servicemembers who apply after the 240-day period must submit evidence of insurability. The initial VGLI coverage available is equal to the amount of SGLI coverage at the time of separation from service.

Effective April 11, 2011, VGLI insureds who are under age 60 and have less than $400,000 in coverage can purchase up to $25,000 of additional coverage on each five-year anniversary of their coverage, up to the maximum $400,000. No medical underwriting is required for the additional coverage.

SGLI Disability Extension
Servicemembers who are totally disabled at the time of separation (unable to work or have certain statutory conditions), can apply for the SGLI Disability Extension, which provides free coverage for up to two years from the date of separation. To apply, Servicmembers must complete and return SGLV 8715, the SGLI Disability Extension Application.

Those covered under the SGLI Disability Extension are automatically converted to VGLI at the end of their extension period, subject to the payment of premiums. VGLI is convertible at any time to a permanent plan policy with any participating commercial insurance company.

Accelerated Death Benefits
Like many private life insurance companies, the SGLI, FSGLI and VGLI programs offer an accelerated benefits option to terminally ill insured members. An insured member is considered to be terminally

ill if he or she has a written medical prognosis of nine months or less to live. All terminally ill members are eligible to receive up to 50 percent of their SGLI or VGLI coverage, and terminally ill spouses can receive up to 50 percent of their FSGLI, in a lump sum. Payment of an accelerated benefit reduces the amount payable to the beneficiaries at the time of the insured's death. To apply, an insured member must submit SGLV 8284, Servicemember/Veteran Accelerated Benefit Option Form, and spouses must complete SGLV 8284A, Servicemember Family Coverage Accelerated Benefits Option Form.

Service-Disabled Veterans' Insurance (S-DVI)

Veterans who separated from service on or after Apr. 25, 1951, under other than dishonorable conditions who have service-connected disabilities, even zero percent, but are otherwise in good health, may apply to VA for up to $10,000 in life insurance coverage under the S-DVI program. Applications must be submitted within two years from the date of being notified of the approval of a new service-connected disability by VA.

Veterans who are totally disabled may apply for a waiver of premiums. If approved for waiver of premiums, the Veteran can apply for additional supplemental insurance coverage of up to $30,000. However, premiums cannot be waived on the additional supplemental insurance. To be eligible for this type of supplemental insurance, Veterans must meet all of the following three requirements:

1.   Be under age 65.
2.   Be eligible for a waiver of premiums due to total disability.
3.   Apply for additional insurance within one year from the date of notification of waiver approval on the basic S-DVI policy.

Veterans' Mortgage Life Insurance (VMLI)

VMLI is mortgage protection insurance available to severely disabled Veterans who have been approved by VA for a Specially Adapted Housing (SAH) Grant. Maximum coverage is the smaller of the existing mortgage balance or $200,000, and is payable only to the mortgage company. Protection is issued automatically following SAH approval, provided the Veteran submits mortgage information required to establish a premium and does not decline coverage. Coverage automatically terminates when the mortgage is paid off. If a mortgage is disposed of through sale of the property, VMLI may be obtained on the mortgage of another home.

Other Insurance Information
The following information applies only to policies issued to World War II, Korean-era, and Vietnam-era Veterans and any Service-Disabled Veterans' Insurance policies. Policies in this group are prefixed by the letters K, V, RS, W, J, JR, JS, or RH.

Insurance Dividends Issued Annually: World War II and Korean-era Veterans with active policies beginning with the letters V, RS, W, J, JR, JS, or K earn tax-free dividends annually on the policy anniversary date. (Policies prefixed by RH do not earn dividends.) Policyholders do not need to apply for dividends, but may select from among the following dividend options:
1. **Cash:** The dividend is paid directly to the insured by direct deposit to a bank account or by check.
2. **Paid-Up Additional Insurance:** The dividend is used to purchase additional insurance coverage.
3. **Credit or Deposit:** The dividend is held in an account for the policyholder with interest. Withdrawals from the account can be made at any time. The interest rate may be adjusted.
4. **Net Premium Billing Options:** These options use the dividend to pay the annual policy premium. If the dividend exceeds the premium, the policyholder has options to choose how the remainder is used. If the dividend is not enough to pay an annual premium, the policyholder is billed the balance.
5. **Other Dividend Options:** Dividends can also be used to repay a loan or pay premiums in advance.

Reinstating Lapsed Insurance
Lapsed term policies may be reinstated within five years from the date of lapse. A five-year term policy that is not lapsed at the end of the term is automatically renewed for an additional five years. Lapsed permanent plans may be reinstated within certain time limits and with certain health requirements. Reinstated permanent plan policies require repayment of all back premiums, plus interest.

Converting Term Policies
Term policies are renewed automatically every five years, with premiums increasing at each renewal. Premiums do not increase after age 70. Term policies may be converted to permanent plans, which have fixed premiums for life and earn cash and loan values.

Dividends on Capped Term Policies

Effective Sept. 2000, VA provides either a cash dividend or paid-up insurance on term policies whose premiums have been capped. Veterans with National Service Life Insurance (NSLI) term insurance that has renewed at age 71 or older and who stop paying premiums on their policies will be given a "termination dividend." This dividend can either be received as a cash payment or used to purchase a reduced amount of paid-up insurance, which insures the Veteran for life with no premium payments required. The amount of the reduced paid-up insurance remains level. This does not apply to S-DVI (RH) policies.

Borrowing on Policies

Policyholders with permanent plan policies may borrow up to 94 percent of the cash surrender value of their insurance after the insurance is in force for one year or more. Interest is compounded annually. The loan interest rate is variable and may be obtained by calling toll-free 1-800-669-8477.

Chapter 8
Burial and Memorial Benefits

Veterans discharged from active duty under conditions other than dishonorable; Service members who die while on active duty, active duty for training, or inactive duty training; and spouses and depen dent children of Veterans and active duty service members, may be eligible for VA burial and memorial benefits. (For the purposes of this chapter, the term "Veteran" includes eligible persons who die during active duty service.) The Veteran does not have to die before a spouse or dependent child can be eligible for burial or memorial benefits.

Burial in VA National Cemeteries
Burial in a VA national cemetery is available for eligible Veterans, spouses and dependents at no cost and includes the gravesite, grave-liner, opening and closing of the grave, a headstone or marker, and perpetual care as part of a national shrine. For Veterans, ben efits may also include a burial flag and military funeral honors.

With certain exceptions, active duty service beginning after Sept 7, 1980, as an enlisted person, and after Oct 16, 1981, as an officer, must be for a minimum of 24 consecutive months or the full period of active duty (as in the case of reservists or National Guard members called to active duty for a limited duration). Active duty for training, by itself, while serving in the reserves or National Guard, is not suf ficient to confer eligibility. Reservists and National Guard members, as well as their spouses and dependent children, are eligible if they were entitled to retired pay at the time of death, or would have been upon reaching requisite age.

Certain otherwise eligible individuals found to have committed fed eral or state capital crimes or certain sex offenses are barred from burial in a VA national cemetery and from receipt of a Government-furnished headstone, marker, medallion, burial flag, and Presidential Memorial Certificate. Veterans and other claimants for VA burial benefits have the right to appeal decisions made by VA regarding eligibility for national cemetery burial or other memorial benefits. Chapter 13 discusses the procedures for appealing VA claims. This chapter contains information on the full range of VA burial and memorial benefits. Readers with questions may contact the nearest national cemetery, listed by state in VA Facilities section of this book, call1-800-827-1000, or visit the website at www.cem.va.gov/.

Surviving spouses of Veterans who died on or after Jan. 1, 2000, do not lose eligibility for burial in a national cemetery if they remarry. Unmarried dependent children of Veterans who are under 21 years of age, or under 23 years of age if a full-time student at an approved educational institution, are eligible for burial. Unmarried adult children who become physically or mentally disabled and incapable of self-support before age 21, or age 23 if a full-time student may also be eligible.

Certain parents of Servicemembers who die as a result of hostile activity or from combat training-related injuries may be eligible for burial in a national cemetery with their child. The biological or adopt ed parents of a servicemember who died in combat or while perform ing training in preparation for a combat mission, who leaves no sur viving spouse or dependent child, may be buried with the deceased servicemember if there is available space. Eligibility is limited to servicemembers who died on or after Oct. 7, 2001, and biological or adoptive parents who died on or after Oct. 13, 2010.

The next of kin or authorized representative (e.g., funeral director) makes interment arrangements at time of need by contacting the National Cemetery Scheduling Office (see information available at http://www.cem.va.gov/bbene/need.asp) or, in some cases, the na tional cemetery in which burial is desired. VA normally does not con duct burials on weekends. Gravesites cannot be reserved; however, VA will honor reservations made before 1973 by the Department of the Army.

VA's National Cemetery Scheduling Office or local national cemetery directors verify eligibility for burial. A copy of the Veteran's discharge document that specifies the period(s) of active duty and character of service is usually sufficient to determine eligibility. A copy of the deceased's death certificate and proof of relationship to the Veteran (for eligible family members) may be required.

VA operates 131 national cemeteries, of which 72 are currently open for both new casket and cremation interments and 18 may accept new interment of cremated remains only. Burial options are limited to those available at a specific cemetery and may include in ground casket, or interment of cremated remains in a columbarium, in-ground, or in a scattering area. Contact the national cemetery directly, or visit our website at http://www.cem.va.gov to determine if a particular cemetery is open for new burials, and what other options are available.

Headstones, Markers and Medallions Veterans, active duty service members, and retired Reservists and National Guard service members, are eligible for an inscribed headstone or marker for their unmarked grave at any cemetery- national, state veterans, tribal, or private. VA will deliver a headstone or marker at no cost, anywhere in the world.

For eligible Veterans or service members buried in a private ceme tery whose deaths occurred on or after Nov. 1, 1990, VA may furnish a government headstone or marker (even if the grave is already marked with a private one); or VA may furnish a medallion to affix to an already existing privately-purchased headstone or marker.

Spouses and dependent children are eligible for a government head stone or marker only if they are buried in a national or State Veterans cemetery.

Flat markers are available in bronze, granite or marble. Upright headstones come in granite or marble. The style provided will be consistent with existing monuments at the place of burial. Niche markers are available to mark columbaria used for inurnment of cremated remains. Medallions are made of bronze and are available in three sizes: 5-inch, 3-inch, and 1 1/2 inches. Headstones, mark ers and medallions previously furnished by the government may be replaced at the government's expense if badly deteriorated, illegible, vandalized or stolen.

Headstones or markers for VA national cemeteries will be ordered by the cemetery director using information provided by the next of kin or authorized representative. Headstones or Markers for private cemeteries: Before ordering, the next of kin or authorized representative should check with the cemetery to ensure that the Government-furnished headstone or marker will be accepted. All installation fees at private cemeteries are the responsibility of the applicant.

To submit a claim for a head stone or marker for a gravesite in a private cemetery, use VA Form 40-1330, Application for Standard Government Headstone or Marker (available at http://www.va.gov/vaforms/. A copy of the Veteran's military discharge document is required. Mail forms to Memorial Pro grams Service, Department of Veterans Affairs, 5109 Russell Road, Quantico, VA 22134-3903. The form and supporting documents may also be faxed toll free to 1-800-455-7143.

"In Memory Of" Markers: VA provides memorial headstones and markers with "In Memory Of" as the first line of inscription for those whose remains have not been recovered or identified, were buried at sea, donated to science or cremated and scattered. Eligibility is the same as for regular headstones and markers. There is no fee when the "In Memory Of" marker is placed in a national cemetery. All installation fees at private cemeteries are the responsibility of the ap plicant. Memorial headstones/markers for spouses and dependents can be provided only for placement in a national or state Veterans cemetery.

Inscriptions: Headstones and markers must be inscribed with the name of the deceased, branch of service, and year of birth and death. They also may be inscribed with other optional information, including an emblem of belief and, space permitting, additional text including military rank; war service such as "World War II;" complete dates of birth and death; military awards; military organizations; civilian or Veteran affiliations; and personalized words of endearment.

Medallion in lieu of government headstone or marker for private cemeteries: For Veterans or service members whose death occurred on or after Nov. 1, 1990, VA is authorized to provide a me dallion instead of a headstone or marker if the grave is in a private cemetery and already marked with a privately-purchased headstone or marker.

To submit a claim for a medallion to be affixed to a private headstone/marker in a private cemetery, use VA Form 40-1330M, Claim for Government Medallion (available at http://www.va.gov/vaforms). A copy of the Veteran's military discharge document is required. Mail forms to Memorial Programs Service, Department of Veterans Affairs, 5109 Russell Road, Quantico, VA 22134-3903. The form and supporting documents may also be faxed toll free to 1-800-455-7143.

To check the status of a claim for a headstone or marker for place
ment in a national, state, or tribal Veterans cemetery, please call the
cemetery. To check the status of one being placed in a private
cemetery, please contact the Applicant Assistance Unit at 1-800-697-
6947 or via email at mps.headstones@va.gov.

Other Memorialization

Presidential Memorial Certificates are issued to recognize the military service of honorably discharged deceased Veterans and per
sons who died in the active military, naval, or air service. Next of kin,
relatives and other loved ones may apply for a certificate by mailing,
or faxing a completed and signed VA Form 40-0247, Presidential
Memorial Certificate Request Form (available at http://www.va.gov/
vaforms), along with a copy of the Veteran's military discharge
documents or proof of honorable military service. The processing
of requests sent without supporting documents will be delayed until
eligibility can determined. Eligibility requirements can be found at
http://www.cem.va.gov.

Burial Flags: Generally, VA will furnish a U.S. burial flag to memori
alize Veterans who received other than dishonorable discharge. This
includes certain persons who served in the organized military forces
of the Commonwealth of the Philippines while in service of
the U.S armed forces and who died on or after April 25, 1951. Also
eligible for a burial flag are Veterans who were entitled to retired pay
for service in the Reserve or National Guard, or would have been
entitled if over age 60; and members or former members of the
Selected Reserve who served their initial obligation, or were discharged for a disability incurred or aggravated in the line of duty, or
died while a member of the Selected Reserve. The next of kin may
apply for the flag at any VA Regional Office or U.S. Post Office by
completing VA Form 21-2008, Application for United States Flag for
Burial Purposes (available at http://www.va.gov/vaforms/. In most
cases, a funeral director will help the family obtain the flag.

Reimbursement of Burial Expenses: VA will pay a burial allowance
up to $2,000 if the Veteran's death is service-connected. In such
cases, the person who bore the Veteran's burial expenses may claim
reimbursement from VA.

In some cases, VA will pay the cost of transporting the remains of a
Veteran whose death was service-connected to the nearest national

cemetery with available gravesites. There is no time limit for filing reimbursement claims in service-connected death cases.

Burial Allowance: VA will pay a burial and funeral allowance of up to $2,000 for Veterans who die from service-connected injuries. VA will pay a burial and funeral allowance of up to $300 for Veterans who, at the time of death from nonservice-connected injuries were entitled to receive pension or compensation or would have been entitled if they were not receiving military retirement pay. VA will pay a burial and funeral allowance of up to $734 when the Veteran's death occurs in a VA facility, a VA-contracted nursing home or a state Veterans nursing home. In cases in which the Veteran's death was not service con nected, claims must be filed within two years after burial or crema tion.

Plot Allowance: VA will pay a plot allowance of up to $734 when a Veteran is buried in a cemetery not under U.S. government jurisdiction if: the Veteran was discharged from active duty because of disability incurred or aggravated in the line of duty; the Veteran was receiving compensation or pension or would have been if the Veteran was not receiving military retired pay; or the Veteran died in a VA facility. The plot allowance may be paid to the state for the cost of a plot or interment in a state-owned cemetery reserved solely for Veteran burials if the Veteran is buried without charge. Burial expenses paid by the deceased's employer or a state agency will not be reimbursed.

Veterans Cemeteries Administered by Other Agencies Department of the Army: Administers Arlington National Cemetery and other Army installation cemeteries. Eligibility is generally more re- strictive than at VA national cemeteries. For information, call (703) 607-8000, write Superintendent, Arlington National Cemetery, Arling ton, VA 22211, or visit www.arlingtoncemetery.mil/.

Department of the Interior: Administers two active national cem- eteries- Andersonville National Cemetery in Georgia and Andrew Johnson National Cemetery in Tennessee. Eligibility is similar to VA national cemeteries. For information, call (202) 208-4747, write Department of Interior, National Park Service 1849 C. St. NW, Washing ton, D. C. 20240.

State and Tribal Veterans Cemeteries: There are currently 90 VA grant-funded Veterans cemeteries operating in 45 states and U.S. Territories that offer burial options for Veterans and their families. Two of these cemeteries are operated by federally recognized tribal organizations. VA grant-funded cemeteries have similar eligibility requirements and certain states/tribal organizations may require state or tribal residency/membership. Some services, particularly for family members, may require a fee. Contact the state or tribal Veterans cemetery or the state Veterans Affairs office for information. To locate a state or tribal Veterans cemetery, visit www.cem.va.gov/grants/veterans_cemeteries.asp

Military Funeral Honors: Upon request, DoD will provide military funeral honors consisting of folding and the presentation of the United States flag and the playing of "Taps." A funeral honors detail consists of two or more uniformed members of the armed forces, with at least one member from the deceased's branch of service.

Family members should inform their funeral director if they want military funeral honors. DoD maintains a toll-free number (1-877-M IL HONR) for use by funeral directors only to request honors. VA can help arrange honors for burials at VA national cemeteries. Veteran's service organizations or volunteer groups may help provide honors. For more information, visit www.militaryfuneralhonors.osd.mil/.

Chapter 9

Reserve and National Guard

Eligibility for VA Benefits

Generally, all Reserve and National Guard members discharged or released under conditions that are not dishonorable are eligible for some VA benefits. The length of your service, service commitment and/or your duty status may determine your eligibility for specific benefits.

Eligibility requirements for several VA benefits include a certain length of active service. Active service in the National Guard or Reserve includes:

Active duty (Title 10) - full-time duty in the Armed Forces, such as unit deployment during war, including travel to and from such duty, except active duty for training, OR

Full-time National Guard duty (Title 32) – duty performed for which you are entitled to receive pay from the federal government, such as responding to a national emergency or performing duties as an Active Guard Reserve (AGR) member.

Note: A state or territory's governor may activate National Guard members for State Active Duty, such as in response to a natural or man-made disaster. State Active Duty is based on state law and does not qualify as "active service" for VA benefits. Unlike full-time National Guard duty, National Guard members on State Active Duty are paid with state funds as opposed to federal funds.

Qualifying for VA Health Care

Under the "Combat Veteran" authority, Combat Veterans who were discharged or released from active service on or after Jan. 28, 2003, are eligible for enrollment in Priority Group 6, unless eligible for enrollment in a higher priority group. This authority provides a 5-year enrollment period, which begins on the discharge or separation date. These Combat Veterans are eligible for health care services and community living care for conditions possibly related to their military service, and are not required to disclose their income information unless they would like to be considered for a higher priority status, beneficiary travel benefits, or exemption of co-pays for care unrelated to their military service.

Activated Reservists and members of the National Guard are eligible if they served on active duty in a theater of combat operations after Nov. 11, 1998, and were discharged under other than dishonorable conditions.

Veterans who enroll with VA under this authority will continue to be enrolled even after their enhanced eligibility period ends. At the end of their enhanced eligibility period, Veterans enrolled in Priority Group 6 may be shifted to a lower priority group depending on their income level. For additional information, call 1-877-222-VETS (8387).

OEF/OIF/OND Veterans may be eligible for a one-time dental evaluation and treatment following separation from service, if they did not have a dental exam prior to separation. Veterans must request a dental appointment within the first 180 days post separation from active duty.

Disability Benefits
VA pays monthly compensation benefits for disabilities incurred or aggravated during active duty, or active duty for training for disabilities as a result of injury or disease, or inactive duty training for disabilities due to injury, heart attack, or stroke. Additionally, the discharge must be under other than dishonorable conditions. For additional information see Chapter 2, "Service-connected Disabilities."

Post-9/11 GI Bill
The Post-9/11 GI Bill is an education benefit program for Servicemembers and Veterans who served on active duty after Sept. 10, 2001. Benefits are payable for training pursued on or after Aug. 1, 2009. No payments can be made under this program for training pursued before that date.

To be eligible, the Servicemember or Veteran must serve at least 90 aggregate days on active duty after Sept. 10, 2001, and remain on active duty or be honorably discharged. Active duty includes active service performed by National Guard members under title 32 U.S.C. for the purposes of organizing, administering, recruiting, instructing, or training the National Guard; or under section 502(f) for the purpose of responding to a national emergency.

Eligibility for benefits expires 15 years from the last period of active duty of at least 90 consecutive days. If released for a service-connected disability after at least 30 days of continuous service, eligibility ends 15 years from when the member is released for the service-connected disability. If, on August1, 2009, the Servicemember or Veteran is eligible for the Montgomery GI Bill; the Montgomery GI Bill – Selected Reserve; or the Reserve Educational Assistance Program, and qualifies for the Post-9/11 GI Bill, an irrevocable election must be made to receive benefits under the Post-9/11 GI Bill.

Montgomery GI Bill – Selected Reserve
Members of reserve elements of the Army, Navy, Air Force, Marine Corps and Coast Guard, and members of the Army National Guard and the Air National Guard, may be entitled to up to 36 months of educational benefits under the Montgomery GI Bill (MGIB) – Selected Reserve. To be eligible, the participant must:

1. Have a six-year obligation in the Selected Reserve or National Guard signed after June 30, 1985, or, if an officer, agree to serve six years in addition to the original obligation.
2. Complete initial active duty for training (IADT).
3. Meet the requirement to receive a high school diploma or equivalency certificate before Completing IADT.
4. Remain in good standing in a Selected Reserve or National Guard unit.

Reserve components determine eligibility for benefits. VA does not make decisions about eligibility and cannot make payments until the Reserve component has determined eligibility and notified VA.

Period of Eligibility
Benefits generally end the day a reservist or National Guard member separates from the military. Additionally, if in the Selected Reserve and called to active duty, VA can generally extend the eligibility period by the length of time on active duty plus four months for each period of active duty. Once this extension is granted, it will not be taken away after leaving the Selected Reserve.

Eligible members separated because of unit deactivation, a disability that was not caused by misconduct, or otherwise involuntarily separated during Oct. 1, 1991, through Dec. 31, 2001, have 14 years after their eligibility date to use benefits. Similarly, members involuntarily separated from the Selected Reserve due to a deactivation of their unit between Oct.1, 2007, and Sept. 30, 2014, may receive a 14-year period of eligibility.

Payments
The rate for full-time training effective Oct.1, 2013, is $362.00 a month for 36 months. Part-time benefits are reduced proportionately. For complete current rates, visit www.www.benefits.va.gov/gibill/. DoD may make additional contributions.

Training
Participants may pursue training at a college or university, or take technical training at any approved facility. Training includes undergraduate, graduate, or post-graduate courses; state licensure and certification; courses for a certificate or diploma from business, technical or vocational schools; cooperative training; apprenticeship or on-the-job training; correspondence courses; independent study programs; flight training; entrepreneurship training; remedial, deficiency or refresher courses needed to complete a program of study; or preparatory courses for tests required or used for admission to an institution of higher learning or graduate school.

Accelerated payments for certain high-cost programs are authorized effective Jan.28, 2008

Education and Career Counseling: Refer to Chapter 11, "Transition Assistance," for detailed information on available services.

Reserve Educational Assistance Program (REAP)
This program provides educational assistance to members of National Guard and Reserve components who are called or ordered to active duty service in response to a war or national emergency as declared by the President or Congress. Visit www.benefits.va.gov/gibill/ for more information.

Eligibility
Eligibility is determined by DoD or the Department of Homeland Security. Generally, a Servicemember who serves on active duty on or after Sept.11, 2001, for at least 90 consecutive days, or accumulates a total of three or more of years of service is eligible.

Payments

Reserve or National Guard members whose eligibility is based upon continuous service receive a payment rate based upon their number of continuous days on active duty. Members who qualify after the accumulation of three or more years of aggregate active duty service receive the full payment allowable.

Reserve Educational Assistance Rates

Active Duty Service	Monthly Payment Rate for Full-Time Students
90 days but less than one year	$625.60
One year but less than two years	$938.40
Two or more continuous years	$1,251.20

Training

Participants may pursue training at a college or university, or take technical training at any approved facility. Training includes undergraduate, graduate, or post-graduate courses; state licensure and certification courses; courses for a certificate or diploma from business, technical or vocational schools; cooperative training; apprenticeship or on-the-job training; correspondence courses; independent study programs; flight training; entrepreneurship training; remedial, deficiency, or refresher courses needed to complete a program of study; or preparatory courses for tests required or used for admission to an institution of higher learning or graduate school. Accelerated payments for certain high-cost programs are authorized.

Period of Eligibility

Prior to Jan. 28, 2008, members of the Selected Reserve called to active duty were eligible as long as they continued to serve in the Selected Reserve. They lost eligibility if they went into the Inactive Ready Reserve (IRR). Members of the IRR called to active duty were eligible as long as they stayed in the IRR or Selected Reserve.

Effective Jan. 28, 2008, members who are called up from the Selected Reserve, complete their REAP-qualifying period of active duty service, and then return to the Selected Reserve for the remainder of their service contract, have 10 years to use their benefits after separation.

In addition, members who are called up from the IRR or Inactive National Guard (ING), complete their REAP-qualifying period of active duty service, and then enter the Selected Reserve to complete their service contract, have 10 years to use their benefits after separation.

Education and Career Counseling: Refer to Chapter 101, "Transition Assistance",, for detailed information on available services.

Home Loan Guaranty
National Guard members and reservists are eligible for a VA home loan if they have completed at least six years of honorable service, are mobilized for active duty service for a period of at least 90 days, or are discharged because of a service-connected disability.

Reservists who do not qualify for VA housing loan benefits may be eligible for loans on favorable terms insured by the federal Housing Administration (FHA), which is a part of HUD. Additional information can be found in Chapter 6.

Life Insurance
National Guard members and reservists are eligible to receive SGLI, VGLI, and FSGLI. They may also be eligible for SGLI Traumatic Injury Protection if severely injured and suffering a qualifying loss, Service-Disabled Veterans Insurance if they receive a service-connected disability rating from VA, and Veterans' Mortgage Life Insurance if approved for a Specially Adapted Housing Grant. Complete details can be found in Chapter 7 – "VA Life Insurance."

Burial and Memorial Benefits
VA provides a burial flag to memorialize members or former members of the Selected Reserve who served their initial obligation, or were discharged for a disability incurred or aggravated in the line of duty, or died while a member of the Selected Reserve.

Reservists and National Guard members may be eligible for additional burial benefits if their death was due to an injury or disease that developed during, or was aggravated during, active duty, active duty for training, or inactive duty for training. Burial benefits may include burial in a national cemetery; an inscribed headstone, marker, or medallion; a Presidential Memorial Certificate; and an allowance to partially reimburse burial and funeral costs. Additional information about burial benefits that may be available can be found in Chapter

7 – "Burial and Memorial Benefits".

Re-employment Rights

A person who left a civilian job to enter active duty in the armed forces is entitled to return to the job after discharge or release from active duty if they:

1. Gave advance notice of military service to the employer.
2. Did not exceed five years cumulative absence from the civilian job (with some exceptions).
3. Submitted a timely application for re-employment.
4. Did not receive a dishonorable or other punitive discharge.

The law calls for a returning Veteran to be placed in the job as if he/she had never left, including benefits based on seniority such as pensions, pay increases and promotions. The law also prohibits discrimination in hiring, promotion, or other advantages of employment on the basis of military service. Veterans seeking re-employment should apply, verbally or in writing, to the company's hiring official and keep a record of their application. If problems arise, contact the Department of Labor's Veterans' Employment and Training Service (VETS) in the state of the employer.

Federal employees not properly re-employed may appeal directly to the Merit Systems Protection Board. Non-federal employees may file complaints in U.S. District Court. For information, visit www.dol.gov/vets/programs/userra/main.htm.

Transition Assistance Advisor Program

The Transition Assistance Advisor (TAA) program is a partnership between the National Guard and VA to assist Veterans. The TAA Program, housed within the National Guard (NG) Office of Warrior Support, places an NG/VA trained expert at the NG Headquarters in each of the 50 states as well as PR, GU, VI, and the District of Columbia. The advisor serves as an advocate for Guard members and their families, as well as other geographically dispersed military members and families.

In collaboration with state and local coalition partners, the TAA Program provides VA benefit enrollment assistance, referrals, and assists in facilitating access for Veterans through the overwhelming maze of programs, with the compassion of someone who knows what it is like to transition from the Guard to active duty and then back to civilian status.

Advisors receive annual training from VA experts in VA health care and benefits to assist Guard members and their families with access to VA health care facilities and TRICARE facilities within their network. To find a local Transition Assistance Advisor call 1-877-577-6691 or go to http://www.taapmo.com.

Outreach for OEF/OIF/OND Veterans

VA's OEF/OIF/OND Outreach Teams focus on improving outreach to members of the National Guard and Reserve by engaging them throughout the deployment cycle with targeted messages and face-to-face encounters with VA staff. These outreach teams are located at VAMCs to help ease the transition from military to civilian life. To learn more, visit www.oefoif.va.gov. Veterans can also call the toll-free OEF/OIF/OND Help Line at 1-866-606-8216 for answers to questions about VA benefits, health care, and enrollment procedures.

Air Reserve Personnel Center

The Air Reserve Personnel Center (ARPC) is available to assist with various personnel issues, including requests for personnel records, copies of DD Form 214, or other military documents. Many Veterans file an Air Force Board Correction of Military Records (AFBCMR) or write their Congressman to get these basic issues resolved which requires that the request be routed through appropriate authorities, sometimes taking up to 180 days. Alternately, the ARPC routinely handles these actions on a much quicker basis. Members should call the ARPC for assistance at 1-800-525-0102 or logon to https://gum-crm.csd.disa.mil.

Chapter 10

Special Groups of Veterans

Veterans Needing Fiduciary Services

The fiduciary program provides oversight of VA's most vulnerable beneficiaries who are unable to manage their VA benefits because of injury, disease, the infirmities of advanced age, or being under 18 years of age. VA appoints fiduciaries who manage VA benefits for these beneficiaries and conducts oversight of VA-appointed fiduciaries to ensure that they are meeting the needs of the beneficiaries they serve.

VA closely monitors fiduciaries for compliance with program responsibilities to ensure that VA benefits are being used for the purpose of meeting the needs, security, and comfort of beneficiaries and their dependents. In deciding who should act as fiduciary for a beneficiary, VA will always select the most effective and least restrictive fiduciary arrangement.

This means that VA will first consider whether the beneficiary can manage his/her VA benefits with limited supervision. VA will consider the choice of the beneficiary as well as any family, friends and caregivers who are qualified and willing to provide fiduciary services for the beneficiary without a fee.

As a last resort, VA will consider appointment of a paid fiduciary. For more information about VA's fiduciary program, please visit our website at http://benefits.va.gov/fiduciary/index.asp.

Homeless Veterans

VA's homeless programs constitute the largest integrated network of homeless assistance programs in the country, offering a wide array of services to help Veterans recover from homelessness and live as self-sufficiently and independently as possible.

VA Health Care for Homeless Veterans (HCHV) Program provides a gateway to VA and community supportive services for eligible Veterans. Through the HCHV Program, Veterans are provided with case management and residential treatment in the community. The program also conducts outreach to homeless Veterans who are not likely to come to VA facilities on their own.

Homeless Veterans Supported Employment Program (HVSEP)
provides vocational assistance, job development and placement, and
ongoing employment supports designed to improve employment out-
comes among homeless Veterans. HVSEP is coordinated between
CWT and the continuum of Homeless Veterans Programs for the
purpose of providing community-based vocational and employment
services. All of the HVSEP vocational rehabilitation specialists (VRS)
hired to provide employment services for the program consists of
homeless, formerly homeless, or at risk of homelessness Veterans.
For more information, please visit: http://www.va.gov/homeless/em-
ployment_programs.asp

The National Call Center for Homeless Veterans (NCCHV) assists
homeless Veterans, at-risk Veterans, their families, and other interested parties with linkages to appropriate VA and community-based
resources. The call center provides trained VA staff members 24
hours a day, seven days a week to assess a caller's needs and connect them to appropriate resources. The call center can be accessed
by dialing 1-877-4AID VET (1-877-424-3838). NCCHV Chat services are also available through the National Call Center's website
at www.va.gov/HOMELESS. NCCHV Chat enables Veterans, their
families and friends to go on-line where they can anonymously chat
with an information and referral specialist by visiting the www.va.gov/
HOMELESS webpage, clicking on the Help for Homeless Veteran
badge, and then the Chat Online tab on the right side of the webpage.

VA's Homeless Providers Grant and Per Diem Program provides
funds to non-profit community agencies providing transitional housing (up to 24 months) and/or offering services to homeless Veterans,
such as case management, education, crisis intervention, counseling, and services targeted towards specialized populations including
homeless women Veterans. The goal of the program is to help homeless Veterans achieve residential stability, increase their skill levels
and/or income, and obtain greater self-determination. For more
information, please visit: http://www.va.gov/homeless/gpd.asp

**The Housing and Urban Development-Veterans Affairs Support-
ive Housing** (HUD-VASH) Program provides permanent housing
aand case management for eligible homeless Veterans who need

community-based support to keep stable housing. This program allows eligible Veterans to live in Veteran-selected housing units with a "Housing Choice" voucher. These vouchers are portable to support the Veteran's choice of housing in communities served by their VA medical facility where case management services can be provided. HUD-VASH services include outreach and case management to ensure integration of services and continuity of care. This program enhances the ability of VA to serve homeless women Veterans, and homeless Veterans with families. For more information, please visit: http//www.va.gov/homeless/hud-vash.asp

The Supportive Services for Veterans Families (SSVF) Program is designed to rapidly re-house homeless Veteran families and prevent homelessness for those at imminent risk due to a housing crisis. Funds are granted to private non-profit organizations and consumer cooperatives that will assist very low-income Veteran families by providing a range of supportive services designed to promote housing stability. To meet this goal, grantees (private non-profit organizations and consumer cooperatives) provide eligible Veteran families with outreach, case management, and assistance in obtaining VA and other benefits, which may include: health care services; daily living services; personal financial planning services ; transportation services; fiduciary and payee services; legal services; child care services; and housing counseling services .

In addition, grantees also provide time-limited payments to third parties (e.g., landlords, utility companies, moving companies, and licensed child care providers) if these payments help Veterans' families stay in or acquire permanent housing on a sustainable basis. To locate a SSVF provider in your community, please visit http://www.va.gov/homeless/ssvf.asp and look for the list of current year SSVF providers or call VA's National call Center for Homeless Veterans at 1-888-4AIDVET (1-888-424-3838).

In VA's Compensated Work Therapy/Transitional Residence (CWT/TR) Program, disadvantaged, at-risk, and homeless Veterans live in CWT/TR community-based supervised group homes while working for pay in VA's CWT Program. While in this program, they learn new job skills, relearn successful work habits, and regain a sense of self-esteem and self-worth.

The Veterans Justice Outreach Program (VJO) offers outreach and case management to Veteran involved in law enforcement encounters, overseen by treatment courts, and incarcerated in local jails who may be at risk for homelessness upon their release.

The **Health Care for Re-Entry Veterans** (HCRV) Program offers outreach, referrals, and short-term case management assistance for incarcerated Veterans who may be at risk for homelessness upon their release. Visit www.va.gov/homeless/ to locate an outreach worker

For more information on VA homeless programs and services, Veterans currently enrolled in VA health care can speak with their VA mental health or health care provider. Other Veterans and interested parties can find a complete list of VA health care facilities at www.va.gov, or they can call VA's general information hotline at 1-800-827-1000. If assistance is needed when contacting a VA facility, ask to speak to the Health Care for Homeless Veterans Program or the Mental Health service manager. Information is also available on VA Homeless program website at www.va.gov/homeless.

Filipino Veterans

World War II era Filipino Veterans are eligible for certain VA benefits. Generally, Old Philippine Scouts are eligible for VA benefits in the same manner as U.S. Veterans. Commonwealth Army Veterans, including certain organized Filipino guerrilla forces and New Philippine Scouts residing in the United States who are citizens or lawfully admitted for permanent residence, are also eligible for VA health care in the United States on the same basis as U.S. Veterans.

Certain Commonwealth Army Veterans and new Philippine Scouts may be eligible for disability compensation and burial benefits. Other Veterans of recognized guerrilla groups also may be eligible for certain VA benefits. Survivors of World War II era Filipino Veterans may be eligible for dependency and indemnity compensation. Eligibility and the rates of benefits vary based on the recipient's citizenship and place of residence. Call 1-800-827-1000 for additional information.

VA Benefits for Veterans Living Overseas

VA monetary benefits, including disability compensation, pension, educational benefits, and burial allowances, are generally payable overseas. Some programs are restricted. Home loan guaranties are available only in the United States and selected U.S. territories and possessions. Educational benefits are limited to approved, degree-granting programs in institutions of higher learning. Beneficiaries living in foreign countries should contact the nearest American embassy or consulate for help. In Canada, contact an office of Veterans Affairs Canada. For information, visit http://www.vba.va.gov/bln/21/Foreign/index.htm.

World War II Era Merchant Marine Seamen
Certain Merchant Marine seamen who served in World War II may qualify for Veterans benefits. When applying for medical care, Merchant Marine seamen must present their discharge certificate from the Department of Defense. Call 1-800-827-1000 for help obtaining a certificate.

Allied Veterans Who Served During WWI or WWII
VA may provide medical care to certain Veterans of nations allied or associated with the United States during World War I or World War II if authorized and reimbursed by the foreign government. VA also may provide hospitalization, outpatient care, and domiciliary care to former members of the armed forces of Czechoslovakia or Poland who fought in World War I or World War II in armed conflict against an enemy of the United States if they have been U.S. citizens for at least 10 years.

World War Service by Particular Groups
A number of groups who provided military-related service to the United States can receive VA benefits. A discharge by the Secretary of Defense is needed to qualify. Service in the following groups has been certified as active military service for benefits purposes:
1. Women Air Force Service Pilots (WASPs).
2. World War I Signal Corps Female Telephone Operators Unit.
3. World War I Engineer Field Clerks.
4. Women's Army Auxiliary Corps (WAAC).
5. Quartermaster Corps female clerical employees serving with the American Expeditionary Forces in World War I.
6. Civilian employees of Pacific naval air bases who actively participated in defense of Wake Island during World War II.
7. Reconstruction aides and dietitians in World War I.
8. Male civilian ferry pilots.
9. Wake Island defenders from Guam.
10. Civilian personnel assigned to OSS secret intelligence.
11. Guam Combat Patrol.
12. Quartermaster Corps members of the Keswick crew on Corregi-

dor during World War II.

13. U.S. civilians who participated in the defense of Bataan.

14. U.S. merchant seamen on block ships in support of Operation Mulberry in the World War II invasion of Normandy.

15. American merchant marines in oceangoing service during World War II.

16. Civilian Navy IFF radar technicians who served in combat areas of the Pacific during World War II.

17. U.S. civilians of the American Field Service who served overseas in World War I.

18. U.S. civilians of the American Field Service who served overseas under U.S. armies and U.S. army groups in World War II.

19. U.S. civilian employees of American Airlines who served overseas in a contract with the Air Transport Command between Dec. 14, 1941, and Aug. 14, 1945.

20. Civilian crewmen of U.S. Coast and Geodetic Survey vessels who served in areas of immediate military hazard while conducting cooperative operations with and for the U.S. armed forces between Dec. 7, 1941, and Aug. 15, 1945. Qualifying vessels are: the Derickson, Explorer, Gilber, Hilgard, E. Lester Jones, Lydonia Patton, Surveyor, Wainwright, Westdahl, Oceanographer, Hydrographer and Pathfinder.

21. Members of the American Volunteer Group (Flying Tigers) who served between Dec. 7, 1941, and July 18, 1942.

22. U.S. civilian flight crew and aviation ground support employees of United Air Lines who served overseas in a contract with Air Transport Command between Dec. 14, 1941, and Aug. 14, 1945.

23. U.S. civilian flight crew, including pursers, and aviation ground support employees of Transcontinental, and Western Air, Inc. who served overseas in a contract with the Air Transport Command between Dec. 14, 1941, and Aug. 14, 1945.

24. U.S. civilian flight crew and aviation ground support employees of Consolidated Vultee Aircraft Corp. who served overseas in a contract with Air Transport Command between Dec. 14, 1941, and Aug. 14, 1945.

25. U.S. civilian flight crew and aviation ground support employees of Pan American World Airways and its subsidiaries and affiliates, who served overseas in a contract with the Air Transport Command and Naval Air Transport Service between Dec. 14, 1941, and Aug. 14, 1945.

26. Honorably discharged members of the American Volunteer Guard, Eritrea Service Command, between June 21, 1942, and Mar.

31, 1943.

27. U.S. civilian flight crew and aviation ground support employees of Northwest Airlines who served overseas under the airline's contract with Air Transport Command from Dec. 14, 1941, through Aug. 14, 1945.

28. U.S. civilian female employees of the U.S. Army Nurse Corps who served in the defense of Bataan and Corregidor between Jan. 2, 1942, and Feb. 3, 1945.

29. U.S. flight crew and aviation ground support employees of Northeast Airlines Atlantic Division, who served overseas as a result of Northeast Airlines' contract with the Air Transport Command from Dec. 7, 1941, through Aug. 14, 1945.

30. U.S. civilian flight crew and aviation ground support employees of Braniff Airways, who served overseas in the North Atlantic or under the jurisdiction of the North Atlantic Wing, Air Transport Command, as a result of a contract with the Air Transport Command between Feb. 26, 1945, and Aug. 14, 1945.

31. Chamorro and Carolina former native police who received military training in the Donnal area of central Saipan and were placed under command of Lt. Casino of the 6th Provisional Military Police Battalion to accompany U.S. Marines on active, combat patrol from Aug. 19, 1945, to Sept. 2, 1945.

32. Three scouts/guides, Miguel Tenorio, Penedicto Taisacan, and Cristino Dela Cruz, who assisted the United States Marines in the offensive operations against the Japanese on the Northern Mariana Islands from June 19, 1944, through Sept. 2, 1945.

33. The operational Analysis Group of the Office of Scientific Research and Development, Office of Emergency Management, which served overseas with the U.S. Army Air Corps from Dec. 7, 1941, through Aug. 15, 1945.

34. Service as a member of the Alaska Territorial Guard during World War II or any individual who was honorably discharged under section 8147 of the Department of Defense Appropriations Act of 2001.

Incarcerated Veterans
VA benefits are affected if a beneficiary is convicted of a felony and imprisoned for more than 60 days. Disability or death pension paid to an incarcerated beneficiary must be discontinued. Disability compensation paid to an incarcerated Veteran rated 20 percent or more disabled is limited to the 10 percent rate. For a Veteran whose disability rating is 10 percent, the payment is reduced to half of the rate payable to a Veteran evaluated as 10 percent disabled.

Any amounts not paid to the Veteran while incarcerated may be apportioned to eligible dependents. Payments are not reduced for participants in work-release programs, residing in halfway houses, or under community control. Failure to notify VA of a Veteran's incarceration can result in overpayment of benefits and the subsequent loss of all VA financial benefits until the overpayment is recovered. VA benefits will not be provided to any Veteran or dependent wanted for an outstanding felony warrant.

The **Health Care for Reentry Veterans Program (HCRV)** offers outreach to Veterans incarcerated in state and federal prisons, and referrals and short-term case management assistance upon release from prison. he Veterans Justice Outreach Program (VJO) offers outreach and case management to Veterans involved in law enforcement encounters, overseen by treatment courts, and incarcerated in local jails. Visit www.va.gov/homeless/ to locate an outreach worker.

The Veterans Justice Outreach (VJO) Program offers outreach and linkage to needed treatment and services to Veterans involved in law enforcement encounters, seen in the court system, and/or incarcerated in local jails who may be at risk for homelessness upon their release. Visit http://www.va.gov/HOMELESS/VJO.asp to locate a Veterans Justice Outreach Specialist.

The Health Care for Re-Entry Veterans (HCRV) Program offers outreach, linkage to needed treatment and services, and short-term case management assistance for Veterans incarcerated in state or federal prison who may be at risk for homelessness upon their release. Visit http://www.va.gov/HOMELESS/Reentry.asp to locate a Reentry Specialist.

Chapter 11
Transition Assistance

Joint Transition Assistance
The Departments of Veterans Affairs, Defense, and Labor re-launched a new and improved website for wounded warriors – the National Resource Directory (NRD). This directory (www.nrd.gov) provides access to thousands of services and resources at the national, state and local levels to support recovery, rehabilitation and community reintegration. The NRD is a comprehensive online tool available nationwide for wounded, ill and injured Servicemembers, Veterans and their families. The NRD includes extensive information for Veterans seeking resources on VA benefits such as disability benefits, pensions for Veterans and their families, VA health care insurance and the GI Bill. The NRD's design and interface is simple, easy-to-navigate and intended to answer the needs of a broad audience of users within the military, Veteran and caregiver communities.

Transition from Military to VA
VA has personnel stationed at major military hospitals to help seriously injured Servicemembers returning from Operations Enduring Freedom, Iraqi Freedom, and New Dawn (OEF/OIF/OND) as they transition from military to civilian life. OEF/OIF/OND Servicemembers who have questions about VA benefits or need assistance in filing a VA claim or accessing services can contact the nearest VA office or call 1-800-827-1000.

eBenefits
The eBenefits portal (www.ebenefits.va.gov) provides Servicemembers, Veterans, their families, and caregivers with self-service access to benefit applications, benefits information, and access to personal information such as official military personnel file documents. The portal provides two main services: 1. it catalogs links to information on other websites about military and Veteran benefits, 2. and it provides a personalized workspace called My Dashboard, which gives quick access to all the online tools currently integrated into eBenefits.

Transition Assistance Program
This consists of comprehensive workshops at military installations designed to assist Servicemembers as they transition from military

to civilian life. The program includes job search, employment and training information, as well as VA benefits information for Service-members who are within 18 months of separation or retirement. VA Benefit Briefings are comprised of two briefings focusing on edu-cation, benefits, and VA health care and disability compensation. Servicemembers can sign up for one-on-one appointments with a VA representative. Interested Servicemembers should contact their local TAP Manager to sign up for this program.

VOW to Hire Heroes Act
Improving the Transition Assistance Program (TAP): The VOW to Hire Heroes Act of 2011 ("the Act") made TAP, including attendance at VA Benefit Briefings, mandatory for most Servicemembers tran-sitioning to civilian status, upgraded career counseling options, and tailored TAP for the 21st Century job market.

Facilitating Seamless Transition
The Act allows Servicemembers to begin the federal employment process prior to separation or retirement from military service. This allows a truly seamless transition from the military to jobs at VA, De-partment of Homeland Security, and the many other federal agencies seeking to hire Veterans.

Expanding Education and Training
The Act provides nearly 100,000 unemployed Veterans of past eras and wars with up to one year of assistance (equal to the full-time payment rate under the Montgomery GI Bill-Active Duty program) to qualify for jobs in high-demand sectors. It also provides disabled Veterans up to one year of additional Vocational Rehabilitation and Employment benefits.

Translating Military Skills and Training
The Act requires the Department of Labor take a hard look at military skills and training equivalencies that are transferrable to the civilian sector, and make it easier to obtain licenses and certifications.

Veterans Tax Credits
The Act provides tax credits for hiring Veterans and disabled Veter-ans who are out of work

The inTransition
Servicemembers and Veterans may receive assistance from the in-

Transition Program when they are receiving mental health treatment and are making transitions from military service, location or a health care system. This program provides access to transitional support, motivation, and healthy lifestyle assistance and advice from qualified coaches through the toll-free telephone number 1-800-424-7877. For more information about the inTransition Program, please log onto www.health.mil/inTransition.

Pre-Discharge Program
The Pre-Discharge Program is a joint VA and DoD program that affords Servicemembers the opportunity to file claims for disability compensation and other benefits up to 180 days prior to separation or retirement. The two primary components of the Pre-Discharge Program, Benefits Delivery at Discharge (BDD) and Quick Start, may be utilized by separating and retiring Servicemembers on active duty, including members of the Coast Guard, and members of the National Guard and Reserves (activated under Titles 10 or 32) in CONUS and some overseas locations. BDD is offered to accelerate receipt of VA disability benefits after release or discharge from active duty.

To participate in the BDD program, Servicemembers must:
1. Have at least 60 days, but not more than 180 days, remaining on active duty.
2. Have a known date of separation or retirement.
3. Provide VA with a complete copy of service treatment records for the current period of service.
4. Be available to complete all necessary examinations prior to leaving the point of separation.

Quick Start is offered to Servicemembers who have less than 60 days remaining on active duty or are unable to complete the necessary examinations prior to leaving the point of separation.

To participate in the Quick Start Program, Servicemembers must:
1. Have at least one day remaining on active duty.
2. Have a known date of separation or retirement.
3. Provide VA with a complete copy of service treatment records, for the current period of service.

Servicemembers should contact the local Transition Assistance Office or Army Career Alumni Program Center to schedule appointments to attend VA benefits briefings and learn how to initiate a pre-discharge claim. Servicemembers can obtain more information by calling VA toll-free at 1-800-827-1000 or by visiting www.vba.va.gov/predischarge.

Integrated Disability Evaluation System (IDES)

The Integrated Disability Evaluation System (IDES) is a joint VA and DoD program designed to improve the process for Servicemembers who face potential medical discharges. IDES participants are referred into the program by the respective service departments when an injury or disability calls into question the member's ability to continue serving.

IDES promotes efficiency and consistency by utilizing a single set of disability examinations and a single disability rating. Examinations and ratings completed in IDES meet the requirements of both VA and DoD and are used by both Departments in their respective disability determinations.

IDES serves to provide timely, accurate and fair determinations regarding Servicemembers' fitness for continued military service and entitlement to military disability benefits, as well as entitlement to VA Compensation. Further, since processing is initiated while the Servicemember is still serving on active duty, IDES allows the expeditious payment of VA benefits following the member's separation from service.

Federal Recovery Coordination Program

The Federal Recovery Coordination Program (FRCP), a joint program of DoD and VA, helps coordinate and access federal, state and local programs, benefits and services for seriously wounded, ill, and injured Servicemembers, and their families through recovery, rehabilitation, and reintegration into the community.

Federal Recovery Coordinators (FRCs) have the delegated authority for oversight and coordination of the clinical and non-clinical care identified in each client's Federal Individual Recovery Plan (FIRP). Working with a variety of case managers, FRCs assist their clients in reaching their FIRP goals. FRCs remain with their clients as long as they are needed regardless of the client's location, duty or health status. In doing so, they often serve as the central point of contact and provide transition support for their clients.

Military Services Provide Pre-Separation Counseling

Servicemembers may receive pre-separation counseling 24 months prior to retirement or 12 months prior to separation from active duty. These sessions present information on education, training, employment assistance, National Guard and Reserve programs, medical benefits, and financial assistance.

Verification of Military Experience and Training (VMET)

The VMET Document, DD Form 2586, helps Servicemembers verify previous experience and training to potential employers, negotiate credits at schools, and obtain certificates or licenses. VMET documents are available only through each military branch's support office and are intended for Servicemembers who have at least six months of active service. Servicemembers should obtain VMET documents from their Transition Support Office within 12 months of separation or 24 months of retirement.

Transition Bulletin Board

To find business opportunities, a calendar of transition seminars, job fairs, information on Veterans associations, transition services, training and education opportunities, as well as other announcements visit www.turbotap.org

DoD Transportal

To find locations and phone numbers of all Transition Assistance Offices as well as mini-courses on conducting successful job-search campaigns, writing resumes, using the internet to find a job, and links to job search and recruiting Websites, visit the DoD Transportal at www.Veteranprograms.com/index.html

Education and Career Counseling

The Vocational Rehabilitation and Employment (VR&E) Program provides education and career counseling services to Servicemembers, Veterans, and certain dependents (U.S.C. Title 38, Section 3697) at no charge. These services provide an opportunity for transitioning Servicemembers and Veterans to receive personalized counseling and support to guide their careers, ensure the most effective use of VA benefits, and achieve their goals. Services include assisting the Servicemember or Veteran with:
• **Career Choice**: Understand the best career options based on interests and capabilities;
• **Benefits Coaching:** Guidance on the effective use of VA benefits

and other resources available to assist in achieving education and career goals; and
• **Personalized Support:** Academic or adjustment counseling and personalized support to help remove any barriers to success.

Eligibility: Education and career counseling services are available during the period the individual is on active duty with the armed forces and within 180 days of the estimated date of his or her discharge or release from active duty. The projected discharge must be under conditions other than dishonorable.

Servicemembers are eligible even if they are only considering whether or not they will continue as members of the armed forces. Veterans are eligible if not more than one year has elapsed since the date they were last discharged or released from active duty.

Servicemembers, Veterans, Survivors and dependents who are eligible for VA education benefits may receive education and career counseling at any time during their eligibility period. This service is based on having eligibility for a VA program such as Chapter 30 (Montgomery GI Bill); Chapter 31 (Vocational Rehabilitation and Employment); Chapter 32 (Veterans Education Assistance Program – VEAP); Chapter 33 (Post-9/11 GI Bill); Chapter 35 (Dependents' Educational Assistance Program) for certain spouses and dependent children; Chapter 18 (Spina Bifida Program) for certain dependent children; and Chapter 1606 and 1607 of Title 10.

Servicemembers, Veterans, Survivors and dependents may apply for counseling services using VA Form 28-8832, Application for Counseling. Veterans and Servicemembers may also write a letter expressing a desire for counseling services.

Upon receipt of either type of request for counseling from an eligible individual, an appointment for counseling will be scheduled. Counseling services are provided to eligible persons at no charge.

Veterans' Workforce Investment Program
Recently separated Veterans and those with service-connected disabilities, significant barriers to employment, or who served on active duty during a period in which a campaign or expedition badge was authorized, can contact the nearest state employment office for employment help through the Veterans Workforce Investment Program.

The program may be conducted through state or local public agencies, community organizations or private, nonprofit organizations.

State Employment Services
Veterans can find employment information, education and training opportunities, job counseling, job search workshops, and resume preparation assistance at state Workforce Career or One-Stop Centers. These offices also have specialists to help disabled Veterans find employment.

Unemployment Compensation
Veterans who do not begin civilian employment immediately after leaving military service may receive weekly unemployment compensation for a limited time. The amount and duration of payments are determined by individual states. Apply by contacting the nearest state employment office listed in the local telephone directory.

Veterans Preference for Federal Jobs
Since the time of the Civil War, Veterans of the U.S. armed forces have been given some degree of preference in appointments to federal jobs. Veterans' preference in its present form comes from the Veterans' Preference Act of 1944, as amended, and now codified in Title 5, United States Code (U.S.C.). By law, Veterans who are disabled or who served on active duty in the U.S. armed forces during certain specified time periods or in military campaigns are entitled to preference over others when hiring from competitive lists of eligible candidates, and also in retention during a reduction in force (RIF).

To receive preference, a Veteran must have been discharged or released from active duty in the U.S. armed forces under honorable conditions (honorable or general discharge). Preference is also provided for certain widows and widowers of deceased Veterans who died in service, spouses of service-connected disabled Veterans, and mothers of Veterans who died under honorable conditions on active duty or have permanent and total service-connected disabilities. For each of these preferences, there are specific criteria that must be met in order to be eligible to receive the Veterans' preference.

Recent changes in Title 5 clarify Veterans preference eligibility criteria for National Guard and Reserve members. Veterans eligible for preference include Reservists and National Guard members who served on active duty as defined by Title 38 at any time in the armed forces for a period of more than 180 consecutive days, any part of which occurred during the period beginning on Sept. 11, 2001, and ending on the date prescribed by Presidential proclamation or by law as the last date of OEF/OIF/OND. Reservists and National Guardsmen must have been discharged or released from active duty in the armed forces under honorable conditions.

Another recent change involves Veterans who earned the Global War on Terrorism Expeditionary Medal for service in OEF/OIF/OND. Under Title 5, service on active duty in the armed forces during a war or in a campaign or expedition for which a campaign badge has been authorized, also qualifies for Veterans preference. Any Armed Forces Expeditionary medal or campaign badge qualifies for preference. Medal holders must have served continuously for 24 months or the full period called or ordered to active duty. For additional information, visit the Office of Personnel Management (OPM) website at www. fedshirevets.gov.

In 2011, President Obama signed the VOW (Veterans Opportunity to Work) To Hire Heroes Act. VOW amends Chapter 21 of Title 5, U.S.C. by adding section 2108a, "Treatment of certain individuals as Veterans, disabled Veterans, and preference eligibles." Section 2108a requires federal agencies to treat active duty Servicemembers as Veterans, disabled Veterans, or preference eligibles for purposes of appointment in the competitive service when these Servicemembers submit a certification of expected discharge or release from active duty under honorable conditions, along with their applications for federal employment. A certification is any written document from the armed forces that certifies the Servicemember is expected to be discharged or released from active duty service in the armed forces under honorable conditions not later than 120 days from the date the certification is signed.

Veterans' preference does not require an agency to use any particular appointment process. Agencies can pick candidates from a number of different special hiring authorities or through a variety of different sources. For example, the agency can reinstate a former federal employee, transfer someone from another agency, reassign someone from within the agency, make a selection under merit promotion procedures or through open, competitive exams, or appoint someone noncompetitively under special authority such as a Veterans Readjustment Appointment or special authority for 30 percent or more disabled Veterans. The decision on which hiring authority the agency desires to use rests solely with the agency. When applying for federal jobs, eligible Veterans should claim preference on their application or resume. Veterans should apply for a federal job by contacting the personnel office at the agency in which they wish to work. For more information, visit www.usajobs.gov for job openings or help creating a federal resume.

Veterans' Employment Opportunities Act
When an agency accepts applications from outside its own work-force, the Veterans' Employment Opportunities Act of 1998 allows preference eligible candidates or Veterans to compete for these vacancies under merit promotion procedures. Veterans who are se-lected are given career or career-conditional appointments. Veterans are those who have been separated under honorable conditions from the U.S. armed forces with three or more years of continuous active service. For more information, visit www.usajobs.gov or www.fedshirevets.gov.

Veterans' Recruitment Appointment
Allows federal agencies to appoint eligible Veterans to jobs without competition. These appointments can be converted to career or career-conditional positions after two years of satisfactory work. Vet-erans should apply directly to the agency where they wish to work. For information,www.fedshirevets.gov/.

Small Businesses
VA's Center for Veterans Enterprise helps Veterans interested in forming or expanding small businesses, and helps VA contracting offices identify Veteran-owned small businesses. For information, write the U.S. Department of Veterans Affairs (OOVE), 810 Vermont Avenue, N.W., Washington, DC 20420-0001, call toll-free 1-866-584-2344, or visit www.vetbiz.gov. Like other federal agencies, VA is required to place a portion of its contracts and purchases with small and disadvantaged businesses. VA has a special office to help small and disadvantaged businesses get information on VA acquisition opportunities. For information, write the U.S. Department of Veterans Affairs (OOSB), 810 Vermont Avenue, N.W., Washington, DC 20420-0001, call toll-free 1-800-949-8387, or visit www.va.gov/osdbu/.

Chapter 12
Dependents & Survivors Health Care

Civilian Health and Medical Program of the Department of Veterans Affairs (CHAMPVA). Under CHAMPVA, certain dependents and survivors can receive reimbursement for most medical expenses – inpatient, outpatient, mental health, prescription medication, skilled nursing care and durable medical equipment.

Eligibility: To be eligible for CHAMPVA, an individual cannot be eligible for TRICARE (the medical program for civilian dependents provided by DoD) and must be one of the following:
1. The spouse or child of a Veteran whom VA has rated permanently and totally disabled due to a service-connected disability.
2. The surviving spouse or child of a Veteran who died from a VA-rated service-connected disability, or who, at the time of death, was rated permanently and totally disabled.
3. The surviving spouse or child of a Veteran who died on active duty service and in the line of duty, not due to misconduct. However, in most of these cases, these family members are eligible for TRICARE, not CHAMPVA.

A surviving spouse under age 55 who remarries loses CHAMPVA eligibility at midnight of the date on remarriage. He/she may re-establish eligibility if the remarriage ends by death, divorce or annulment effective the first day of the month following the termination of the remarriage or December 1, 1999, whichever is later. A surviving spouse who remarries after age 55 does not lose eligibility upon remarriage.

For those who have Medicare entitlement or other health insurance, CHAMPVA is a secondary payer. Beneficiaries with Medicare must be enrolled in Parts A&B to maintain CHAMPVA eligibility. For additional information, contact the Chief Business Office Purchased Care at the VA Health Administration Center, CHAMPVA, P.O. Box 469028, Denver, CO 80246, call 1-800-733-8387 or visit www.va.gov/hac/forbeneficiaries/champva/champva.asp.

Many VA health care facilities provide services to CHAMPVA beneficiaries under the CHAMPVA In-house Treatment Initiative (CITI) program. Contact the nearest VA health care facility to determine if it participates. Beneficiaries who use a CITI facility incur no cost for services; however, services are provided on a space-available basis, after the needs of Veterans are met. Not all services are available at all times. The coverage of services is dependent upon the CHAMP-VA benefit coverage. CHAMPVA beneficiaries who are covered by Medicare cannot use CITI.

VA's Comprehensive Assistance for Family Caregivers Program entitles the designated Primary Family Caregiver, who is without health insurance coverage, CHAMPVA benefits. Some of the health plans that would make a Primary Family Caregiver ineligible for CHAMPVA benefits include Medicare, Medicaid, commercial health plans through employment and individual plans.

Children Born with Spina Bifida to Certain Vietnam or Korea Veterans: The Spina Bifida (SB) Health Care Benefits Program is a health care benefits program administered by the Department of Veterans Affairs for birth children of certain Vietnam and Korea Veterans who have been diagnosed with spina bifida (except spina bifida occulta). The SB Health Care Benefits Program provides reimbursement for covered medical services and supplies, such as inpatient and outpatient medical services, pharmacy, durable medical equipment, and supplies. The Chief Business Office Purchased Care in Denver, Colorado manages the SB Health Benefits Program, including the authorization of benefits and the subsequent processing and payment of health care claims. For more information about spina bifida health care benefits, call 1-888-820-1756 or visit www.va.gov/hac/forbeneficiaries/spina/spina.asp

Eligibility: To be eligible for the SB Health Care Benefits Program, the child must have received a monetary award under the Veterans Benefits Administration (VBA). The Denver VA Regional Office makes the determination regarding this entitlement. VBA notifies the Chief Business Office Purchased Care after an award is made and the eligible child is enrolled in the SB Health Care Benefits Program.

Children of Women Vietnam Veterans (CWVV) Born with Certain Birth Defects: The CWVV Health Care Program is a federal health benefits program administered by the Department of Veterans Affairs for children of women Vietnam Veterans born with certain birth defects. The CWVV Program provides reimbursement for medical care related to covered birth defects and conditions associated with the covered birth defect except for spina bifida. For more information about benefits for children with birth defects, call 1-888-820-1756 or visit www.va.gov/hac/forbeneficiaries/spina/spina.asp

Eligibility: To be eligible for the CWVV Program, the child must have received a monetary award under VBA. The Denver VA Regional Office makes determination regarding this entitlement. VBA notifies the Chief Business Office Purchased Care after an award is made and the eligible child is enrolled in CWVV.

Bereavement Counseling: VA Vet Centers provide bereavement counseling to all family members including spouses, children, parents, and siblings of Servicemembers who die while on active duty. This includes federally activated members of the National Guard and reserve components. Bereavement services may be accessed by calling (202) 461-6530.

Bereavement Counseling related to Veterans: Bereavement counseling is available through any VA medical center to immediate family members of Veterans who die unexpectedly or while participating in a VA hospice or similar program, as long as the immediate family members had been receiving family support services in connection with or in furtherance of the Veteran's treatment. (In other cases, bereavement counseling is available to the Veteran's legal guardian or the individual with whom the Veteran had certified an intention to live, as long as the guardian or individual had been receiving covered family support services.) This bereavement counseling is of limited duration and may only be authorized up to 60 days. However, VA medical center directors have authority to approve a longer period of time when medically indicated. Contact the Social Work Service at the nearest VA medical center to access bereavement counseling.

Dependents/Survivors and the Health Care Law

The Affordable Care Act, also known as the health care law, was created to expand access to affordable health care coverage to all Americans, lower costs, and improve quality and care coordination. Under the health care law, people will:
- have health coverage that meets a minimum standard (called "minimum essential coverage") by January 1, 2014;
- qualify for an exemption; or

- pay a fee when filing their taxes if they have affordable options but remain uninsured.

Key Information for Family Members about the Health Care Law

- VA wants all Veterans and their families to receive health care that improves their health and well-being.
- Family members are a key part of Veterans' good health and support network.
- Dependents/survivors enrolled in the Civilian Health and Medical Program of the Department of Veterans Affairs (CHAMPVA) or the Spina Bifida Health Care Program meet the requirement to have health care coverage under the health care law and do not need to take any additional steps. The health care law does not change CHAMPVA or Spina Bifida benefits, access to care, or out-of-pocket costs.

Veterans' family members who do not have coverage that meets the health care law's standard should consider their options through the Health Insurance Marketplace, which is a new way to shop for and purchase private health insurance. Family members may also get lower costs on monthly premiums or out-of-pocket costs or be eligible for free or low-cost coverage through Medicaid or the Children's Health Insurance Program (CHIP). For more information about the Health Insurance Marketplace, visit www.healthcare.gov or call 1-800-318-2596. For additional information about the VA and the health care law, visit www.va.gov/aca or call 1-877-222-VETS (8387).

Chapter 13
Dependents & Survivors Benefits

Death Gratuity Payment
Military services provide payment, called a death gratuity, in the amount of $100,000 to the next of kin of Servicemembers who die while on active duty (including those who die within 120 days of separation) as a result of service-connected injury or illness.

If there is no surviving spouse or child, then parents or siblings designated as next of kin by the Servicemember may be provided the payment. The payment is made by the last military command of the deceased. If the beneficiary is not paid automatically, application may be made to the military service concerned.

Dependency and Indemnity Compensation
Eligibility: For a survivor to be eligible for Dependency and Indemnity Compensation (DIC), one of the following must have directly caused or contributed to the Veteran's death:
1. A disease or injury incurred or aggravated in the line of duty while on active duty or active duty for training.
2. An injury, heart attack, cardiac arrest, or stroke incurred or aggravated in the line of duty while on inactive duty for training.
3. A service-connected disability or a condition directly related to a service-connected disability.

2014 DIC Payment Rates for Surviving Spouses DIC rates
(Veteran died on or after Jan. 1, 1993.)

Allowances	Monthly Rate
Basic Payment Rate	$1,233.23
Additional Allowances	
Each Dependent Child	$305.52
Aid and Attendance	$305.52
Housebound	$143.12

Special Allowances
Add $261.87 if the Veteran was totally disabled eight continuous

DIC also may be paid to certain survivors of Veterans who were to-tally disabled from service-connected conditions at the time of death, even though their service-connected disabilities did not cause their deaths. The survivor qualifies if the Veteran was:
1. Continuously rated totally disabled for a period of 10 years immediately preceding death; or
2. Continuously rated totally disabled from the date of military discharge and for at least 5 years immediately preceding death; or
3. A former POW who was continuously rated totally disabled for a period of at least on a year immediately preceding death.

Payments will be offset by any amount received from judicial pro-ceedings brought on by the Veteran's death. When the surviving spouse is eligible for payments under the military's Survivor Benefit Plan (SBP), only the amount of SBP greater than DIC is payable. If DIC is greater than SBP, only DIC is payable. The Veteran's dis-charge must have been under conditions other than dishonorable.

Payments for Deaths After Jan. 1, 1993: Surviving spouses of Veterans who died on or after Jan. 1, 1993, receive a basic rate, plus additional payments for dependent children, for the aid and attendance of another person if they are patients in a nursing home or require the regular assistance of another person, or if they are permanently housebound.

Aid and Attendance and Housebound Benefits
Surviving spouses who are eligible for DIC or survivors pension may also be eligible for Aid and Attendance or Housebound benefits. They may apply for these benefits by writing to their VA regional office. They should include copies of any evidence, preferably a report from an attending physician or a nursing home, validating the need for aid and attendance or housebound care. The report should contain suf-ficient detail to determine whether there is disease or injury produc-ing physical or mental impairment, loss of coordination, or conditions affecting the ability to dress and undress, to feed oneself, to attend to sanitary needs, and to keep oneself ordinarily clean and presentable. In addition, it is necessary to determine whether the surviving spouse is confined to the home or immediate premises.

Special Allowances
Add $261.87 if the Veteran was totally disabled eight continuous

years prior to death. Add $266 if there are dependent children under age 18 for the initial two years of entitlement for DIC awards commencing on or after Jan. 1, 2005.

Payments for Deaths Prior to Jan. 1, 1993: Surviving spouses of Veterans who died prior to Jan. 1, 1993, receive an amount based

Parents' DIC: VA provides an income-based monthly benefit to the surviving parent(s) of a Servicemember or Veteran whose death was service-related. When countable income exceeds the limit set by law, no benefits are payable. The spouse's income must also be included if living with a spouse.

A spouse may be the other parent of the deceased Veteran, or a spouse from remarriage. Unreimbursed medical expenses may be used to reduce countable income. Benefit rates and income limits change annually.

Restored Entitlement Program for Survivors: Survivors of Veterans who died of service-connected causes incurred or aggravated prior to Aug. 13, 1981, may be eligible for a special benefit payable in addition to any other benefits to which the family may be entitled. The amount of the benefit is based on information provided by the Social Security Administration.

Survivors Pension
VA provides pension benefits to qualifying surviving spouses and unmarried dependent children of deceased Veterans with wartime service.

Eligibility
To be eligible, spouses must not have remarried (with an exception that remarriage of surviving spouse terminated prior to Nov. 1, 1990), and children must be under age 18, or under age 23 if attending a VA-approved school, or have become permanently incapable of self-support because of disability before age 18. Surviving spouses and children must have qualifying income.

The Veteran must have been discharged under conditions other than dishonorable and must have had 90 days or more of active military service, at least one day of which was during a period of war, or a service-connected disability justifying discharge. Longer periods of service may be required for Veterans who entered active duty on or after Sept. 8, 1980, or Oct. 16, 1981, if an officer. If the Veteran died in service but not in the line of duty, survivors pension may be payable if the Veteran completed at least two years of honorable service.

Children who become incapable of self-support because of a disability before age 18 may be eligible for survivors pension as long as the condition exists, unless the child marries or the child's income exceeds the applicable limit.

Payment: Survivors pension provides a monthly payment to bring an eligible person's income to a level established by law. The payment is reduced by the annual income from other sources such as Social Security. The payment may be increased if the recipient has unreimbursed medical expenses that can be deducted from countable income.

2014 Survivors Pension Rates

Recipient of Pension	Maximum Annual Rate
Surviving spouse	$8,485
(With dependent child)	$11,107
Permanently housebound	$10,371
(With dependent child)	$12,988
Needs regular aid & attendance	$13,563
(With dependent child)	$16,180
Each additional dependent child	$2,161
Pension for each surviving child	$2,161

Aid and Attendance and Housebound Benefits

Surviving spouses who are eligible for VA survivors pension are eligible for a higher maximum pension rate if they qualify for aid and attendance or housebound benefits. An eligible individual may qualify if he or she requires the regular aid of another person in order to perform personal functions required for everyday living, or is bedridden, a patient in a nursing home due to mental or physical incapacity, blind, or permanently and substantially confined to his/her immediate premises because of a disability.

Surviving spouses who are ineligible for basic survivors pension based on annual income may still be eligible for survivors pension if they are eligible for aid and attendance or housebound benefits because a higher income limit applies. In addition, unreimbursed medical expenses for nursing-home or home-health care may be used to reduce countable annual income, which may result in a higher pension benefit.

To apply for aid and attendance or housebound benefits, write to a VA regional office. Please include copies of any evidence, preferably a report from an attending physician or a nursing home, validating the need for aid and attendance or housebound type care. The report should contain sufficient detail to determine whether there is disease or injury producing physical or mental impairment, loss of coordination, or conditions affecting the ability to dress and undress, to feed oneself, to attend to sanitary needs, and to keep oneself ordinarily clean and presentable. In addition, it is necessary to determine whether the claimant is confined to the home or immediate premises.

Survivors' & Dependents' Educational Assistance
Eligibility: VA provides educational assistance to qualifying dependents as follows:
1. The spouse or child of a Servicemember or Veteran who either died of a service-connected disability, or who has permanent and total service-connected disability, or who died while such a disability existed.
2. The spouse or child of a Servicemember listed for more than 90 days as currently Missing in Action (MIA), captured in the line of duty by a hostile force, or detained or interned by a foreign government or power.
3. The spouse or child of a Servicemember who is hospitalized or receives outpatient care or treatment for a disability that is determined to be totally and permanently disabling, incurred or aggravated due to active duty, and for which the service member is likely to be discharged from military service.

Surviving spouses lose eligibility if they remarry before age 57 or are living with another person who has been recognized publicly as their spouse. They can regain eligibility if their remarriage ends by death or divorce or if they cease living with the person. Dependent children do not lose eligibility if the surviving spouse remarries. Visit www.benefits.va.gov/gibill// for more information.

Period of Eligibility: The period of eligibility for Veterans' spouses expires 10 years from either the date they become eligible or the date of the Veteran's death. Children generally must be between the ages of 18 and 26 to receive educational benefits. VA may grant extensions to both spouses and children.

The period of eligibility for spouses of Servicemembers who died on active duty expires 20 years from the date of death. This is a change in law that became effective Dec. 10, 2004. Spouses of Servicemembers who died on active duty whose 10-year eligibility period expired before Dec. 10, 2004, now have 20 years from the date of death to use educational benefits.

Effective Oct. 10, 2008, Public Law 110-389 provides a 20-year period of eligibility for spouses of Veterans with a permanent and total service-connected disability rating effective within 3 years of release from active duty.

Payments: The payment rate effective Oct. 1, 2013, is $1,003 a month for full-time school attendance, with lesser amounts for part-time. Benefits are paid for full-time training up to 45 months or the equivalent in part-time training.

Training Available: Benefits may be awarded for pursuit of associate, bachelor, or graduate degrees at colleges and universities; independent study; cooperative training; study abroad; certificate or diploma from business, technical, or vocational schools; apprenticeships; on-the-job training programs; farm cooperative courses; and preparatory courses for tests required or used for admission to an institution of higher learning or graduate school.

Benefits for correspondence courses under certain conditions are available to spouses only. Beneficiaries without high-school degrees can pursue secondary schooling, and those with a deficiency in a subject may receive tutorial assistance if enrolled half-time or more.

Special Benefits: Dependents over age 14 with physical or mental disabilities that impair their ability to pursue an education may receive specialized vocational or restorative training, including speech and voice correction, language retraining, lip reading, auditory training, Braille reading and writing, and similar programs. Certain disabled or surviving spouses are also eligible.

Marine Gunnery Sergeant John David Fry Scholarship
Children of those who died in the line of duty on or after Sept. 11, 2001, are potentially eligible to use Post-9/11 GI Bill benefits. Refer to Chapter 4, "Education and Training", for more details.

Counseling: VA may provide counseling to help participants pursue an educational or vocational objective.

Montgomery GI Bill (MGIB) Death Benefit: VA will pay a special MGIB death benefit to a designated survivor in the event of the service-connected death of a Servicemember while on active duty or within one year after discharge or release. The deceased must either have been entitled to educational assistance under the MGIB program or a participant in the program who would have been so entitled but for the high school diploma or length-of-service require-ment. The amount paid will be equal to the participant's actual mili-tary pay reduction, less any education benefits paid.

Children of Vietnam or Korean Veterans Born with Spina Bifida:
Biological children of male and female Veterans who served in Viet-nam at any time during the period beginning Jan. 9, 1962, and end-ing May 7, 1975, or who served in or near the Korean demilitarized zone (DMZ) during the period beginning Sept. 1, 1967, and ending Aug. 31, 1971, born with spina bifida may be eligible for a monthly monetary allowance and vocational training if reasonably feasible. The law defines "child" as the natural child of a Vietnam Veteran, regardless of age or marital status. The child must have been con-ceived after the date on which the Veteran first entered the Republic of Vietnam.

2014 VA Benefits for Children of Vietnam or Korean Veterans Born with Spina Bifida

	Level I	Level II	Level III
Monthly Rate	$308	$1,054	$1,796

For more information about benefits for children with birth defects, visit www.va.gov/hac/forbeneficiaries/spina/spina.asp. A monetary allowance is paid at one of three disability levels based on the neurological manifestations that define the severity of disability: impairment of the functioning of extremities, impairment of bowel or bladder function, and impairment of intellectual functioning.

Children of Women Vietnam Veterans Born with Certain Birth Defects: Biological children of women Veterans who served in Vietnam at any time during the period beginning on Feb. 28, 1961, and ending on May 7, 1975, may be eligible for certain benefits because of birth defects associated with the mother's service in Vietnam that resulted in a permanent physical or mental disability.

The covered birth defects do not include conditions due to family disorders, birth-related injuries, or fetal or neonatal infirmities with well-established causes. A monetary allowance is paid at one of four disability levels based on the child's degree of permanent disability.

Vocational Training: VA provides vocational training, rehabilitation services, and employment assistance to help these children prepare for and attain suitable employment. To qualify, an applicant must be a child receiving a VA monthly allowance for spina bifida or another covered birth defect and for whom VA has determined that achievement of a vocational goal is reasonably feasible. A child may not begin vocational training before his/her 18th birthday or the date he/she completes secondary schooling, whichever comes first. Depending on need and eligibility, a child may be provided up to 24 months of full-time training with the possibility of an extension of up to 24 months if it is needed to achieve the identified employment goal.

Other Benefits for Survivors

VA Home Loan Guaranty
A VA loan guaranty to acquire a home may be available to an unmarried spouse of a Veteran or Servicemember who died as a result of service-connected disabilities, a surviving spouse who remarries after age 57, or to a spouse of a Servicemember officially listed as MIA or who is currently a POW for more than 90 days. Spouses of those listed MIA/POW are limited to one loan. Surviving spouses of certain totally disabled Veterans, whose disability may not have been the cause of death, may also be eligible for VA loan guaranty.

"No-Fee" Passports
"No-fee" passports are available to immediate family members (spouse, children, parents, brothers and sisters) for the expressed purpose of visiting their loved one's grave or memorialization site

at an American military cemetery on foreign soil. For additional information, write to the American Battle Monuments Commission, Courthouse Plaza II, Suite 500, 2300 Clarendon Blvd., Arlington, VA 22201, or telephone 703-696-6897, or visit www.abmc.gov

Burial and Memorial Benefits for Survivors
The Department of Veterans Affairs offers several burial and memorial benefits for eligible survivors and dependents. These benefits may include interment at a state, tribal or national Veterans cemetery, plot, marker and more. To learn more about these and other benefits please refer to Chapter 8 of this guide.

Chapter 14

Appeals of VA Claims Decisions

Veterans and other claimants for VA benefits have the right to appeal decisions made by a VA regional office, medical center or National Cemetery Administration (NCA) office. Typical issues appealed are disability compensation, pension, education benefits, recovery of overpayments, reimbursement for unauthorized medical services, and denial of burial and memorial benefits.

A claimant has one year from the date of the notification of a VA decision to file an appeal. The first step in the appeal process is for a claimant to file a written notice of disagreement with VA regional office, medical center or national cemetery office that made the decision. Following receipt of the written notice, VA will furnish the claimant a "Statement of the Case" describing what facts, laws, and regulations were used in deciding the case. To complete the request for appeal, the claimant must file a "Substantive Appeal" within 60 days of the mailing of the Statement of the Case, or within one year from the date VA mailed its decision, whichever period ends later.

Board of Veterans' Appeals
The Board of Veterans' Appeals ("the Board") makes decisions on appeals on behalf of the Secretary of Veterans Affairs. Although it is not required, a veterans service organization, an agent, or an attorney may represent a claimant. Appellants may present their cases in person to a member of the Board at a hearing in Washington, D.C., at a VA regional office or by videoconference.

Decisions made by the Board can be found at www.index.va.gov/search/va/bva.html. The pamphlet, "Understanding the Appeal Process," is available on the website or may be requested by writing: Mail Process Section (014), Board of Veterans' Appeals, 810 Vermont Avenue, NW, Washington, DC 20420.

U.S. Court of Appeals for Veterans Claims
A final Board of Veterans' Appeals decision that does not grant a claimant the benefits desired may be appealed to the U.S. Court of

Appeals for Veterans Claims. The court is an independent body, not part of the Department of Veterans Affairs.

Notice of an appeal must be received by the court with a postmark that is within 120 days after the Board of Veterans' Appeals mailed its decision. The court reviews the record considered by the Board of Veterans' Appeals. It does not hold trials or receive new evidence.

Appellants may represent themselves before the court or have lawyers or approved agents as representatives. Oral argument is held only at the direction of the court. Either party may appeal a decision of the court to the U.S. Court of Appeals for the Federal Circuit and may seek review in the Supreme Court of the United States.

Published decisions, case status information, rules and procedures, and other special announcements can be found at http://www.us-courts.cavc.gov/. The court's decisions can also be found in West's Veterans Appeals Reporter, and on the Westlaw and LEXIS online services. For questions, write the Clerk of the Court, 625 Indiana Ave. NW, Suite 900, Washington, DC 20004, or call (202) 501-5970.

Chapter 15

Military Medals and Records

Replacing Military Medals

Medals awarded while in active service are issued by the individual military services if requested by Veterans or their next of kin. Requests for replacement medals, decorations, and awards should be directed to the branch of the military in which the Veteran served. However, for Air Force (including Army Air Corps) and Army Veterans, the National Personnel Records Center (NPRC) verifies awards and forwards requests and verification to appropriate services.

Requests for replacement medals should be submitted on Standard Form 180, "Request Pertaining to Military Records," which may be obtained at VA offices or the Internet at www.va.gov/vaforms/. Forms, addresses, and other information on requesting medals can be found on the Military Personnel Records section of NPRC's Website at www.archives.gov/st-louis/military-personnel/index.html. For questions, call Military Personnel Records at (314) 801-0800, or e-mail questions to: MPR.center@nara.gov.

When requesting medals, type or clearly print the Veteran's full name, include the Veteran's branch of service, service number or Social Security number, and provide the Veteran's exact or approximate dates of military service. The request must contain the signature of the Veteran or next of kin if the Veteran is deceased. If available, include a copy of the discharge or separation document, WDAGO Form 53-55 or DD Form 214.

If discharge or separation documents are lost, Veterans or the next of kin of deceased Veterans may obtain duplicate copies through the eBenefits portal (www.ebenefits.va.gov) or by completing forms found on the Internet at www.archives.gov/research/index.html and mailing or faxing them to the NPRC.

Alternatively, write the National Personnel Records Center, Military Personnel Records, One Archives Drive, St. Louis, MO 63138-1002. Specify that a duplicate separation document is needed. The Veteran's full name should be printed or typed so that it can be read clearly, but the request must also contain the signature of the Veteran or the signature of the next of kin, if the Veteran is deceased. Include the Veteran's branch of service, service number or Social Security number, and exact or approximate dates and years of service. Use Standard Form 180, "Request Pertaining To Military Records."

It is not necessary to request a duplicate copy of a Veteran's discharge or separation papers solely for the purpose of filing a claim for VA benefits. If complete information about the Veteran's service is furnished on the application, VA will obtain verification of service.

Correcting Military Records

The Secretary of a military department, acting through a Board for Correction of Military Records, has authority to change any military record when necessary to correct an error or remove an injustice. A correction board may consider applications for correction of a military record, including a review of a discharge issued by court-martial.

The Veteran, survivor, or legal representative must file a request for correction within three years of discovering an alleged error or injustice. The board may excuse failure to file within this time, however, if it finds it would be in the interest of justice. It is an applicant's responsibility to show why the filing of the application was delayed and why it would be in the interest of justice for the board to consider it despite the delay. To justify a correction, it is necessary to show to the satisfaction of the board that the alleged entry or omission in the records was in error or unjust. Applications should include all available evidence, such as signed statements of witnesses or a brief of arguments supporting the correction. Application is made with DD Form 149, available at VA offices, Veterans organizations or visit www.dtic.mil/whs/directives/infomgt/forms/formsprogram.htm.

Review of Discharge from Military Service

Each of the military services maintains a discharge review board with authority to change, correct or modify discharges or dismissals not issued by a sentence of a general court-martial. The board has no authority to address medical discharges.

The Veteran or, if the Veteran is deceased or incompetent, the surviving spouse, next of kin or legal representative, may apply for a review of discharge by writing to the military department concerned, using DD Form 293, "Application for the Review of Discharge from the Armed Forces of the United States." This form may be obtained at a VA regional office, from Veterans organizations or online at www. dtic.mil/whs/directives/infomgt/forms/formsprogram.htm.

However, if the discharge was more than 15 years ago, a Veteran must petition the appropriate Service's Board for Correction of Military Records using DD Form 149, "Application for Correction of Military Records Under the Provisions of Title 10, U.S. Code, Section 1552." A discharge review is conducted by a review of an applicant's record and, if requested, by a hearing before the board.

Discharges awarded as a result of a continuous period of unauthorized absence in excess of 180 days make persons ineligible for VA benefits regardless of action taken by discharge review boards, unless VA determines there were compelling circumstances for the absence. Boards for the Correction of Military Records also may consider such cases.

Veterans with disabilities incurred or aggravated during active duty may qualify for medical or related benefits regardless of separation and characterization of service. Veterans separated administratively under other than honorable conditions may request that their discharge be reviewed for possible re-characterization, provided they file their appeal within 15 years of the date of separation. Questions regarding the review of a discharge should be addressed to the appropriate discharge review board at the address listed on DD Form 293.

Physical Disability Board of Review

Veterans separated due to disability from Sept. 11, 2001, through Dec. 31, 2009, with a combined rating of 20 percent or less, as determined by the respective branch of service Physical Evaluation Board (PEB), and not found eligible for retirement, may be eligible for a review by the Physical Disability Board of Review (PDBR).

The PDBR was established to reassess the accuracy and fairness of certain PEB decisions, and where appropriate, recommend the correction of discrepancies and errors. A PDBR review will not lower the disability rating previously assigned by the PEB, and any correction may be made retroactively to the day of the original disability separation. As a result of the request for review by the PDBR, no further relief from the Board of Corrections of Military Records may be sought, and the recommendation by the PDBR, once accepted by the respective branch of service, is final. A comparison of these two boards, along with other PDBR information, can be viewed at www. health.mil/pdbr.

The Veteran or, if the Veteran is deceased or incompetent, the spouse or surviving spouse, next of kin or legal representative, may apply for a review using DD Form 294, "Application for a Review by the Physical Disability Board of Review (PDBR) of the Rating Awarded Accompanying a Medical Separation from the Armed Forces of the United States." As part of the review process, the PDBR considers the rating(s) previously awarded by VA. The completion of VA Form 3288, "Request for and Consent to Release of Information from Individual's Records," along with DD Form 294, allows the PDBR to request VA records. Both forms can be downloaded from the PDBR website at www.health.mil/pdbr. These forms may also be obtained at a VA Regional Office (VARO), from a veterans service organization (VSO) or online at www.dtic.mil/whs/directives/infomgt/forms/formsprogram.htm.

Chapter 16

Benefits Provided by Other Federal Agencies

Internal Revenue Service

Disabled Military Retirees may be eligible to claim a federal tax refund based on an increase in their disability rating percentage from VA, or, if combat disabled, applying for and being granted Combat-Related Special Compensation after an award for Concurrent Retirement and Disability. To do so, the disabled Military Retiree needs to file the amended return, Form 1040X, Amended U.S. Individual Income Tax Return, to correct a previously filed Form 1040, 1040A or 1040EZ. An amended return cannot be e-filed. It must be filed as a paper return. The filer should include all documents received from VA and any information received from Defense Finance and Accounting Service explaining proper tax treatment for the current year.

If needed, Military Retirees should seek assistance from a competent tax professional before filing amended returns based on a disability determination. Refund claims based on an incorrect interpretation of the tax law could subject the taxpayer to interest and/or penalty charges. Complete information and requirements can be found at http://www.irs.gov/Individuals/Military/Special-Tax-Considerations-for-Veterans.

USDA Provides Loans for Farms and Homes

The U.S. Department of Agriculture (USDA) provides loans and guaranties to buy, improve or operate farms. Loans and guaranties are generally available for housing in towns with a population up to 20,000. Applications from Veterans have preference. For further information, contact Farm Service Agency or Rural Development, USDA, 1400 Independence Ave., S.W., Washington, DC 20250, or apply at local Department of Agriculture offices, usually located in county seats.

HUD Veteran Resource Center (HUDVET)

Housing and Urban Development (HUD) sponsors the Veteran Resource Center (HUDVET), which works with national Veterans service organizations to serve as a general information center on all

HUD-sponsored housing and community development programs and services. To contact HUDVET, call 1-800-998-9999, TDD 800-483-2209, or visit www.hud.gov/hudvet.

Veterans Receive Naturalization Preference
Honorable active duty service in the U.S. armed forces during a designated period of hostility allows an individual to naturalize without being required to establish any periods of residence or physical presence in the United States. A Servicemember who was in the United States, certain territories, or aboard an American public vessel at the time of enlistment, re-enlistment, extension of enlistment or induction, may naturalize even if he or she is not a lawful permanent resident.

On July 3, 2002, the President issued Executive Order 13269 establishing a new period of hostility for naturalization purposes beginning Sept. 11, 2001, and continuing until a date designated by a future Executive Order. Qualifying members of the armed forces who have served at any time during a specified period of hostility may immediately apply for naturalization using the current application, Form N-400, "Application for Naturalization". Additional information about filing and requirement fees and designated periods of hostility are available on the U.S. Citizenship and Immigration Services Website at www.uscis.gov.

Individuals who served honorably in the U.S. armed forces, but were no longer serving on active duty status as of Sept. 11, 2001, may still be naturalized without having to comply with the residence and physical presence requirements for naturalization if they filed Form N-400 while still serving in the U.S. armed forces or within six months of termination of their active duty service.

An individual who files the application for naturalization after the six-month period following termination of active-duty service is not exempt from the residence and physical presence requirements, but can count any period of active-duty service towards the residence and physical presence requirements. Individuals seeking naturalization under this provision must establish that they are lawful permanent residents (such status not having been lost, rescinded, or abandoned) and that they served honorably in the U.S. armed forces for at least one year.

If a Servicemember dies as a result of injury or disease incurred or aggravated by service during a time of combat, the Servicemember's survivor(s) can apply for the deceased Servicemember to receive posthumous citizenship at any time within two years of the Servicemember's death. The issuance of a posthumous certificate of citizenship does not confer U.S. citizenship on surviving relatives. However, a non-U.S. citizen spouse or qualifying family member may file for certain immigration benefits and services based upon their relationship to a Servicemember who died during hostilities or a non-citizen Servicemember who died during hostilities and was later granted posthumous citizenship.

For additional information, USCIS has developed a web page, www.uscis.gov/military, that contains information and links to services specifically for the military and their families. Members of the U.S. military and their families stationed around the world can also call USCIS for help with immigration services and benefits using a dedicated, toll-free help line at 1-877-CIS-4MIL (1-877-247-4645).

Small Business Administration (SBA)

Historically, Veterans do very well as small business entrepreneurs. Veterans interested in entrepreneurship and small business ownership should look to the U.S. Small Business Administration's Office of Veterans Business Development (OVBD) for assistance. OVBD conducts comprehensive outreach to Veterans, service-disabled Veterans, and Reservists of the U.S. military. OVBD also provides assistance to Veteran- and Reservist-owned small businesses. SBA is the primary federal agency responsible for assisting Veterans who own or are considering starting their own small businesses.

Among the services provided by SBA are business-planning assistance, counseling, and training through community based Veterans Business Outreach Centers. For more information, go to www.sba.gov/aboutsba/sbaprograms/ovbd/OVBD_VBOP.html. There are more than 1,000 university-based Small Business Development Centers; nearly 400 SCORE chapters (www.score.org/Veteran.html) with 11,000 volunteer counselors, many of whom are Veterans; and 100 Women's Business Centers.

SBA also manages a range of special small business lending programs at thousands of locations, ranging from Micro Loans to the Military-community-targeted Patriot Express Pilot Loan, to venture capital and Surety Bond Guarantees (www.sba.gov/services/financi-alassistance/index.html). Veterans also participate in all SBA federal procurement programs, including a special 3 percent federal procurement goal specifically for service-connected disabled Veterans, and SBA supports Veterans and others participating in international trade.

A special Military Reservist Economic Injury Disaster Loan (www.sba.gov/reservists) is available for self-employed Reservists whose small businesses may be damaged through the absence of the owner or an essential employee as a result of Title 10 activation to Active Duty.

A Veterans Business Development Officer is stationed at every SBA District Office to act as a guide to Veterans, and SBA offers a full range of self-paced small business planning assistance at www.sba.gov/survey/checklist/index.cgi for Veterans, Reservists, discharging Servicemembers, and their families. Information about the full range of services can be found at http://www.sba.gov/about-offices-content/1/2985, or by calling 202-205-6773 or 1-800-U-ASK-SBA (1-800-827-5722).

Social Security Administration
Monthly retirement, disability, and survivor benefits under Social Security are payable to Veterans and dependents if the Veteran has earned enough work credits under the program. Upon the Veteran's death, a one-time payment of $255 may be made to the Veteran's spouse or child. In addition, a Veteran may qualify at age 65 for Medicare's hospital insurance and medical insurance. Medicare protection is available to people who have received Social Security disability benefits for 24 months, and to insured people and their dependents who need dialysis or kidney transplants, or who have amyotrophic lateral sclerosis (more commonly known as Lou Gehrig's disease).

Since 1957, military service earnings for active duty (including active duty for training) have counted toward Social Security, and those earnings are already on Social Security records. Since 1988, inactive duty service in the Reserve Component (such as weekend drills) has also been covered by Social Security. Servicemembers and Veterans are credited with $300 in additional earnings for each calendar quarter in which they received active duty basic pay after 1956 and before 1978.

Veterans who served in the military from 1978 through 2001 are credited with an additional $100 in earnings for each $300 in active duty basic pay, up to a maximum of $1,200 a year. No additional Social Security taxes are withheld from pay for these extra credits. Veterans who enlisted after Sept. 7, 1980, and did not complete at least 24 months of active duty or their full tour of duty, may not be able to receive the additional earnings. Check with Social Security for details. Additional earnings will no longer be credited for military service periods after 2001.

Also, non-contributory Social Security earnings of $160 a month may be credited to Veterans who served after Sept. 15, 1940, and before 1957, including attendance at service academies. For information, call 1-800-772-1213 or visit www.socialsecurity.gov/. (Note: Social Security cannot add these extra earnings to the record until an application is filed for Social Security benefits).

Armed Forces Retirement Homes
Veterans are eligible to live in the Armed Forces Retirement Homes located in Gulfport, Miss., or Washington, D.C., if their active duty military service is at least 50 percent enlisted, warrant officer or limited duty officer if they qualify under one of the following categories:

1. Are 60 years of age or older; and were discharged or released under honorable conditions after 20 or more years of active service.
2. Are determined to be incapable of earning a livelihood because of a service-connected disability incurred in the line of duty.
3. Served in a war theater during a time of war declared by Congress or were eligible for hostile-fire special pay and were discharged or released under honorable conditions; and are determined to be incapable of earning a livelihood because of injuries, disease or disability.
4. Served in a women's component of the armed forces before June 12, 1948; and are determined to be eligible for admission due to compelling personal circumstances.

Eligibility determinations are based on rules prescribed by the Home's Chief Operating Officer. Veterans are not eligible if they have been convicted of a felony or are not free from alcohol, drug or psychiatric problems. Married couples are welcome, but both must be eligible in their own right. At the time of admission, applicants must be capable of living independently. The Armed Forces Retirement Home is an independent federal agency. For information, call 1-800-332-3527 or 1-800-422-9988, or visit www.afrh.gov/.

Commissary and Exchange Privileges

Unlimited commissary and exchange store privileges in the United States are available to honorably discharged Veterans with a service-connected disability rated at 100 percent or totally disabling, and to the un-remarried surviving spouses and dependents of Servicemembers who die on active duty, military retirees, recipients of the Medal of Honor, and Veterans whose service-connected disability was rated 100 percent or totally disabling at the time of death. Certification of total disability is done by VA. National Guard Reservists and their dependents may also be eligible. Privileges overseas are governed by international law and are available only if agreed upon by the foreign government concerned

Though these benefits are provided by DOD, VA does provide assistance in completing DD Form 1172, "Application for Uniformed Services Identification and Privilege Card." For detailed information, contact the nearest military installation.

U.S. Department of Health and Human Services

The U.S. Department of Health and Human Services provides funding to states to help low-income households with their heating and home energy costs under the Low Income Home Energy Assistance Program (LIHEAP). LIHEAP can also assist with insulating homes to make them more energy efficient and reduce energy costs. The LIHEAP program in your community determines if your household's income qualifies for the program. To find out where to apply call 1-866-674-6327 or e-mail energy@ncat.org 7 a.m.- 5 p.m. (Mountain Time). More information can be found at www.acf.hhs.gov/programs/ocs/liheap/#index.html

VA Facilities

Patients should call the telephone numbers listed to obtain clinic hours of operation and services.

For more information or to search for a facility by ZIP code, visit www1. va.gov/directory/guide/home.asp?isFlash=1

ALABAMA

Regional Office:
Montgomery 36109 (345 Perry Hill Rd., statewide 1-800-827-1000)

VA Medical Centers:
Birmingham, VA Medical Center (521), 700 South 19th Street, Birmingham, AL, 35233, 205-933-8101
Montgomery, Central Alabama Veterans HCS-VAMC, 215 Perry Hill Road, Montgomery, AL, 36109, 334-260-4100
Tuscaloosa, VA Medical Center, 3701 Loop Road, Tuscaloosa, AL, 35404, 205-554-2000
Tuskegee, Ctrl. Alabama Veterans HCS-VAMC, 2400 Hospital Road, Tuskegee, AL, 36083, 334-725-3085

Clinics:
Anniston/Oxford AL, Anniston/Oxford Primary Care Clinic, 96 Ali Way, Creekside South, Oxford, AL, 36203, 256-832-4141
Bessemer, Medical West Office Complex, 975 Ninth Avenue SW, Suite 400, Bessemer, AL, 35020, 205-428-3495
Childersburg, 151 9th Ave NW, Childersburg, AL, 35044, 256-378-9026
Decatur AL/Madison, 8075 Madison Blvd., Suite 101, Madison, AL, 35758, 256-772-6220
Dothan, 2020 Alexander Drive, Dothan, AL, 36301, 334-673-4166
Florence AL (Shoals Area), Shoals Area Veterans Health Clinic, 422 DD Cox Boulevard, Sheffield, AL, 35660, 256-381-9055
Guntersville, 101 Judy Smith Drive, Guntersville, AL, 35976, 205-933-8101
Huntsville AL, 301 Governor's Drive SW, Huntsville, AL, 35801, 256-535-3100
Jasper AL, Jasper Primary Care Clinic, is 1454 Jones Dairy Road, Jasper, AL 35501 Jasper, AL, 35501, 205-221-7384
Mobile, Mobile Outpatient Clinic, 1504 Springhill Avenue, Mobile, AL, 36604, 251-219-3900
Monroe County, Monroe County CBOC, 159 Whetstone Street, Monroeville, AL, 36460, 251-743-5860
Rainbow City, Gadsden Primary Care Clinic, 206 Rescia Ave., Gadsden, AL, 35906, 256-413-7154
Wiregrass, 301 Andrews Ave., Ft. Rucker, AL, 36362, 334-503-7831

Vet Centers:
Birmingham Vet Center, Birmingham Vet Center, 1201 2nd Avenue South, Birmingham, AL, 35233, 205-212-3122
Huntsville Vet Center, Huntsville Vet Center, Depot Professional Center, 415 Church Street Bldg H, Suite 101, Huntsville, AL, 35801, 256-539-5775
Mobile Vet Center, Mobile Vet Center, 3221 Springhill Ave, Bldg 2, Suite C, Mobile, AL, 36607, 251-478-5906
Montgomery Vet Center, Montgomery Vet Center, 4405 Atlanta Highway, Montgomery, AL, 36109, 334-273-7796

National Cemeteries:
Alabama 35115 (3133 Hwy. 119, Montevallo, 205-665-9039)
Fort Mitchell 36856 (553 Hwy. 165, Fort Mitchell, 334-855-4731)
Mobile 36604 (1202 Virginia St., 850-453-4846)

ALASKA

VA Medical Center:
Alaska VA HCS, Alaska VA HCS, 1201 North Muldoon Road, Anchorage, AK, 99504, 907-257-4700

Clinics:
Fairbanks, Fairbanks VA CBOC, 4076 Neeley Road, Room 1J-101, Fort Wainwright, AK, 99703, 907-361-6370
Kenai, Kenai VA CBOC, 11312 Kenai Spur Highway, Suite 39, Kenai, AK, 99611, 907-395-4100
Mat-Su, 865 N Seward Meridian Parkway, Suite 105, Wasilla, AK, 99654, 907-631-3100

Regional Office:
Anchorage 99508-2989 (1201 N. Muldoon Rd., statewide 1-800-827-1000)

Vet Centers:
Anchorage Vet Center, 4400 Business Park Blvd, Suite B-34, Anchorage, AK, 99503, 907-563-6966
Fairbanks Vet Center, 540 4th Ave., Suite 100, Fairbanks, AK, 99701, 907-456-4238
Wasilla Vet Center, 851 E. West Point Drive, Suite 111, Wasilla, AK, 99654, 907-376-4318

National Cemeteries:
Fort Richardson 99505-5498 (Building 997, Davis Hwy., 907-384-7075)
Sitka 99835 (803 Sawmill Creek Rd., 907-384-7075)

AMERICAN SAMOA

Clinics:
American Samoa, VA American Samoa CBOC, Fiatele Teo Army Reserve Building, Pago Pago, AS, 96799, 684-699-3730

Benefits Office:
Pago Pago 96799 (PO Box 1005, 684-633-5073)

Vet Centers:
American Samoa Vet Center, American Samoa Vet Center, Ottoville Road, Equator Bldg, Pago Pago, AS, 96799, 684-699-3760

ARIZONA

VA Medical Centers:
Northern Arizona HCS, VA Medical Center, 500 Highway 89 North, Prescott, AZ, 86313, 928-445-4860
Phoenix, VA Medical Center, 650 E. Indian School Road, Phoenix, AZ, 85012, 602-277-5551
Southern Arizona HCS, VA Medical Center, 3601 South Sixth Avenue, Tucson, AZ, 85723, 520-792-1450

Clinics:
Anthem, 3618 Anthem Way, Building D, Suite 120, Anthem, AZ, 85086, 623-551-6092
Casa Grande, Casa Grande CBOC, 1876 E Sabin Dr., Bldg A, Casa Grande, AZ, 85222, 520-836-2536
Cottonwood (Yavapai County), Cottonwood CBOC, 501 S Willard Street, Cottonwood, AZ, 86326, 928-649-1532
1338 West Forest Meadows St. # 130, Flagstaff, AZ 86001 (Phone 928-226-1845)
Globe, 5860 S. Hospital Dr., Suite 111, Globe, AZ, 85501, 928-425-0027
Green Valley, Green Valley CBOC, 380 West Vista Hermosa Drive, Suite 140, Green Valley, AZ, 85614, 520-399-2291
Kingman, Kingman CBOC, 1726 East Beverly Avenue, Kingman, AZ, 86409, 928-692-0080
Lake Havasu, 2035 Mesquite Avenue, Suite D, Lake Havasu City, AZ, 86403, 928-680-0090
Mesa, Mesa CBOC, 6950 East Williams Field Road, Mesa, AZ, 85212, 602-222-6568
NW Tucson Urban 1, VA Northwest Tucson Urban Clinic, 2945 W. Ina Road, Tucson, AZ, 85741, 520-219-2418
Payson (Gila County), Payson CBOC, 903 E Highway 260, Suite 2, Payson, AZ, 85541, 928-472-3148
Safford, Safford CBOC, 355 N. 8th Avenue, Safford, AZ, 85546, 928-428-8010
Show Low, Show Low CBOC, 5171 Cub Lake Road, Bldg C, Show Low, AZ, 85901, 928-532-1069
Sierra Vista, Sierra Vista CBOC, 101 N. Coronado Dr., Suite A, Sierra Vista, AZ, 85635, 520-459-1529
Southeast Tucson , VA Southeast Tucson CBOC, 7395 S. Houghton Road, Suite 129, Tucson, AZ, 85747, 520-664-1836
Southwest VA Health Care Clinic, Southwest VA Health Care Clinic, 213 E

Monroe Avenue, Buckeye, AZ, 85326, 623-386-6093
Sun City, Sun City CBOC, 13985 W. Grand Avenue, Suite 101, Surprise, AZ, 85374, 623-251-2884
Thunderbird, Thunderbird CBOC, 9424 N 25th Avenue, Phoenix, AZ, 85021, 602-633-6900
Yuma, Yuma CBOC, 3111 South 4th Avenue, Yuma, AZ, 85364, 928-317-9973)

Regional Office:
Phoenix 85012 (3333 N. Central Ave., statewide 1-800-827-1000)

Benefits Offices:
Tucson 85746 Voc Rehab (1360 W. Irvington Rd., Ste. 150, 602-627-0020)
Flagstaff 86001 Voc Rehab (123 N. San Francisco, Suite 103, 928-226-1845)

Vet Centers:
Lake Havasu Vet Center, Lake Havasu Vet Center, 1720 Mesquite Avenue, Suite 101, Lake Havasu City, AZ, 86403, 928-505-0394
Mesa Vet Center, Mesa Vet Center, 1303 S. Longmore, Suite 5, Mesa, AZ, 85202, 480-610-6727
Phoenix Vet Center, 4020 N. 20th Street, Suite 110, Phoenix, AZ, 85016, 602-640-2981
Prescott Vet Center, 3180 Stillwater Drive, Suite A, Prescott, AZ, 86305, 928-778-3469
Tucson Vet Center,(Readjustment Counseling Service, RCS) 2525 E. Broadway Suite 100, Tucson, AZ 85716 520-882-0333
Yuma County Vet Center, Yuma County Vet Center, 1450 E. 16th Street, Suite 103, Yuma, AZ, 85365, 928-271-8700

National Cemeteries:
Nat. Mem. Cem. of Arizona 85024 (23029 N. Cave Creek Rd., Phoenix, 480-513-3600)
Prescott 86301 (500 Hwy. 89 N., 480-513-3600)

ARKANSAS
VA Medical Centers:
Central AR. Veterans HCS LR, 4300 West Seventh Street, Little Rock, AR, 72205, 501-257-1000
Central AR. Veterans HCS NLR, 2200 Fort Roots Drive, North Little Rock, AR, 72114, 501-257-1000
Fayetteville AR, VA Medical Center, 1100 N. College Avenue, Fayetteville, AR, 72703, 479-443-4301

Clinics:
Conway, 1520 East Dave Ward Drive, Conway, AR, 72032, 501-548-0500
El Dorado CBOC, 460 W. Oak Street, El Dorado, AR, 71730, 870-881-4488
Ft. Smith, Sparks Medical Plaza, 1500 Dodson Avenue, Fort Smith, AR,

72917, 479-441-2600
Harrison, Main Street Medical Clinic, 707 N. Main Street, Harrison, AR, 72601, 870-741-3592
Helena, 812A Newman Drive, Helena, AR, 72342, 870-338-8308
Hot Springs CBOC, 177 Sawtooth Oak Street, Hot Springs, AR, 71901, 501-520-62500
Jonesboro, 1901 Wood Springs Road, Jonesboro, AR, 72401, 870-268-6962
Mena, 1706 Highway 71 North, Mena, AR, 71953, 479-394-4800
Mountain Home CBOC, 10 Medical Plaza, Mountain Home, AR, 72653, 870-424-410
Ozark, Ozark VA Outpatient Clinic, 2713 W. Commercial, Ozark, AR, 72949, 877-760-8387
Paragould, 2420 Linwood Drive, Suite #3, Paragould, AR, 72450, 870-236-9756
Pine Bluff CBOC, 4747 Dusty Lake Drive Suite 203, Pine Bluff, AR, 71603, 870-541-9300
Pocahontas –300 Camp Road, Pocahontas, AR 72455 (870)-248-0571
Russellville, 3106 West 2nd Court, Russellville, AR, 72801, 479-880-5100
Searcy, 1120 South Main Street, Searcy, AR, 72143, 501-207-4700
Texarkana, Texarkana Community Based Outpatient Clinic, 910 Realtor Road, Texarkana, AR, 71854, 870-779-2750

Regional Office:
North Little Rock 72114 (2200 Fort Roots Dr., Bldg. 65, statewide 1-800-827-1000

Vet Center:
Fayetteville Vet Center, 1416 North College Avenue, Fayetteville, AR, 72703, 479-582-7152
Little Rock Vet Center, 201 W. Broadway St., Suite A, North Little Rock, AR, 72114, 501-324-6395

National Cemeteries:
Fayetteville 72701 (700 Government Ave., 479-444-5051)
Fort Smith 72901 (522 Garland Ave., 479-783-5345)
Little Rock 72206 (2523 Confederate Blvd., 501-324-6401)

CALIFORNIA
Benefits Office:
Sacramento 95827 (10365 Old Placerville Rd., 916-364-6500)

VA Medical Centers:
Fresno, VA Medical Center, 2615 E. Clinton Avenue, Fresno, CA, 93703, 559-225-6100
Greater Los Angeles HCS, 11301 Wilshire Blvd., West Los Angeles, CA, 90073, 310-478-3711

Livermore, VA Palo Alto HCS Livermore Div., 4951 Arroyo Road, Livermore, CA, 94550, 925-455-7402

Loma Linda HCS, 11201 Benton Street, Loma Linda, CA, 92357, 909-825-7084

Long Beach HCS, 5901 E. Seventh Street, Long Beach, CA, 90822, 562-826-8000

N. California HCS-Martinez, VA Northern California Health Care System, 150 Muir Rd, Martinez, CA, 94553, 925-372-2000

N. California HCS-Sacramento, Sacramento VA Medical Center, 10535 Hospital Way, Mather, CA, 95655, 916-843-7000

Palo Alto-Menlo Pk, Palo Alto HCS Menlo Park Div., 795 Willow Road, Menlo Park, CA, 94025, 650-858-3939

Palo Alto-Palo Alto, VA Palo Alto HCS VAMC Palo Alto CA Div, 3801 Miranda Avenue, Palo Alto, CA, 94304, 650-493-5000

San Diego HCS, 3350 La Jolla Village Drive, San Diego, CA, 92161, 858-552-8585

San Francisco, VA Medical Center, 4150 Clement Street, San Francisco, CA, 94121, 415-281-5100

Sepulveda, 16111 Plummer Street, Sepulveda, CA, 91343, 818-891-7711

Clinics:

Anaheim, Anaheim CBOC, 2569 W. Woodland Drive, Anaheim, CA, 92801, 714-763-5300

Antelope Valley, 547 W. Lancaster Blvd., Lancaster, CA, 93534, 661-729-8655

Bakersfield, 1801 Westwind Drive, Bakersfield, CA, 93301, 661-632-1800

Blythe, 1273 West Hobson Way, Blythe, CA 92225, 760-921-1224

Chico, Chico VA Outpatient Clinic, 280 Cohasset Road, Chico, CA, 95926, 530-879-5000

Chico-Annex, Chico VA Outpatient Clinic, 254 Cohasset Road, Suite 20, Chico, CA, 95926, 530-879-5057

Chula Vista, 835 3rd Avenue, Suite B, Chula Vista, CA, 91910, 619-409-1600

Clearlake, 15145 Lakeshore Drive, Clearlake, CA, 95422, 707-995-7200

Corona, 800 Magnolia Street, Suite 101, Corona, CA, 92879, 951-817-8820

Diamond View, Diamond View CBOC, 110 Bella Way, Susanville, CA, 96130, 530-251-4550

East Los Angeles Clinic, 5426 E. Olympic Blvd., Suite 150, Commerce, CA, 90022, 323-725-7372

Escondido, 815 East Pennsylvania Ave., Escondido, CA, 92025, 760-466-7020

Eureka, Eureka CBOC, 930 W. Harris Street, Eureka, CA, 95503, 707-269-7500

Fairfield, Fairfield VA Outpatient Clinic, 103 Bodin Circle, Building 778, Travis AFB, CA, 94535, 707-437-1800

Fremont/East Bay (Alameda County), 39199 Liberty Street, Fremont, CA, 94538, 510-791-4000

Gardena, 1251 Redondo Beach Blvd., Third Floor, Gardena, CA, 90247, 310-851-4705

Imperial Valley, 1600 S Imperial Dr., El Centro, CA, 92243, 760-352-1506

Laguna Hills, Laguna Hills Veterans Health, 25292 McIntyre Street, Laguna Hills, CA, 92653, 949-269-0700

Long Beach Clinic, Villages at Cabrillo Clinic, 2001 River Avenue, Building 28, Long Beach, CA, 90810, 562-826-8414

Los Angeles, 351 East Temple Street, Los Angeles, CA, 90012, 213-253-2677

Martinez, Martinez VA Outpatient Clinic, 150 Muir Road, Martinez, CA, 94553, 925-372-2000

McClellan, McClellan VA Outpatient Clinic, 5342 Dudley Blvd., Building 88, McClellan Park, CA, 95652, 916-561-7400

Merced, Merced CBOC, 340 E Yosemite Ave., Suite D, Merced, CA, 95340, 209-381-0105

Mission Valley, 8810 Rio San Diego Drive, San Diego, CA, 92108, 619-400-5000

Modesto, Modesto CBOC, 1225 Oakdale Road, Modesto, CA, 95355, 209-557-6200

Monterey, VA Monterey Outpatient Clinic, 3401 Engineer Lane, Seaside, CA, 93955, 831-883-3800

Murrieta, 28078 Baxter Road, Suite 540, Murrieta, CA, 92563, 951-290-6500

Oakhurst, 40597 Westlake Drive, Oakhurst, CA, 93644, 559-683-5300

Oakland, Oakland VA Outpatient Clinic, 2221 Martin Luther King Jr. Way, Oakland, CA, 94612, 510-267-7820

Oakland-Behavioral Health, Oakland Behavioral Health Clinic, 525 21st Street, Oakland, CA, 94612, 510-587-3400

Oceanside, 1300 Rancho del Oro Drive, Oceanside, CA, 92056, 760-643-2000

Palm Desert, 41-990 Cook Street, Bldg F Suite 1004, Palm Desert, CA, 92211, 760-341-5570

Palo Alto HCS- Capitola, VA Capitola Outpatient Clinic, 1350 N. 41st Street, Suite 102, Capitola, CA, 95010, 831-464-5519

Pasadena, 420 W. Las Tunas Drive, San Gabriel, CA, 91776, 626-289-5973

Port Hueneme (Oxnard), 2000 Outlet Center Drive, Suite 225, Oxnard, CA, 93036, 805-604-6960

Rancho Cucamonga, 8599 Haven Avenue, Suite 102, Rancho Cucamonga, CA, 91730, 909-946-5348

Redding, Redding VA Outpatient Clinic, 351 Hartnell Ave., Redding, CA, 96002, 530-226-7555

Redding-Annex, Redding Clinic Annex, 760 Cypress Avenue, Suite 100, Redding, CA, 96001, 530-244-8800

San Bruno, 1001 Sneath Lane, San Bruno, CA, 94066, 650-615-6000

San Francisco, SFVAMC Downtown Clinic - 662GF, 401 3rd Street, San Francisco, CA, 94107, 415-551-7300

San Jose, VA San Jose Outpatient Clinic, 80 Great Oaks Blvd., San Jose, CA, 95119, 408-363-3011

San Luis Obispo, 1288 Morro St., #200, San Luis Obispo, CA, 93401, 805-543-1233

Santa Ana, Brookhollow Business Park, 1506 Brookhollow Drive, Suite 100, Santa Ana, CA, 92705, 714-434-4600

Santa Barbara, 4440 Calle Real, Santa Barbara, CA, 93110, 805-683-1491

Santa Fe Springs/Whittier, Whittier/Santa Fe Springs Clinic, 10210 Orr & Day Road, Santa Fe Springs, CA, 90670, 562-466-6080
Santa Maria, 1550 East Main Street, Santa Maria, CA, 93454, 805-354-6000
Santa Rosa, Santa Rosa Outpatient Clinic, 3841Brickway Blvd., Santa Rosa, CA, 95403, 707-569-2300
Sepulveda, 16111 Plummer Street, Sepulveda, CA, 91343, 818-891-7711
Sierra Foothills, VA Sierra Foothills Outpatient Clinic, 11985 Heritage Oaks Place, Suite 1, Auburn, CA, 95603, 530-889-0872
Sonora (Tuolumne County), VA Sonora Outpatient Care, 13663 Mono Way, Sonora, CA, 95370, 209-588-2600
South Central LA, 3737 E. Martin Luther King Jr Blvd., Suite 515, Lynwood, CA, 90262, 310-537-6825
Stockton, VA Stockton Outpatient Clinic, 7777 South Freedom Road, French Camp, CA, 95231, 209-946-3400
Tulare, South Valley Outpatient Clinic, 1050 N. Cherry, Tulare, CA, 93274, 559-684-8703
Ukiah, VA Ukiah Outpatient Clinic, 238B Hospital Drive, Ukiah, CA, 95482, 707-468-7700
Vallejo/Mare Island, Mare Island VA Outpatient Clinic, 201 Walnut Avenue, Building 201, Mare Island, CA, 94592, 707-562-8200
Victorville, 12138 Industrial Blvd., Suite 120, Victorville, CA, 92395, 760-951-2599
Yuba City, Yuba City VA Outpatient Clinic, 425 Plumas Blvd, Yuba City, CA, 95991, 530-751-4500

Regional Office:
Los Angeles 90024 (Fed. Bldg., 11000 Wilshire Blvd., serving counties of Inyo, Kern, Los Angeles, San Bernardino, San Luis Obispo, Santa Barbara and Ventura, statewide 1-800-827-1000)
Oakland 94612 (1301 Clay St., Rm. 1300 North, serving all CA counties not served by the Los Angeles, San Diego, or Reno VA Regional Offices, 1-800-827-1000)
San Diego 92108 (8810 Rio San Diego Dr., serving Imperial, Orange, Riverside and San Diego, statewide 1-800-827-1000). The counties of Alpine, Lassen, Modoc, and Mono are served by the Reno, NV, Regional Office.

Benefits Office:
Sacramento 95827 (10365 Old Placerville Rd., 1-800-827-1000)
Camp Pendleton 92055 (Family Services, Bldg 13150, Rm 226, 760-385-0416, VR&E 619-980-6113)
Camp Pendleton 92055 (Wounded Warrior Transition Ctr, Santa Margarita Rd, 760-870-4428, VR&E 760-909-7291)
Hemet 92543 (VR&E, Work Force Development Center, 1075 N. State Street, 951-791-3503)
Laguna Hills 92653 (Outbased Clinic, 25292 McIntyre St, 949-269-0700, VR&E 562-826-8582)
Riverside 92507 (VR&E Riverside County Government Offices, 1153 Spruce

Street, Suite A, 951-955-3032)
San Diego 92134 (Balboa Career Transition Ctr, Naval Medical Ctr, Bldg 26, 619-532-5122, VR&E 619-532-8194)
San Diego 92136 (Naval Station San Diego, Dolphin Alley, Bldg 270, 619-230-0393, VR&E 619-230-0390)
San Diego 92140 (Marine Corps Recruit Depot, 4025 Tripoli Ave, Bldg 14, 619-524-8233)
San Diego 92145 (MCAS Miramar, Bldg 5305, 858-689-2141)
San Diego 92182 (VR&E San Diego State University, Student Services West, 5500 Campanile Dr, 619-594-2444)

Vet Centers:
Antelope Valley Vet Center, Antelope Valley Vet Center, 38925 Trade Center Drive, Palmdale, CA, 93551, 661-267-1026
Bakersfield Vet Center, Bakersfield Vet Center, 1110 Golden State Ave., Bakersfield, CA, 93301, 661-323-8387
Chatsworth Vet Center, Chatsworth Vet Center, 20946 Devonshire Street, Suite 101, Chatsworth, CA, 91311, 818-576-0201
Chico Vet Center, Chico Vet Center, 250 Cohasset Road, Suite 40, Chico, CA, 95926, 530-899-6300
Chula Vista Vet Center, Chula Vista Vet Center, 180 Otay Lakes Road, Suites 107-108, Bonita, CA, 91902, 858-404-8380
Citrus Heights Vet Center, Citrus Heights Vet Center, 5650 Sunrise Boulevard, Suite 150, Citrus Heights, CA, 95610, 916-535-0420
Concord Vet Center, Concord Vet Center, 1333 Willow Pass Road, Suite 106, Concord, CA, 94520, 925-680-4526
Corona Vet Center, 800 Magnolia Avenue, Suite 110, Corona, CA, 92879, 951-734-0525
East Los Angeles Vet Center, 5400 E. Olympic Blvd., Suite 140, Commerce, CA, 90022, 323-728-9966
Eureka Vet Center, Eureka Vet Center, 2830 G Street, Suite A/B, Eureka, CA, 95501, 707-444-8271
Fresno Vet Center, 1320 E. Shaw Avenue, Suite 125, Fresno, CA, 93710, 559-487-5660
High Desert Vet Cente 15095 Amargosa Road, Suite 107, Victorville, CA, 92394, 760-261-5925
Los Angeles Vet Center, 1045 W. Redondo Beach Blvd., Suite150, Gardena, CA, 90247, 310-767-1221
Modesto Vet Center, Modesto Vet Center, 1219 N. Carpenter Road, Suite 12, Modesto, CA, 95351, 209-569-0713
North Orange County Vet Center, 12453 Lewis Street, Suite 101, Garden Grove, CA, 92840, 714-776-0161
Northbay Vet Center, 6225 State Farm Drive, Suite 101, Rohnert Park, CA, 94928, 707-586-3295
Oakland Vet Center, 2221 Martin Luther King Jr. Way, Oakland, CA, 94612, 510-763-3904
Peninsula Vet Center, 2946 Broadway St., Redwood City, CA, 94062, 650-299-

0672

Sacramento Vet Center, 1111 Howe Ave., Suite 390, Sacramento, CA, 95825, 916-566-7430

San Bernardino Vet Center, 1325 E Cooley Dr., Suite 101, Colton, CA, 92324, 909-801-5762

San Diego Vet Center, San Diego Vet Center, 2790 Truxtun Road, Suite 130, San Diego, CA, 92106, 858-642-1500

San Francisco Vet Center, 505 Polk Street, San Francisco, CA, 94102, 415-441-5051

San Jose Vet Center, 278 North 2nd Street, San Jose, CA, 95112, 408-993-0729

San Luis Obispo Vet Center, San Luis Obispo Vet Center, 1070 Southwood Drive, San Luis Obispo, CA, 93401, 805-782-9101

San Marcos Vet Center, San Marcos Vet Center, One Civic Center Drive, Suite 150, San Marcos, CA, 92069, 855-898-6050

Santa Cruz County Vet Center, Santa Cruz County Vet Center, 1350 41st Ave., Suite 104, Capitola, CA, 95010, 831-464-4575

South Orange County Vet Center, South Orange County Vet Center, 26431 Crown Valley Parkway, Suite 100, Mission Viejo, CA, 92691, 949-348-6700

Temecula Vet Center, T40935 County Center Drive, Suite A, Temecula, CA, 92591, 951-302-4849

Ventura Vet Center, 790 East Santa Clara Ave., Suite 100, Ventura, CA, 93001, 805-585-1860

West Los Angeles Vet Center, 5730 Uplander Way, Suite 100, Culver City, CA, 90230, 310-641-0326

National Cemeteries:
Bakersfield 93203 (30338 E. Bear Mountain Blvd., Arvin, 661-867-8850)
Fort Rosecrans 92106 (P.O. Box 6237, Point Loma, San Diego, 619-553-2084)
Golden Gate 94066 (1300 Sneath Ln., San Bruno, 650-589-7737)
Los Angeles 90049 (950 South Sepulveda Blvd., 310-268-4675)
Miramar 92122 (5795 Nobel Dr.., San Diego, 619-553-2084)
Riverside 92518 (22495 Van Buren Blvd., 951-653-8417)
Sacramento Valley VA 95620 (5810 Midway Rd., Dixon, 707-693-2460)
San Francisco 94129 (1 Lincoln Blvd., Presidio of San Francisco, 650-589-7737)
San Joaquin Valley 95322 (32053 West McCabe Rd., Santa Nella, 209-854-1040)

COLORADO
Medical centers:
Eastern Colorado HCS, VA Medical Center, 1055 Clermont Street, Denver, CO, 80220, 303-399-8020

Eastern Colorado HCS- Southern Colorado, VA Nursing Home Unit, 2600 Oak-shire Lane, Pueblo, CO, 81001, 719-295-7275

Grand Junction, VA Medical Center, 2121 N. Avenue,, Grand Junction, CO, 81501, 970-242-0731

Clinics:
Alamosa, Alamosa Clinic, 622 Del Sol Drive, Alamosa, CO, 81101, 719-587-6800
Aurora, Aurora Clinic, 13701 East Mississippi Ave, Gateway Medical Bldg Ste 200, Aurora, CO, 80012, 303-398-6340
Burlington, Burlington VA CBOC, 1177 Rose Avenue, Burlington, CO, 80807, 719-346-5239
Colorado Springs, Colorado Springs Clinic, 25 North Spruce, Colorado Springs, CO, 80905, 719-327-5660
Colorado Springs-Fontanero, 320 East Fontanero St., Colorado Springs, CO, 80905, 719-327-5660
Major William Adams Veterans' Telehealth Clinic, 785 Russell St. Suite 400, Craig , CO 81625. Phone: 970-824-6721 Fax: 970-824-9439
Durango, Durango CBOC, 1970 E Third Ave., Suite 102, Durango, CO, 81301, 970-247-2214
Fort Collins, Fort Collins Outpatient Clinic, 2509 Research Blvd., Fort Collins, CO, 80526, 970-224-1550
Glenwood Springs VA Telehealth Clinic, 2425 S. Grand Ave Ste 101, Glenwood Springs CO 81601. 970-945-100
Greeley, Greeley Outpatient Clinic, 2001 70th Avenue, Suite 200, Greeley, CO, 80634, 970-313-0027
Golden VA Community Clinic 1020 Johnson Road Golden, CO 80401, 303-914-2680
La Junta, La Junta Clinic, 1100 Carson Ave., Suite 204, La Junta, CO, 81050, 719-383-5195
Lamar, Lamar Clinic, 403 Kendal Drive, Lamar, CO, 81052, 719-336-7155
Montrose, Montrose Outpatient Clinic, 4 Hillcrest Plaza Way, Montrose, CO, 81401, 970-249-7791
Pueblo, Pueblo Clinic, 4776 Eagleridge Circle, Pueblo, CO, 81008, 719-553-1000

Regional Office:
Denver 80225 (Mailing Address: PO Box 25126. Physical Address: 155 Van Gordon St., Lakewood, 80228, statewide 1-800-827-1000)

Vet Centers:
Boulder Vet Center, 2336 Canyon Blvd., Suite 103, Boulder, CO, 80302, 303-440-7306
Colorado Springs Vet Center, 602 South Nevada Ave., Colorado Springs, CO, 80903, 719-471-9992
Denver Vet Center, 7465 East First Ave., Suite B, Denver, CO, 80230, 303-326-0645
Fort Collins Vet Center, Fort Collins Vet Center, 702 W. Drake, Building C, Fort Collins, CO, 80526, 970-221-5176
Grand Junction Vet Center, Grand Junction Vet Center, 2472 Patterson Road, Unit #16, Grand Junction, CO, 81505, 970-245-4156

Pueblo Vet Center, Pueblo Vet Center, 1515 Fortino Blvd, Suite 130, Pueblo, CO, 81008, 719-583-4058

VHA Chief Business Office:
Health Administration Center: Denver 80209 (3773 Cherry Creek North Dr., 303-331-7500)
Project HERO: Denver 80209 (3773 Cherry Creek North Dr., 303-370-7755)

National Cemeteries:
Fort Logan 80236 (4400 W. Kenyon Ave., Denver, 303-761-0117)
Fort Lyon 81504 (15700 County Road HH, Las Animas, 303-761-0117)

CONNECTICUT
VA Medical Centers:
Newington Campus, VA Connecticut Health care System, 555 Willard Avenue, Newington, CT, 6111, 860-666-6951
West Haven, VA Connecticut Health care System, 950 Campbell Avenue, West Haven, CT, 6516, 203-932-5711

Clinics:
Danbury, 7 Germantown Road, Suite 2B, Danbury, CT, 6810, 203-798-8422
New London VA Primary Care Center, 4 Shaw's Cove, 1st Floor Suite 101, New London, CT, 6320, 860-701-5996
Stamford VA Primary Care Center, 1275 Summer Street, Suite 102, Stamford, CT, 6905, 203-325-0649
Waterbury VA Primary Care Center, Croft Building, 95 Scovill Street, Waterbury, CT, 6706, 203-465-5292
Willimantic CBOC, Willimantic CBOC, 1320 Main Street, Willimantic, CT, 6226, 860-450-7583
Winsted VA Primary Care, Winsted Health Center, 115 Spencer Street, Winsted, CT, 6098, 860-738-6985

Regional Office:
Hartford (PO Box 310909, Newington, CT 06131),1-800-827-1000)
For UPS shipments :
VA Regional Office – 308, Building 2E - Room 5137, 555 Willard Ave., Newington, CT 06111
Vet Centers:
Danbury Vet Center, Danbury Vet Center, 457 North Main Street, Danbury, CT, 6831, 203-790-4000
Hartford Vet Center, 25 Elm Street, Suite A, Rocky Hill, CT, 6067, 860-563-8800
New Haven Vet Center, 141 Captain Thomas Blvd., West Haven, CT, 6516, 203-932-9899
Norwich Vet Center, 2 Cliff Street, Norwich, CT, 6360, 860-887-1755

DELAWARE

VA Medical Center:
Wilmington, VA Medical Center, 1601 Kirkwood Highway, Wilmington, DE, 19805, 302-994-2511

Clinics:
Kent County, Kent County VA Outpatient Clinic, 1198 S. Governors Avenue, Suites 201, Dover, DE, 19901, 302-994-2511 x2400
Sussex County, Sussex County CBOC, 15 Georgetown Plaza, Georgetown, DE, 19947, 302-994-2511 x2300

Regional Office:
Wilmington 19805 (1601 Kirkwood Hwy., local, 1-800-827-1000)

Vet Center:
Sussex County Vet Center, Sussex County Vet Center, 20653 DuPont Blvd., Georgetown, DE, 19947, 302-225-9110
Wilmington Vet Center, Wilmington Vet Center, 2710 Centerville Road, Suite 103, Wilmington, DE, 19808, 302-994-1660

DISTRICT OF COLUMBIA

VA Medical Center:
Washington, VA Medical Center, 50 Irving Street NW, Washington, DC, 20422, 202-745-8000

Clinic:
Southeast Washington, 820 Chesapeake St. SE, Washington, DC, 20032, 202-745-8685

Appeals Management Center:
Washington, D.C., 20421 (1722 I St., N.W., local, 1-800-827-1000)

Regional Office:
Washington, D.C., 20421 (1722 I St., N.W., local, 1-800-827-1000)

Vet Center:
Washington Vet Center, 1250 Taylor Street, NW, Washington, DC, 20011, 202-726-5212

Community Resource and Referral Center 1500 Franklin St., NE Washington, DC 20018, 202-636-7660

FLORIDA

VA Medical Centers:
Bay Pines, VA Health care System, 10000 Bay Pines Blvd., Bay Pines, FL, 33708, 727-398-6661

Miami, VA Health care System, 1201 N W 16th Street, Miami, FL, 33125, 305-575-7000
North Florida/South Georgia HCS-Gainesville, 1601 S W Archer Road, Gainesville, FL, 32608, 352-376-1611
North Florida/South Georgia HCS-Lake City, VA Medical Center, 619 S. Marion Ave., Lake City, FL, 32025, 386-755-3016
North Florida/South Georgia VHS Domiciliary, 1604 SE 3rd Avenue, Gaines-ville, FL, 32641, 352-548-1800
Orlando, Orlando VA Health care Center, 5201 Raymond Street, Orlando, FL, 32803, 407-629-1599
Tampa, James A. Haley VA Medical Center, 13000 Bruce B Downs Blvd., Tampa, FL, 33612, 813-972-2000
West Palm Beach, VA Medical Center, 7305 N. Military Trail, West Palm Beach, FL, 33410, 561-422-8262

Clinics:
Boca Raton, VA Clinic, 901 Meadows Road, Boca Raton, FL, 33433, 561-416-8995
Bradenton, VA Clinic, 5520 SR 64, Bradenton, FL, 34208, 941-721-0649
Brooksville, VA Clinic, 14540 Cortez Blvd., Suite 108, Brooksville, FL, 34613, 352-597-8287
Broward County, VA Outpatient Clinic, 9800 West Commercial Blvd., Sunrise, FL, 33351, 954-475-5500
Clermont, 805 Oakley Seaver Drive, Clermont, FL, 34711, 352-536-8200
Daytona Beach, William V. Chappell Jr. VA OPC, 551 National Health Care Drive, Daytona Beach, FL, 32114, 386-323-7500
Daytona Beach-South, Daytona Beach VA OPC Day Treatment Program, 721 Beville Road, Daytona Beach, FL, 32119, 386-323-7500
Deerfield Beach, VA Clinic, 2100 SW 10th Street, Deerfield, FL, 33442, 954-570-5572
Delray Beach, VA Clinic, 4800 Linton Blvd., Suite E300, Delray Beach, FL, 33445, 561-495-1973
Eglin AFB, Eglin CBOC, 100 Veterans Way, Eglin AFB, FL, 32542, 850-609-2600
Ft Pierce, VA Clinic, 1901 South 25th Street, Suite 103, Fort Pierce, FL, 34950, 772-595-5150
Hollywood (Southeast Broward Co.), Hollywood CBOC, 3702 Washington Street, Suite 201, Hollywood, FL, 33021, 954-986-1811
Homestead, VA Clinic, 950 Krome Avenue, Suite 401, Homestead, FL, 33030, 305-248-0874
Jacksonville, 1536 N. Jefferson Street, Jacksonville, FL, 32209, 904-475-5800
Joint Ambulatory Care Center, Pensacola Outpatient Clinic, 790 Veterans Way, Pensacola, FL, 32507, 850-912-2000
Key Largo, VA Clinic, 105662 Overseas Highway, Key Largo, FL, 33037, 305-451-0164
Key West, VA Clinic, 1300 Douglas Circle, Key West, FL, 33040, 305-293-4609

Kissimmee, Kissimmee CBOC, 2285 North Central Avenue, Kissimmee, FL, 34741, 407-518-5004

Lake Baldwin OPC, 5201 Raymond Street, Orlando, FL, 32803, 407-629-1599

Lake Nona Annex, 10415 Moss Park Road, Orlando FL 32832 407-304-2500

Lakeland, VA Clinic, 4237 South Pipkin Road, Lakeland, FL, 33811, 863-701-2470

Lecanto, Lecanto CBOC, 2804 W Marc Knighton Court, Suite A, Lecanto, FL, 34461, 352-746-8000

Lee County, 2489 Diplomat Parkway East, Cape Coral, FL, 33909, 239-652-1800

Leesburg (Lake County), VA Clinic, 711 W. Main Street, Leesburg, FL, 34748, 352-435-4000

Marianna, 4970 Highway 90, Marianna, FL, 32446, 850-718-5620

Miami, Miami OSAC, 1(1201 NW 16th Street, Room 1E107A Miami, FL 33215) (305) 575-7000

Naples/Collier County, VA Clinic, 2685 Horseshoe Drive S., Suite 101, Naples, FL, 34104, 239-659-9188

New Port Richey, VA Clinic, 9912 Little Road, New Port Richey, FL, 34654, 727-869-4100

Ocala, VA Clinic, 1515 East Silver Springs Blvd., Suite 226, Ocala, FL, 34470, 352-369-3320

Ocala-West, Ocala West, 3307 SW 26th Avenue, Ocala, FL, 34474, 352-861-3940

Okeechobee, VA Clinic, 1201 N. Parrot Ave., Okeechobee, FL, 34972, 863-824-3232

Orange City CBOC 2583 South Volusia Avenue (US 17-92) Orange City FL 32763, 386-456-2080

Palatka, 400 North State Road 19, Palatka, FL, 32177, 386-329-8800

Palm Harbor, Palm Harbor CBOC, 35209 US Hwy 19 North, Palm Harbor, FL, 34684, 727-734-5276

Panama City, Naval Support Activity, 101 Vernon Avenue, Bld 387, Panama City Beach, FL, 32407, 850-636-7000

Pembroke Pines, VA Clinic, 7369 Sheridan Street, Suite 102, Hollywood, FL, 33024, 954-894-1668

Port Charlotte/Charlotte County, 4161 Tamiami Trail, Unit 4, Port Charlotte, FL, 33952, 941-235-2710

Port St. Lucie 34986 (126 S.W. Chamber Court, Port St. Lucie Phone: 772-878-7876 (PCT Clinic) 772-344-9288 (Expanded Services)

Sarasota, VA CLINIC, 5682 Bee Ridge Road, Suite 100, Sarasota, FL, 34233, 941-371-3349

Sebring, Sebring CBOC - VA Primary Care Clinic, 5901 US Highway 27 South, Sebring, FL, 33870, 863-471-6227

St Petersburg, St. Petersburg CBOC, 840 Dr. MLK Jr. Street North, St. Petersburg, FL, 33705, 727-502-1700

St. Augustine, VA Clinic, 1955 Highway US1 South, Suite 200, St. Augustine, FL, 32086, 904-829-0814

Stuart, VA Clinic, 3501 SE Willoughby Blvd., Stuart, FL, 34997, 772-288-0304

Tallahassee, VA Clinic, 1607 St. James Court, Tallahassee, FL, 32308, 850-878-0191

The Villages CBOC, The Villiages CBOC, 8900 SE 165th Mulberry Lane, The Villages, FL, 32162, 352-674-5000

Vero Beach, VA Clinic, 372 17th Street, Vero Beach, FL, 32960, 772-299-4623

Viera OPC, VA Clinic, 2900 Veterans Way, Viera, FL, 32940, 321-637-3788

Zephyrhills, VA Clinic, 6937 Medical View Lane, Zephyrhills, FL, 33542, 813-780-2550

Regional Office:
St. Petersburg 33708 (mailing address: P.O. Box 1437, 33731; physical address: 9500 Bay Pines Blvd., statewide 1-800-827-1000)

Benefits Offices:
Fort Lauderdale 33301 (VR&E - 9800 W. Commercial Blvd., Sunrise, FL 33351 1-800-827-1000)

Jacksonville 32256 (VR&E, 7825 Baymeadows Way, Suite 120-B, 1-800-827-1000)

Orlando 32801 (1000 Legion Pl., VRE-Suite 1500, C&P-Suite 1550, 1-800-827-1000)

Pensacola 32503-7492 (C&P, 312 Kenmore Rd., Rm. 1G250, 1-800-827-1000)

West Palm Beach 33410 (C&P, 7305 North Military Tr., Suite 1A-167, 1-800-827-1000)

Vet Centers:
Bay County Vet Center, 3109 Minnesota Avenue, Suite 101, Panama City, FL, 32405, 850-522-6102

Clearwater Vet Center, Clearwater Vet Center, 29259 US Hwy 19 North, Clearwater, FL, 33761, 727-549-3600

Collier County Vet Center (Naples),, 2705 South Horseshoe Drive, Unit 203, Naples, FL, 34104, 239-403-2377

Daytona Beach Vet Center, 1620 Mason Ave, Suite C, Daytona Beach, FL, 32117, 386-366-6600

Fort Lauderdale Vet Center, 713 NE 3rd Ave., Ft. Lauderdale, FL, 33304, 954-356-7926

Ft. Myers Vet Center, 4110 Center Pointe Drive, Suite 204, Ft Myers, FL, 33916, 239-652-1861

Gainesville Vet Center, 105 NW 75th Street, Suite 2, Gainesville, FL, 32607, 352-331-1408

Jacksonville Vet Center, 300 East State St., Suite J, Jacksonville, FL, 32202, 904-232-3621

Jupiter Vet Center, 6650 W Indiantown Road, Suite 120, Jupiter, FL, 33458, 561-422-1220

Lake County Vet Center (Clermont), 1655 East Highway 50, Suite 102, Clermont, FL, 33073, 352-536-6701

Marion County Vet Center (Ocala),), 612 Southwest 1st Avenue, Ocala, FL, 34471, 352-317-2563

Melbourne Vet Center, 2098 Sarno Road, Melbourne, FL, 32935, 321-254-3410

Miami Vet Center, 8280 NW 27th Street, Suite 511, Miami, FL, 33122, 305-718-3712

Okaloosa County Vet Center, Shalimar Centre II, 6 11th Avenue, Suite G 1, Shalimar, FL, 32579, 850-651-1000

Orlando Vet Center, 5575 S. Semoran Blvd., #36, Orlando, FL, 32822, 407-857-2800

Palm Beach Vet Center, Haverhill Plaza, 4669 10th Ave., N. #86, Suite 6, Lake Worth, FL, 33463, 561-422-1201

Pasco County Vet Center, Pasco County Vet Center, 7347 Ridge Road, New Port Richey, FL, 34668, 727-697-5176

Pensacola Vet Center, Office Park West, 4504 Twin Oak Dr., Suite 104, Pensacola, FL, 32506, 850-456-5886

Polk County Vet Center, 1370 Ariana Street, Lakeland, FL, 33803, 863-284-0841

Pompano Beach Vet Center, 2300 West Sample Road, Suite 102, Pompano Beach, FL, 33073, 954-984-1669

Sarasota Vet Center, 4801 Swift Road, Suite A, Sarasota, FL, 34231, 941-927-8285

St. Petersburg Vet Center, Gaslight Square, 6798 Crosswinds Drive N, Building A, St. Petersburg, FL, 33710, 727-549-3633

Tallahassee Vet Center, 548 Bradford Road, Tallahassee, FL, 32303, 850-942-8810

Tampa Vet Center, 36 W. Waters Avenue, Fountain Oaks Business Plaza, Tampa, FL, 33614, 813-228-2621

National Cemeteries:
Barrancas 32508-1054 (1 Cemetery Rd., Naval Air Station Pensacola, 850-453-4846)

Bay Pines 33504-0477 (10000 Bay Pines Blvd., Bay Pines, 727-398-9426)

Florida 33513 (6502 SW 102nd Ave., Bushnell, 352-793-7740)

Jacksonville 32218 (4083 Lannie Rd., 904-766-5222)

St. Aug. ine 32084 (104 Marine St., 352-793-7740)

Sarasota 34241 (9810 State Road 72, Sarasota, 941-922-7200)

South Florida 33467 (6501 South State Road 7, Lake Worth, 561-649-6489)

GEORGIA
VA Medical Centers:
Atlanta, VA Medical Center, 1670 Clairmont Road,, Decatur, GA, 30033, 404-321-6111

Augusta, VA Medical Center, 950 15th Street, Augusta, GA, 30901, 706-733-0188

Carrollton, 180 Martin Drive, Carrollton, GA, 30117, 404-321-6111 x2155

Dublin, Carl Vinson VA Medical Center, 1826 Veterans Boulevard, Dublin, GA, 31021, 478-272-1210

Lenwood (Uptown), VA Medical Center, 1 Freedom Way, Augusta, GA, 30904, 706-733-0188

Clinics:
Albany GA, 526 West Broad Avenue, Albany, GA, 31701, 478-272-1210
Athens, 9249 Hwy 29 S., Athens, GA, 30601, 706-227-4534
Austell, 2041 Mesa Valley Way, Suite 185, Austell, GA, 30106, 404-329-2222
Baldwin County, Peter Wheeler Building, 2249 Vinson Highway, Georgia War Veterans Home, Milledgeville, GA, 31061, 478-414-4540
Blairsville, 1294 Highway 515 East, Blairsville, GA, 30512, 404-321-6111
Brunswick, Summit Professional Plaza 2, 1111 Glynco Parkway, Suite 200, Brunswick, GA, 31525, 912-261-2355
Carrollton, 180 Martin Drive, Carrollton, GA, 30117, 404-321-6111 x2155
Columbus, The Medical Arts Building, 1310 13th Street, Columbus, GA, 31906, 706-257-7200
East Point, 1513 Cleveland Ave., Suite 300 Buggy Works Office Park, East Point, GA, 30344, 404-321-6111
Hinesville, 740 East General Stewart Way, Suite 102, Hinesville, GA, 31313, 912-920-0214
Lawrenceville (Gwinnett County), 455 Philip Boulevard, Suite 200, Lawrenceville, GA, 30046, 404-321-6111
Macon GA, 5398 Thomaston Road, Suite B, Macon, GA, 31220, 478-476-8868
NE Georgia/Oakwood, 3931 Mundy Mill Road, Suite C, Oakwood, GA, 30566, 404-728-8210
Newnan, 39-A Oak Hill Court, Newnan, GA, 30265, 404-728-7601
Savannah, 325 West Montgomery Crossroads, Savannah, GA, 31406, 912-920-0214
St. Marys, 205 Lakeshore Point, St. Marys, GA, 31558, 912-510-3420
Stockbridge, 175 Medical Blvd., Stockbridge, GA, 30281, 404-329-2222
Valdosta, VA Clinic, 2841 N Patterson Street, Valdosta, GA, 31602, 229-293-0132

Regional Office:
Decatur 30033 (1700 Clairmont Rd., statewide 1-800-827-1000)

Vet Centers:
Atlanta Vet Center, 1800 Phoenix Blvd, Building 400, Suite 404, Box 55, Atlanta, GA, 30349, 404-321-6111
Lawrenceville Vet Center, 930 River Centre Place, Lawrenceville, GA, 30043, 404-728-4195
Macon Vet Center, 750 Riverside Drive, Macon, GA, 31201, 478-477-3813
Marietta Vet Center, 40 Dodd Street, Suite 700, Marietta, GA, 30060, 404-327-4954
Muscogee County (Columbus), 2601 Cross Country Drive, Condominium B-2, Suite 900, Columbus, GA, 31901, 706-596-7170
Richmond County Vet Center (Augusta), 2050 Walton Way, Suite 100, Augusta, GA, 30904, 706-729-5762
Savannah Vet Center, 321 Commercial Drive, Savannah, GA, 31406, 912-961-5800

VHA Chief Business Office
Health Eligibility Center: Atlanta, 30329-1647 (2957 Clairmont Rd. NE, STE 200, 404-828-5200)

National Cemeteries:
Georgia 30114 (2025 Mt. Carmel Church Lane, Canton, 866-236-8159)
Marietta 30060 (500 Washington Ave., 866-236-8159)

GUAM
Clinic:
Guam, VA Guam Clinic, 498 Chalan Palasyo, Agana Heights, GU, 96910, 671-472-7250

Benefits Office/Vet Center:
Hagatna 96910 (Reflection Center, Suite 201, 222 Chalan Santo Papa St., 671-472-7161)

Vet Center:
Guam Vet Center, Reflection Center, 222 Chalan Santo Papa, Suite 201, Hagatna, GU, 96910, 671-472-7160

HAWAII
Medical Center:
Pacific Islands HCS (Honolulu), VA Pacific Islands Health Care System, 459 Patterson Road, Honolulu, HI, 96819, 808-433-0100

Clinics:
Hilo, VA Hilo Outpatient Clinic, 1285 Waianuenue, Suite 211, Hilo, HI, 96720, 808-935-3781
Kailua-Kona, VA Kona Outpatient Clinic, 75-377 Hualalai Road, Kailua-Kona, HI, 96740, 808-329-0774
Leeward Oahu, Leeward Oahu CBOC, 91-2135 Fort Weaver Road, Suite 501, Ewa Beach, HI, 96706, 800-214-1306
Lihue, VA Kauai Outpatient Cllinic, 4485 Pahe'e Street, Suite 150, Lihue, HI, 96766, 808-246-0497
Maui, VA Maui Outpatient Clinic, 203 Ho'ohana Street, Suite 303, Kahului, HI, 96732, 808-871-2454

Regional Office:
Honolulu 96819-1522 (459 Patterson Rd., E Wing. Mailing address: PO Box 29020, Honolulu, HI 96820) (toll-free from Hawaii, Guam, Saipan, Rota and Tinian, 1-800-827-1000; toll-free from American Samoa, 684-699-3730)

VR&E Benefits Offices:
Hilo 96720 (1285 Waianuenue, 2nd Floor, 808-935-6691)
Kahului 96732 (203 Ho'ohana St., 808-873-9426)

Vet Centers:
Hilo Vet Center, 70 Lanihuli Street, Suite 102, Hilo, HI, 96720, 808-969-3833
Honolulu Vet Center, 1680 Kapiolani Blvd, Suite F-3, Honolulu, HI, 96814, 808-973-8387
Kailua-Kona Vet Center, Hale Kui Plaza, 73-4976 Kamanu St., Suite 207, Kailua-Kona, HI, 96740, 808-329-0574
Kauai Vet Center, 3-3367 Kuhio Hwy., Suite 101, Lihue, HI, 96766, 808-246-1163
Maui Vet Center, 35 Lunalilo, Suite 101, Wailuku, HI, 96793, 808-242-8557
Western Oahu Vet Center, 885 Kamokila Blvd., Unit 105, Kapolei, HI, 96707, 808-674-2414

National Cemetery:
Nat. Mem. Cem. of the Pacific 96813-1729 (2177 Puowaina Dr., Honolulu, 808-532-3720)

IDAHO

Medical Center:
Boise, VA Medical Center, 500 W. Fort Street, Boise, ID, 83702, 208-422-1000

Clinics:
Canyon County, Canyon County CBOC, 4521 Thomas Jefferson Street, Caldwell, ID, 83605, 208-454-4826
Grangeville, 711 West North Street, Grangeville, ID, 208-983-4671 Lewiston
CBOC , 1630 23rd Avenue, Building 2, Lewiston, ID, 83501, 208-746-7784
North Idaho, North Idaho CBOC, 2177 Ironwood Center Drive, Coeur d'Alene, ID, 83814, 208-665-1700
Mountain Home, Idaho – Mountain Home Outpatient Clinic. 815 North 6th East Mountain Home, ID 83647. (208) 580-2001
Pocatello, Pocatello VA Outpatient Clinic, 444 Hospital Way, Suite 801, Pocatello, ID, 83201, 208-232-6214
Salmon, Idaho – Salmon Outreach Clinic. 705 Lena St. Salmon, ID 83467 (208) 756-8515
Twin Falls, Twin Falls CBOC, 260 2nd Avenue East, Twin Falls, ID, 83301, 208-732-0959

Regional Office:
Boise 83702 (444 W. Fort St., statewide, 1-800-827-1000)

Vet Centers:
Boise Vet Center, 2424 Bank Drive, Suite 100, Boise, ID, 83705, 208-342-3612
Pocatello Vet Center, 1800 Garrett Way, Pocatello, ID, 83201, 208-232-0316

ILLINOIS

VA Medical Centers:
Captain James A. Lovell Federal HCC, VA Medical Center, 3001 Greenbay

Road, North Chicago, IL, 60064, 847-688-1900

Hines, Edward Hines Jr Hospital, 5th Ave. & Roosevelt Ave, Hines, IL, 60141, 708-202-8387

Illiana HCS (Danville), VA Illiana Health Care System, 1900 E. Main, Danville, IL, 61832, 217-554-3000

Jesse Brown VAMC, Jesse Brown VA Medical Center, 820 S Damen Street, Chicago, IL, 60612, 312-569-8387

Marion IL, VA Medical Center, 2401 W. Main Street, Marion, IL, 62959, 618-997-5311

Clinics:

Auburn-Gresham, Auburn-Gresham CBOC, 7731 S Halsted, Chicago, IL, 60620, 773-962-3700

Aurora IL, Aurora Veterans Clinic, 161 South Lincolnway, North Aurora, IL, 60542, 630-859-2504

Belleville, Arcades Center, 6500 W. Main Street, Belleville, IL, 62223, 314-286-6988

Carbondale, 1130 East Walnut Street, Suite 100, Carbondale, IL, 62901, 618-351-1031

Charleston (Mattoon), Mattoon VA Outpatient Clinic, 501 Lakeland Blvd, Suite D, Mattoon, IL, 61938, 217-258-3370

Chicago Heights, Chicago Heights CBOC, 30 East 15th Street, Suite 314, Chicago Heights, IL, 60411, 708-756-5454

Decatur, Decatur VA Outpatient Clinic, 3035 East Mound Road, Decatur, IL, 62526, 217-875-2670

Effingham, 1901 S. 4th Street, Suite 21, Effingham, IL, 62401, 217-347-7600

Elgin, Elgin Veterans Clinic, 450 Dundee Ave, Suite 100, Elgin, IL, 60120, 847-742-5920

Evanston, Evanston CBOC, 1942 Dempster, Evanston, IL, 60202, 847-869-6315

Freeport, Freeport VA Clinic, 1301 S. Kiwanis Drive, Freeport, IL, 61032, 815-235-4881

Galesburg, VA Galesburg Outpatient Clinic, 310 Home Boulevard, Galesburg, IL, 61401, 309-343-0311

Harrisburg, 608 Rollie Moore Dr., Harrisburg, IL, 62946, 618-252-6150

Joliet, Joliet Veterans Clinic, 1201 Eagle St., Joliet, IL, 60432, 815-740-8100

Kankakee, 581 William Latham Drive, Bourbonnais, IL, 60914, 815-932-3823

Lakeside, Lakeside CBOC, 211 East Ontario Street, Chicago, IL, 60611, 312-569-8387

Lasalle, LaSalle Veterans Clinic, 4461 N Progress Village, Peru, IL, 61354, 815-223-9678

Mattoon CBOC 501 Lake Land Blvd. Mattoon, Illinois 61938 217-258-3370

McHenry, McHenry CBOC, 620 South IL Rte 31, Suite 4, McHenry, IL, 60050, 815-759-2306

Mt. Vernon, 4101 N Water Tower Place, Mt. Vernon, IL, 62864, 618-246-2910

Oak Lawn, Oak Lawn Clinic, 10201 S. Cicero Avenue, Oak Lawn, IL, 60453, 708-499-3675

Peoria, Bob Michel VA Outpatient Clinic, 7717 North Orange Prairie Road, Peoria, IL, 61615, 309-589-6800

Quincy, Quincy CBOC, 721 Broadway Street, Quincy, IL, 62301, 217-224-3366

Rockford, Rockford VA Clinic, 816 Featherstone Road, Rockford, IL, 61107, 815-227-0081

Springfield, Springfield VA Outpatient Clinic, 5850 S 6th Street, Frontage Road East Suite A, Springfield, IL, 62703, 217-529-5046

Sterling, Sterling CBOC, 406 Avenue C, Sterling, IL, 61081, 815-632-6200

Regional Office:
Chicago 60612 (2122 W. Taylor St., statewide 1-800-827-1000)

Benefits Office:
North Chicago 60064 (3001 Green Bay Rd.,

Vet Centers:
Chicago Heights Vet Center, Chicago Heights Vet Center, 1010 Dixie Highway, 2nd Floor, Chicago Heights, IL, 60411, 708-754-8885

Chicago Vet Center, Chicago Vet Center, 7731 S Halsted Street, Chicago, IL, 60620, 773-962-3740

DuPage County Vet Center, DuPage County Vet Center, 750 Shoreline Drive, Suite 150, Aurora, IL, 60504, 630-585-1853

East St. Louis Vet Center, East St. Louis Vet Center, 1265 N. 89th Street, Suite 5, East St. Louis, IL, 62203, 618-397-6602

Evanston Vet Center, 565 Howard St., Evanston, IL, 60202, 847-332-1019

Oak Park Vet Center, 1515 South Harlem Ave., Forest Park, IL, 60130, 708-383-3225

Orland Park Vet Center, Orland Park Vet Center, 8651 W 159th Street, Suite 1, Orland Park, IL, 60462, 708-444-0561

Peoria Vet Center, Peoria Vet Center, 8305 N. Allen Road, Suite 1, Peoria, IL, 61615, 309-689-9708

Quad Cities Vet Center, Quad Cities Vet Center, 1529 46th Ave., #6, Moline, IL, 61265, 309-762-6955

Rockford Vet Center, Rockford Vet Center, 7015 Rote Road, Suite 105, Rockford, IL, 61107, 815-395-1276

Springfield Vet Center, 1227 S. Ninth Street, Springfield, IL, 62703, 217-492-4955

National Cemeteries:
Abraham Lincoln 60421 (20953 W. Hoff Rd., Elwood, 815-423-9958)
Alton 62003 (600 Pearl St., 314-845-8320)
Camp Butler 62707 (5063 Camp Butler Rd., Springfield, 217-492-4070)
Danville 61832 (1900 East Main St., 217-554-4550)
Mound City 62963 (Highways 37 & 51, 314-845-8320)
Quincy 62301 (36th and Maine St., 309-782-2094)
Rock Island 61299-7090 (Rock Island Arsenal, Bldg. 118, 309-782-2094)

INDIANA

VA Medical Centers:
Indianapolis, Richard L. Roudebush VA Medical Center, 1481 W. Tenth Street, Indianapolis, IN, 46202, 317-554-0000
VA Northern Indiana Health Care System - Ft. Wayne, 2121 Lake Avenue, Fort Wayne, IN, 46805, 260-426-5431
VA Northern Indiana Health Care System - Marion, 1700 E. 38th Street, Marion, IN, 46953, 765-674-3321

Clinics:
Adams Benjamin Jr. (Crown Point IN), Adam Benjamin Jr Outpatient Clinic, 9301 Madison Street, Crown Point, IN, 46307, 219-662-5000
Bloomington, Bloomington VA Outpatient Clinic, 455 S. Landmark Ave., Bloomington, IN, 47403, 812-336-5723
Bloomington-Mental Health, 1332 Arch Haven, Bloomington, IN, 47403, 812-349-4406
Evansville, 6211 E. Waterford Blvd., Evansville, IN, 47715, 812-465-6202
Goshen, IN, Goshen VA Outpatient Clinic, 2014 Lincolnway East, Goshen, IN, 46526, 574-534-6108
Evanston, IL Vet Center: 1901 Howard St, Evanston, IL 60202, Phone: 847-332-1019 Or 847-332-1019
Lafayette, Lafayette VA Outpatient Clinic, 3851 N. River Road, West Lafayette, IN, 47906, 765-464-2280
Lawrenceburg (Dearborn County), VA Health care Associates-Southeastern Indiana, 1600 Flossie Drive, Greendale, IN, 47025, 812-539-2313
Martinsville, Martinsville Community Based Outpatient Clinic, 2200 John R. Wooden Drive, Martinsville, IN, 46151, 317-988-4498
Muncie, Muncie/Anderson VA Outpatient Clinic, 2600 W White River Blvd., Muncie, IN, 47303, 765-284-6822
New Albany, VA Health care Center New Albany, 811 Northgate Blvd., New Albany, IN, 47150, 502-287-4100
New Albany-Annex, Mental Health Clinic, 821 Mt Tabor Road, New Albany, IN, 47150, 502-287-4100
Peru, Peru Community Based Outpatient Clinic, 750 North Broadway, Peru, IN, 46970, 765-472-8900
Richmond, VA Community Based Outpatient Clinic, 4351 South A Street, Richmond, IN, 47374, 765-973-6915
Scott County, Scott County CBOC, 1467 N Scott Valley Drive, Scottsburg, IN, 47170, 502-287-6900
South Bend, South Bend VA Outpatient Clinic, 333 W. Western Ave., South Bend, IN, 46601, 574-299-4847
Terre Haute-Mental Health, 142 W. Honey Creek Parkway, Terre Haute, IN, 47804, 812-232-8325
Terre Haute, Terre Haute VA Outpatient Clinic, 110 W. Honey Creek Parkway, Terre Haute, IN, 47804, 812-232-2890
Vincennes, 1815 Willow Street, Suite 6A, Vincennes, IN, 47591, 812-882-0894

Vet Centers:
Evansville Vet Center, 311 N. Weinbach Ave., Evansville, IN, 47711, 812-473-5993
Fort Wayne Vet Center, 5800 Fairfield Avenue, Suite265, Fort Wayne, IN, 46807, 260-460-1456
Gary Vet Center, 107 E. 93rd Street, Crown Point, IN, 46307, 219-736-5633
Indianapolis Vet Center, 8330 Naab Road, Suite 103, Indianapolis, IN, 46260, 317-988-1600
South Bend Vet Center, 4727 Miami Street, South Bend, IN, 46601, 574-231-8480

Regional Office:
Indianapolis 46204 (575 North Pennsylvania St. statewide 800-827-1000)

National Cemeteries:
Crown Hill 46208 (700 W. 38th St., Indianapolis, 765-674-0284)
Marion 46952 (1700 E. 38th St., 765-674-0284)
New Albany 47150 (1943 Ekin Ave., 502-893-3852)

IOWA

VA Medical Centers:
Des Moines, VA Central Iowa HCS VAMC Des Moines IA Div, 3600 30th Street, Des Moines, IA, 50310, 515-699-5999
Iowa City VA HCS, VA Medical Center, 601 Highway 6 West, Iowa City, IA, 52246, 319-338-0581

Clinics:
Bettendorf, VA Quad Cities Outpatient Clinic, 2979 Victoria Street, Bettendorf, IA, 52722, 563-332-9274
Carroll, 311 South Clark Street, Suite 275, Carroll, IA, 51401, 712-794-6780
Cedar Rapids, Cedar Rapids CBOC, 2230 Wiley Blvd SW, Cedar Rapids, IA, 52404, 319-369-4340
Decorah, Decorah CBOC, 915 Short Street, Decorah, IA, 52101, 563-387-5840
Dubuque, Dubuque Outpatient Clinic-Mercy Health Center, 200 Mercy Drive, Dubuque, IA, 52001, 563-588-5520
Fort Dodge, Fort Dodge VA Clinic, 2419 2nd Avenue, Fort Dodge, IA, 50501, 515-576-2235
Fort Dodge North, 102 N 25th Street, Fort Dodge, IA, 50501, 515-576-2235
Knoxville, 1515 West Pleasant, Knoxville, IA, 50138, 641-828-5019
Marshalltown, 101 Iowa Ave. West, Marshalltown, IA, 50158, 641-754-6700
Mason City, Mason City VA Clinic, 520 S. Pierce Ave, Suite 150, Mason City, IA, 50401, 641-421-8077
Ottumwa, Ottumwa CBOC, 1009 East Pennsylvania Avenue, Ottumwa, IA, 52501, 641-683-4300
Shenandoah, 512 S. Fremont Street, Shenandoah, IA, 51601, 712-246-0092
Sioux City, Sioux City VA Clinic, 1551 Indian Hills Dr., Suite 206, Sioux City, IA,

51104, 712-258-4700
Spirit Lake, Spirit Lake VA Clinic, 1310 Lake Street, Spirit Lake, IA, 51360, 712-336-6400
Waterloo, VA Outpatient Clinic, 945 Tower Park Drive, Waterloo, IA, 50701, 319-235-1230
Regional Office:
Des Moines 50309 (210 Walnut St., Rm. 1063, statewide 1-800-827-1000)

Vet Centers:
Cedar Rapids Vet Center, Cedar Rapids Vet Center, 4250 River Center Court NE, Suite D, Cedar Rapids, IA, 52402, 319-378-0016
Des Moines Vet Center, 1821 22nd Street, Suite #115, Des Moines, IA, 50266, 515-284-4929
Sioux City Vet Center, 1551 Indian Hills Drive, Suite 214, Sioux City, IA, 51104, 712-255-3808

National Cemetery:
Keokuk 52632 (1701 J St., 309-782-2094)

KANSAS

VA Medical Centers:
Eastern Kansas HCS - Leavenworth Division, 4101 4th Street Trafficway, Leavenworth, KS, 66048, 913-682-2000
Eastern Kansas HCS - Topeka Division, 2200 SW Gage Blvd., Topeka, KS, 66622, 785-350-3111
Robert J. Dole VAM&ROC (Wichita), 5500 East Kellogg Avenue, Wichita, KS, 67218, 316-685-2221
Clinics:
Chanute, 629 South Plummer, Suite D, Chanute, KS, 66720, 1-800-574-8387 Ext. 54750
Dodge City, Fort Dodge OPC, 301 Miles Walk - Hwy 400, Grant Hall, Fort Dodge, KS, 67801, 888-878-6881 x41040
Emporia, 919 West 12th Avenue, Suite D, Emporia, KS, 66801, 1-800-574-8387 Ext. 54750
Fort Riley, 600 Caisson Hill Road, Fort Riley, KS, 66442, 785-350-3111
Ft. Scott (Bourbon Co.), 902 South Horton, Ft. Scott, KS, 66701, 61-800-574-8387 Ext. 54750
Garnett, Garnett - Anderson County Hospital, 421 S. Maple, Garnett, KS, 66032, 1-800-574-8387 Ext. 54750
Hays, 207B E. 7th Street, Hays, KS, 67601, 888-878-6881 x41000
Hutchinson, 1625 E. 30th Street, Hutchinson, KS, 67502, 888-878-6881 x41100
Junction City, 715 Southwind Dr., Junction City, KS, 66441, 1-800-574-8387 Ext. 54750
Lawrence, 2200 Harvard Road, Suite C-103, Lawrence, KS, 66049, 1-800-574-8387 Ext. 54750
Liberal, 2 Rock Island Road, Suite 200, Liberal, KS, 67901, 620-626-5574
Louisburg-Paola, 510 Hospital Dr., Paola, KS, 66071, 913-294-5847 x54260

Parsons, 1907 Harding Drive, Parsons, KS, 67357, 888-878-6881 x41060
Salina, 1410 E. Irons Street, Suite 1, Salina, KS, 67401, 888-878-6881 x41020
Seneca, Nemaha Valley Community Hospital (Seneca), 1600 Community
Drive, Seneca, KS, 66538, 1-800-574-8387 Ext. 54750
Wyandotte County VA Outpatient Clinic, 21 North 12th Street, Suite 110, Kansas City, KS, 66102, 1-800-574-8387 Ext. 54750

Regional Office:
Wichita 67208 (Wichita Regional Office, P.O. Box 21318, 1-800-827-1000)

Benefits Offices:
Leavenworth 66048 (150 Muncie Rd.,)
Ft. Riley 66442 (VA Military Services Coordinators Office)

Vet Center:
Manhattan Vet Center, 205 South 4th Street, Suite B, Manhattan, KS, 66502,
785-587-8257
Wichita Vet Center, 251 N Water Street, Wichita, KS, 67202, 316-265-0889)

National Cemeteries:
Fort Leavenworth 66027 (395 Biddle Blvd., 913-758-4105)
Fort Scott 66701 (900 East National Ave., 620-223-2840)
Leavenworth 66048 (150 Muncie Rd., 913-758-4105)

KENTUCKY

VA Medical Centers:
Lexington-Cooper Division, VA Medical Center, 1101 Veterans Drive, Lexington, KY, 40502, 859-281-4901
Lexington-Leestown, VA Medical Center, 2250 Leestown Rd.,, Lexington, KY,
40511, 859-233-4511
Louisville, VA Medical Center, 800 Zorn Avenue, Louisville, KY, 40206, 502-287-4000

Clinics:
Bellevue, VA CBOC Northern KY Health Care Assoc., 103 Landmark Drive,
3rd Floor, Bellevue, KY, 41073, 859-392-3840
Berea, 209 Pauline Drive, Berea, KY, 40403, 859-986-1259
Bowling Green, CORPCARE, 1110 Wilkinson Trace Circle, Hartland Medical
Plaza, Bowling Green, KY, 42103, 270-796-3590
Carroll County, Carroll County CBOC, 1911 Highway 227, Carrollton, KY,
41008, 502-287-6060
Dupont, Professional Towers, 4010 Dupont Circle, Suite 100, Louisville, KY,
40207, 502-287-6986
Florence, Florence CBOC, 7711 Ewing Blvd, Florence, KY, 41042, 859-282-4480
Fort Knox, VA Health care Center, 289 Ireland Ave., Ireland Army Community

Hospital, Fort Knox, KY, 40121, 502-624-9396
Grayson County, 619 West Main Street, Clarkson, KY, 42726, 866-653-8232
Hanson (Hopkins County) KY, 926 Veterans Drive, Hanson, KY, 42413, 270-322-8019
Hazard/Perry County, 210 Black Gold Boulevard, #107, Hazard, KY, 41701, 606-436-2350
Hopkinsville (Christian County), Hopkinsville CBOC, 1102 S. Virginia Drive, Hopkinsville, KY, 42240, 270-885-2106
Mayfield, 1253 Paris Road, Suite A, Mayfield, KY, 42066, 270-247-2455
Morehead, 333 Beacon Hill Drive, Rd 100, Morehead, KY, 40351, 606-784-3004
Newburg, Newburg CBOC, 3430 Newburg Road, Suite 200 214, Louisville, KY, 40218, 502-287-6223
Owensboro, 3400 New Hartford Road, Owensboro, KY, 42303, 270-684-5034
Paducah, 2620 Perkins Creek Drive, Paducah, KY, 42001, 270-444-8465
Prestonsburg, Prestonsburg Primary Care Clinic, 5230 Kentucky Route 321, Suite 8, Prestonsburg, KY, 41653, 606-886-1970
Shively (Louisville-Jefferson County), 3934 N Dixie Highway, Suite 210, Louisville, KY, 40216, 502-287-6000
Somerset, 163 Tower Circle, Somerset, KY, 42503, 606-676-0786

Regional Office:
Louisville 40202 (321 W. Main St., Ste., 390, statewide 1-800-827-1000)

Benefits Office:
Ft. Knox 40121 (Building 1109-B Room 24, P.O. Box 937)

Vet Centers:
Lexington Vet Center, Lexington Vet Center, 1500 Leestown Road, Suite 104, Lexington, KY, 40511, 859-253-0717
Louisville Vet Center, 1347 S. Third St., Louisville, KY, 40208, 502-634-1916

National Cemeteries:
Camp Nelson 40356 (6980 Danville Rd., Nicholasville, 859-885-5727)
Cave Hill 40204 (701 Baxter Ave., Louisville, 502-893-3852)
Danville 40442 (277 N. First St., 859-885-5727)
Lebanon 40033 (20 Highway 208, 270-692-3390)
Lexington 40508 (833 W. Main St., 859-885-5727)
Mill Springs 42544 (9044 West Highway 80, Nancy, 859-885-5727)
Zachary Taylor 40207 (4701 Brownsboro Rd., Louisville, 502-893-3852)

LOUISIANA
VA Medical Centers:
Alexandria, VA Medical Center, 2495 Shreveport Highway, Pineville, LA, 71360, 318-473-0010
Overton Brooks VAMC, VA Medical Center, 510 East Stoner Avenue, Shreve-

port, LA, 71101, 318-221-8411
Southeast Louisiana Veterans Health Care System - New Orleans, VA Medical Center, 1601 Perdido Street, New Orleans, LA, 70112, 800-935-8387

Clinics:
Baton Rouge, Baton Rouge Outpatient Clinic, 7968 Essen Park Avenue, Baton Rouge, LA, 70809, 225-761-3400
Baton Rouge South, 7850 Anselmo Lane, Baton Rouge, LA, 70810, 225-768-6419
Bogalusa, Bogalusa VA Outpatient Clinic, 319 Memphis Street, Bogalusa, LA, 70427, 985-735-9029
Fort Polk Intake Site 71459 (Bayne-Jones Army Community Hospital, 1585 3rd St. Rm 5109., 800-827-1000) 318-861-3984
Franklin, Franklin VA Outpatient Clinic, 603 Haifleigh Street, Franklin, LA, 70538, 337-828-9092
Hammond, Hammond VA Outpatient Clinic, 1131 South Morrison Blvd, Hammond, LA, 70403, 985-902-5100
Houma, Houma VA Outpatient Clinic, 6433 West Park Avenue, Houma, LA, 70364, 985-851-0188
Jennings, Jennings CBOC, 1907 Johnson Street, Jennings, LA, 70546, 337-785-4700
Lafayette, Lafayette Parish CBOC, 2100 Jefferson Street, Bldg B, Lafayette, LA, 70501, 337-261-0734
Monroe, Monroe Community Based Outpatient Clinic, 250 DeSiard Plaza Drive, Monroe, LA, 71203, 318-343-6100
Natchitoches, Natchitoches CBOC, 740 Keyser Ave, Natchitoches, LA, 71457, 318-357-3300
Slidell, Slidell VA Outpatient Clinic, 60491 Doss Drive, Suite B, Slidell, LA, 70460, 985-690-2626
St. Johns, St. John VA Outpatient Clinic, 4004 West Airline Highway, Reserve, LA, 70084, 985-479-6770

Regional Office:
New Orleans 70113 (1250 Poydras St., Suite 200., 1-800-827-1000)

Benefits Offices:
Fort Polk Intake Site 71459 (Bayne-Jones Army Community Hospital, 1585 3rd St. Rm 1221., 800-827-1000)
Shreveport 71101 (510 E. Stoner Ave.,)
Pineville 71360 (2495 Shreveport Highway, 71 North)

Vet Centers:
Baton Rouge Vet Center, Baton Rouge Vet Center, 7850 Anselmo Lane, Suite B, Baton Rouge, LA, 70810, 225-761-3140
New Orleans, New Orleans Vet Center, 1250 Poydras St., Suite 400, N.O. LA 70113, 504-565-4977
Rapides Parish Vet Center, Rapides Parish Vet Center, 5803 Coliseum Blvd,

Suite D, Alexandria, LA, 71303, 318-466-4327
Shreveport Vet Center, Shreveport Vet Center, 2800 Youree Dr., Building 1, Suite 105, Shreveport, LA, 71104, 318-861-1776

National Cemeteries:
Alexandria 71360 (209 E. Shamrock St., Pineville, 601-445-4981)
Baton Rouge 70806 (220 N. 19th St., 225-654-3767)
Port Hudson 70791 (20978 Port Hickey Rd., Zachary, 225-654-3767)
Zachary, 70791 (303 W. Mount Pleasant Rd LA, 225-654-1988)

MAINE
VA Medical Center:
Maine VA HCS, VAMC, 1 VA Center, Augusta, ME, 4330, 207-623-8411

Clinics:
Caribou VA Clinic, 163 Van Buren Road, Suite 6, Caribou, ME, 04736, 207-493-3800
Bangor VA Clinic, 35 State Hospital Street, Bangor, ME, 04401, 207-561-3600
Calais VA Clinic, 50 Union Street, Calais, ME, 04619, 207-904-3700
Lewiston-Auburn VA Clinic, 15 Challenger Drive, Lewiston, ME, 04240, 207-753-4601
Portland VA Clinic, 144 Fore Street, Suite 200, Portland, ME, 04101, 207-623-8411 x3101
Rumford VA Clinic, 431 Franklin Street, Rumford, ME, 04276, 207-369-3200
Saco VA Clinic, 655 Main Street, Saco, ME, 04072, 207-294-3100

Regional Office:
Togus 04330 (1 VA Center, Augusta, statewide 1-800-827-1000; VR&E Division 207-623-8411 ext 4600)

Vet Centers:
Bangor Vet Center, In-Town Plaza, 352 Harlow St., Bangor, ME, 04401, 207-947-3391
Caribou Vet Center, 456 York Street, York Street Complex, Caribou, ME, 04736, 207-496-3900
Lewiston Vet Center, Parkway Complex, 29 Westminster St., Lewiston, ME, 04240, 207-783-0068
Portland Vet Center, 475 Stevens Ave., Portland, ME, 04103, 207-780-3584
Sanford Vet Center, 628 Main Street, Springvale, ME, o4083, 207-490-1513

National Cemetery:
Togus 04330 (1 VA Center; 508-563-7113/4)

MARYLAND
VA Medical Centers:
Baltimore, VA Maryland HCS VAMC Baltimore MD Div., 10 North Greene Street, Baltimore, MD, 21201, 410-605-7000

Perry Point, VA Maryland Health Care System, VAMC Perry Point, MD Division (512A5), Perry Point, MD, 21902, 410-642-2411

Clinics:
Cambridge, VA Maryland HCS-Cambridge Comm. Outpatient Clinic, 830 Chesapeake Drive, Cambridge, MD, 21613, 410-228-6243
Charlotte Hall, Washington DC-CH CBOC, 29431 Charlotte Hall Road, Charlotte Hall, MD, 20622, 301-884-7102
Cumberland, Cumberland Community Based Outpatient Clinic, 200 Glen Street, Cumberland, MD, 21502, 301-724-0061
Fort Detrick, 1433 Porter Street, Frederick, MD, 21702, 301-624-1200
Fort Howard, VA Maryland HCS-Fort Howard, 9600 North Point Road, Fort Howard, MD, 21052, 410-477-1800
Fort Meade, Fort Meade CBOC, 2479 5th Street, Fort Meade, MD, 20755, 410-305-5300
Glen Burnie Community Based Outpatient Clinic, 808 Landmark Drive, Suite 128, Glen Burnie, MD, 21061, 410-590-4140
Hagerstown, Hagerstown Community Based Outpatient Clinic, 1101 Opal Court, Hagerstown, MD, 21742, 301-665-1462
Landover/Greenbelt (Prince Georges County), Greenway East Professional Center, 7525 Greenway Center Drive, Suite T4, Greenbelt, MD, 20770, 301-345-2463
Loch Raven, Loch Raven VA Outpatient Clinic, 3901 The Alameda, Baltimore, MD, 21218, 410-605-7651
Pocomoke City, Pocomoke City CBOC, 1701 Market Place, Unit 211, Pocomoke City, MD, 21851, 410-957-6718
Southern Prince George's County, 5801 Allentown Road, Suites 103 104 and 106, Camp Springs, MD, 20746, 301-423-3700

Regional Office:
Baltimore 21201 (31 Hopkins Plaza Federal Bldg., 1-800-827-1000)

Vet Centers:
Annapolis Vet Center, 100 Annapolis Street, Suite 102, Annapolis, MD, 21401, 410-605-7826
Baltimore County Vet Center, 1553 Merritt Blvd., Dundalk, MD, 21222, 410-282-6144
Baltimore Vet Center, Commercentre East, 1777 Reisterstown Road, Suite 199, Baltimore, MD, 21208, 410-764-9400
Elkton Vet Center, Upper Chesapeake Center, 103 Chesapeake Blvd., Suite A, Elkton, MD, 21921, 410-392-4485
Prince Georges County Vet Center, 7905 Malcolm Road, Suite 101, Clinton, MD, 20735, 301-856-7173
Silver Spring Vet Center, 2900 Linden Lane, Suite 100, Silver Spring, MD, 20910, 301-589-1073

National Cemeteries:
Annapolis 21401 (800 West St., 410-644-9696/7)
Baltimore 21228 (5501 Frederick Ave., 410-644-9696/7)
Loudon Park 21228 (3445 Frederick Ave., Baltimore, 410-644-9696/7)

MASSACHUSETTS

VA Medical Centers:
Bedford, VA Medical Center, 200 Springs Road, Bedford, MA, 01730, 781-687-2000
Brockton VAMC, VA Boston Health Care System Brockton Division, 940 Belmont Street, Brockton, MA, 02301, 508-583-4500
Central Western Massachusetts HCS, VA Medical Center, 421 N. Main Street, Leeds, MA, 01053, 413-584-4040
VA Boston HCS- Boston Div., VA Medical Center, 150 South Huntington Avenue, Boston, MA, 02130, 617-232-9500
VA Boston Health care System West Roxbury, 1400 VFW Parkway, West Roxbury, MA, 20132, 617-323-7700

Clinics:
Causeway Clinic (Boston), VA Causeway Clinic, 251 Causeway Street, Boston, MA, 02114, 617-248-1000
Fitchburg, VA Fitchburg Clinic, 275 Nichols Road, Fitchburg, MA, 01420, 413-584-4040 800-893-1522
Framingham VA Primary Care Unit, VA Framingham Clinic, 61 Lincoln Street, Suite 112, Framingham, MA, 01702, 508-628-0205
Gloucester, VA Gloucester Clinic, 298 Washington Street, Gloucester, MA, 01930, 978-282-0676
Greenfield , 143 Munson Street, Greenfield, MA, 01301, 413-584-4040 800-893-1522
Haverhill, VA Haverhill Clinic, 108 Merrimack Street, Haverhill, MA, 01830, 978-372-5207
Hyannis Primary Care Center, Hyannis Primary Care Center, 233 Stevens Street, Hyannis, MA, 02601, 508-771-3190
Lowell, VA Lowell Clinic, 130 Marshall Road, Lowell, MA, 1852, 978-671-9000
Lowell, Veterans Community Care Center, 130 Marshall Road, Lowell, MA, 01852, 978-671-9000
Lynn/North Shore, VA North Shore Clinic, 225 Boston Street, Suite 107, Lynn, MA, 01904, 781-595-9818
New Bedford Primary Care Ctr., VA Primary Care Center, 175 Elm Street, New Bedford, MA, 02740, 508-994-0217
Pittsfield, 73 Eagle Street, Pittsfield, MA, 01201, 413-584-4040 800-893-1522
Plymouth, 116 Long Pond Road, Plymouth, MA, 02360, 774-826-3732
Quincy, Quincy Medical Center, 114 Whitwell St, 2nd Floor, Quincy, MA, 02169, 617-376-2010
Springfield, 25 Bond Street, Springfield, MA, 01104, 413-584-4040 800-893-1522
Worcester, VA Worcester Clinic, 605 Lincoln Street, Worcester, MA, 01605, 508-856-0104 800-893-1522

Regional Office:
Boston 02203-0393 (JFK Federal Building, Room 1625, Government Center, statewide 1-800-827-1000) (Towns of Fall River & New Bedford, counties of Barnstable, Dukes, Nantucket, Bristol, part of Plymouth served by Providence, R.I., VA Regional Office)

Vet Centers:
Boston Vet Center, 7 Drydock Avenue, Suite 2070, Boston, MA, 02210, 617-424-0665
Brockton Vet Center, 1041L Pearl St., Brockton, MA, 02301, 508-580-2730
Hyannis Vet Center, 474 West Main Street, Hyannis, MA, 02601, 508-778-0124
Lowell Vet Center, Gateway Center, 10 George Street, Lowell, MA, 10852, 978-453-1151
New Bedford Vet Center, 73 Huttleston Avenue, Unit 2, Fairhaven, MA, 02719, 508-999-6920
Springfield Vet Center, Northgate Plaza, 95 Ashley Avenue, Suite A, West Springfield, MA, 01089, 413-737-5167
Worcester Vet Center, 691 Grafton Street, Worcester, MA, 01604, 508-753-7902
National Cemetery:
Massachusetts 02532 (Connery Ave., Bourne, 508-563-7113/4)

MICHIGAN
VA Medical Centers:
Ann Arbor HCS, VA Ann Arbor Health care System, 20215 Fuller Road, Ann Arbor, MI, 48105, 734-769-7100
Battle Creek, Battle Creek VA Medical Center, 5500 Armstrong Rd., Battle Creek, MI, 49037, 269-966-5600
Detroit (John D. Dingell), John D. Dingell VA Medical Center, 4646 John R Street, Detroit, MI, 48201, 313-576-1000
Iron Mountain MI, VA Medical Center, 325 East H Street, Iron Mountain, MI, 49801, 906-774-3300
Saginaw, Aleda E. Lutz VA Medical Center, 1500 Weiss Street, Saginaw, MI, 48602, 989-497-2500

Clinics:
Alpena County, Clement C. Van Wagoner Outpatient Clinic, 180 N. State Avenue Alpena, MI, 49707, 989-356-8720
Bad Axe, Bad Axe Community Based Outpatient Clinic, 1142 S Van Dyke Road, Suite 100, Bad Axe, MI, 48413, 989-269-7445
Benton Harbor, Benton Harbor VA Outpatient Clinic, 115 W. Main Street, Benton Harbor, MI, 49022, 269-934-9123
Cadillac Community Based Outpatient Clinic, 1909 N Mitchell Street, Cadillac, MI, 49601, 231-775-4401
Cheboygan County Community Based Outpatient Clinic, 14540 Mackinaw Hwy, Mackinaw City, MI, 49701, 231-436-5176

Clare Community Outpatient Clinic, 11775 N Isabella Road, Clare, MI, 48617, 989-386-8113

Flint (Genessee Co.), Flint VA Outpatient Clinic, G2360 South Linden Rd, Flint, MI, 48532, 810-720-2913

Gaylord, Gaylord VA Outpatient Clinic, 806 S. Otsego, Gaylord, MI, 49732, 989-732-7525

Grand Rapids VA Outpatient Clinic, 3019 Coit Street NE, Grand Rapids, MI, 49505, 616-365-9575

Grayling Community Based Outpatient Clinic, 1680 Hartwick Pines Road, Grayling, MI, 49738, 989-344-2002

Hancock, Hancock Clinic, 787 Market Street, Suite 9, Hancock, MI, 49930, 906-482-7762

Ironwood CBOC, 629 W. Cloverland Drive, Suite 1, Ironwood, MI, 49938, 906-932-0032

Jackson VA Outpatient Clinic, 4328 Page Avenue, Michigan Center, MI, 49254, 517-764-3609

Lansing VA Outpatient Clinic, 2025 S Washington Avenue, Lansing, MI, 48910, 517-267-3925

Marquette MI, Marquette CBOC, 1414 W Fair Avenue, Suite 285, Marquette, MI, 49855, 906-226-4618

Menominee CBOC, 1110 10th Avenue, Menominee, MI, 49858, 906-863-1286

Muskegon VA Outpatient Clinic, 5000 Hakes Drive, Muskegon, MI, 49441, 231-798-4445

Oscoda VA Outpatient Clinic, 5671 Skeel Ave., Suite 4, Oscoda, MI, 48750, 989-747-0026

Pontiac VA Outpatient Clinic, 44200 Woodward Avenue, Suite 208, Pontiac, MI, 48341, 248-332-4540

Sault Ste. Marie Area Clinic, 509 Osborn Blvd, Suite 306, Sault Ste Marie, MI, 49783, 906-253-9383

Traverse City VA Outpatient Clinic, 3271 Racquet Club Drive, Traverse City, MI, 49684, 231-932-9720

Yale VA Outpatient Clinic, 7470 Brockway Road, Yale, MI, 48097, 810-387-3211

Regional Office:
Detroit 48226 (Patrick V. McNamara Federal Bldg., 477 Michigan Ave., Rm. 1280, 1-800-827-1000)

Vet Centers:
Dearborn Vet Center, 19855 Outer Drive, Suite 105 W, Dearborn, MI, 48124, 313-277-1428

Detroit Vet Center, 4161 Cass Avenue, Detroit, MI, 48201, 313-576-1514

Escanaba Vet Center, 3500 Ludington Street, Suite #110, Escanaba, MI, 49829, 906-233-0244

Grand Rapids Vet Center, 2050 Breton Road SE, Grand Rapids, MI, 49546, 616-285-5795

Macomb County Vet Center, 42621 Garfield Road, Suite 105, Clinton Town-

ship, MI, 49236, 586-412-0107
Pontiac Vet Center, 44200 Woodward Avenue, Suite 108, Pontiac, MI, 48341, 248-874-1015
Vet Center, 5360 Hampton Place, Saginaw, MI, 48604, 989-321-4650
Traverse City Vet Center, 3766 N US 31 South, Traverse City, MI, 49684, 231-935-0051

National Cemetery:
Fort Custer 49012 (15501 Dickman Rd., Aug. a, 269-731-4164)
Great Lakes 48442 (4200 Belford Rd., Holly,248-348-8603)

MINNESOTA
VA Medical Centers:
Minneapolis VA HCS, Minneapolis VA HCS, One Veterans Drive, Minneapolis, MN, 55417, 612-725-2000
St. Cloud VA HCS, VA Medical Center, 4801 Veterans Drive, St. Cloud, MN 56303, 320-252-1670

Clinics:
Bemidji, 705 5th Street, Bemidji, MN, 56601, 218-755-6360
Brainerd, Brainerd VA Clinic, 722 Northwest 7th Street, Brainerd, MN, 56401, 218-855-1115
Ely VA Outpatient Clinic, Ely Outpatient Clinic, 720 Miners Drive East, Ely, MN, 55731, 218-365-0001
Fergus Falls, C/O MN Veterans Home, 1839 North Park Street, Fergus Falls, MN, 56537, 218-739-1400
Hibbing, Hibbing VA Outpatient Clinic, 990 West 41st Street, Suite 5, Hibbing, MN, 55746, 218-263-9698
Maplewood, Maplewood CBOC, 1725 Legacy Parkway, Suite 100, Maplewood, MN, 55109, 651-290-3040
Max J. Beilke, 515 22nd Avenue E, Alexandria, MN, 56308, 320-759-2640
Montevideo, Montevideo VA Clinic, 1025 North 13th Street, Montevideo, MN, 56265, 320-269-2222
Northwest Metro, Northwest Metro VA Outpatient Clinic, 7545 Veterans Drive, Ramsey, MN, 55303, 612-467-1100
Rochester, Rochester VA Outpatient Clinic, 3900 55th Street NW, Rochester, MN, 55901, 507-252-0885
South Central, St James VA Outpatient Clinic, 1961 Premier Drive, St. James, MN, 56001, 507-375-9670
South Central-St James, St James VA Clinic, 1212 Heckman Court, St James, MN, 56081, 507-375-9670

Regional Office:
St. Paul 55111 (Bishop Henry Whipple Federal Bldg., 1 Federal Dr., Fort Snelling 1-800-827-1000)
    (Counties of Becker, Beltrami, Clay, Clearwater, Kittson, Lake of the Woods,

Mahnomen, Marshall, Norman, Otter Tail, Pennington, Polk, Red Lake, Roseau, Wilkin served by Fargo, N.D., VA Regional Office)

Vet Centers:
Brooklyn Park Vet Center, 7001 78th Ave N, Suite 300, Brooklyn Park, MN, 55445, 763-503-2220
Duluth Vet Center, 405 E. Superier St., Duluth, MN, 55802, 218-722-8654
St. Paul Vet Center, 550 County Road D, Suite 10, New Brighton, MN, 55112, 651-644-4022

National Cemetery:
Fort Snelling NC 55450-1199 (7601 34th Ave. So., Minneapolis, 612-726-1127)

MISSISSIPPI
Medical centers:
G.V. (Sonny) Montgomery VAMC, 1500 E. Woodrow Wilson Drive, Jackson, MS, 39216, 601-362-4471
Gulf Coast HCS, VA Medical Center, 400 Veterans Avenue, Biloxi, MS, 39531, 228-523-5000

Clinics:
Byhalia, Northeastern Mississippi Health care, 12 East Brunswick, Byhalia, MS, 38611, 662-838-2098
Byhalia-Mount Pleasant, 154 Mount Pleasant Road, Mount Pleasant, MS, 38635, 662-838-2098
Columbus, 824 Alabama Street, Columbus, MS, 39702, 662-244-0391
Durant (Kosciusko), Kosciusko Medical Clinic, 332 Highway 12 West, Kosciusko, MS, 39090, 662-289-1800
Greenville, The Greenville Clinic, 1502 S. Colorado St., Greenville, MS, 38703, 662-332-9872
Hattiesburg, VA Clinic, 231 Methodist Blvd., Hattiesburg, MS, 39402, 601-296-3530
McComb, McComb CBOC, 1308 Harrison Avenue, McComb, MS, 39648, 601-250-0965
Meridian, G.V. (Sonny) Montgomery VA OPC, 2103 13th Street, Meridian, MS, 39301, 601-482-3275
Natchez (Adams County), 105 Northgate Drive, Suite 2, Natchez, MS, 39120, 601-442-7141
Smithville, Access Family Health Services Inc., 63420 Hwy 25 North, Smithville, MS, 38870, 662-651-4637
Smithville-Houlka, Access Family Health Services, Inc., 106 Walker St, Houlka, MS, 38850, 662-651-4637
Smithville-Tremont, Access Family Health Services, Inc., 10103 HWY 178 W, Tremont, MS, 38876, 662-651-4637
Smithville-Tupelo, VA CBOC, 499 Gloster Creek Village, Suite D-1, Tupelo, MS, 38801, 662-651-4637

Regional Office:
Jackson 39216 (1600 E. Woodrow Wilson Ave., statewide 1-800-827-1000)

Vet Centers:
Biloxi Vet Center, 288 Veterans Avenue, Biloxi, MS, 39531, 228-388-9938
Jackson Vet Center, 1755 Lelia Drive, Suite 104, Jackson, MS, 39216, 601-965-5727

National Cemeteries:
Biloxi 39535-4968 (P.O. Box 4968, 400 Veterans Ave., 228-388-6668)
Corinth 38834 (1551 Horton St., 901-386-8311)
Natchez 39120 (41 Cemetery Rd., 601-445-4981)

MISSOURI

VA Medical Centers:
Columbia MO, Harry S. Truman Memorial VH, 800 Hospital Drive, Columbia, MO, 65201, 573-814-6000
Kansas City, VA Medical Center, 4801 Linwood Blvd., Kansas City, MO, 64128, 816-861-4700
Poplar Bluff, John J. Pershing VA Medical Center, 1500 N. Westwood Blvd., Poplar Bluff, MO, 63901, 573-686-4151
St Louis-Jefferson Barracks Division, VA Medical Center, 1 Jefferson Barracks Drive, St. Louis, MO, 63125, 314-652-4100
St Louis-John Cochran Division, 915 North Grand, St. Louis, MO, 63106, 314-652-4100

Clinics:
Belton, 17140 Bel-Ray Place, Belton, MO, 64012, 816-922-2161
Branson, Branson VA Outpatient Clinic, 5571 North Gretna Road, Branson, MO, 65616, 417-243-2300
Cameron, 1111 Euclid Drive, Cameron, MO, 64429, 816-861-4700
Cape Girardeau, 3051 William Street, Cape Girardeau, MO, 63703, 573-339-0909
Excelsior Springs, 197 S McCleary Road, Excelsior Springs, MO, 64024, 816-922-2970
Farmington, 1580 West Columbia, Farmington, MO, 63640, 573-760-1365
Ft Leonard Wood MO, 700 GW Lane Street, Waynesville, MO, 65583, 573-774-2285
Gene Taylor, Gene Taylor Community Based Outpatient Clinic, 600 N. Main Street, Mt. Vernon, MO, 65734, 800-253-8387
Jefferson City, 2707 W. Edgewood Dr., Jefferson City, MO, 65109, 573-635-0233
Kirksville, VA Clinic Northeast MO Health Council, 1510 North Crown Drive, Kirksville, MO, 63501, 660-627-8387
Lake of the Ozarks/Camdenton, 940 Executive Drive, Osage Beach, MO, 65065, 573-302-7890
Marshfield, 1240 Banning Street, Marshfield, MO, 65706, 417-468-1963

Mexico, One Veterans Drive, Mexico, MO, 65265, 573-581-9630
Nevada, 322 South Prewitt, Nevada, MO, 64772, 417-448-8905
Salem, Hwy 72 North (Box 774), Salem, MO, 65560, 573-729-6626
Sedalia, 3320 West 10th Street, Sedalia, MO, 65301, 660-826-3800
Sikeston, 903 South Kings Highway, Sikeston, MO, 63801, 573-472-2139
St. Charles County, 844 Waterbury Falls Drive, O'Fallon, MO, 63368, 314-286-6988
St. James, VA Clinic-Missouri Veterans Home, 620 N. Jefferson, St. James, MO, 65559, 573-265-0448
St. Joseph, 3302 South Belt Highway, Suite P, St. Joseph, MO, 64503, 816-676-1044
St. Louis CBOC, 6854 Parker Road, Florissant, MO, 63033, 314-286-6988
Warrensburg, 1300 Veterans Road, Warrensburg, MO, 64093, 660-747-3864
Washington, 1627 A. Roy Drive, Washington, MO, 63090, 314-289-7950
West Plains, 1801 East State Route K, West Plains, MO, 65775, 417-257-2454

Regional Office:
St. Louis 63103 (400 South 18th St., statewide 1-800-827-1000)

Vet Centers:
Columbia Vet Center, 4040 Rangeline Drive, Suite 105, Columbia, MO, 65203, 573-814-6206
Kansas City Vet Center, 4800 Main Street, Suite 107, Kansas City, MO, 64112, 816-753-1866
Springfield Vet Center, 3616 S Campbell, Springfield, MO, 65806, 417-881-4197
St. Louis Vet Center, 2901 Olive Street, St. Louis, MO, 63103, 314-531-5355

National Cemeteries:
Jefferson Barracks 63125 (2900 Sheridan Rd., St. Louis, 314-845-8320)
Jefferson City 65101 (1024 E. McCarty St., 314-845-8320)
Springfield 65804 (1702 E. Seminole St., 417-881-9499)

MONTANA
VA Medical Centers:
Miles City, VA Montana HCS VAMC Miles City MT Div, 210 South Winchester, Miles City, MT, 59301, 406-874-5675
Montana HCS, VA Montana HCS Ft. Harrison MT Div., 3687 Veterans Drive, Fort Harrison, MT, 59636, 406-442-6410

Clinics:
Anaconda, Anaconda Primary Care Clinic, 118 East 7th Street, Anaconda, MT, 59711, 406-496-3000
Billings, Billings Community Based Clinic, 2345 King Avenue West, Billings, MT, 59102, 406-373-3500

Billings-Spring Creek Lane, 1775 Spring Creek Lane, Billings, MT, 59102, 406-373-3500

Billings-Majestic Clinic, 1766 Majestic Lane, Billings MT, 59102

Bozeman, Bozeman Primary Care Clinic, 300 North Wilson, Suite 703G, Bozeman, MT, 59715, 406-582-5300

Cut Bank, 8 Second Ave SE, Cut Bank, MT, 59427, 406-873-9047

Glasgow, Glasgow CBOC, 630 2nd Avenue South, Suite A, Glasgow, MT, 59230, 406-228-4101

Glendive Montana, Eastern Montana Veterans Home, 2000 Montana Ave., Glendive, MT, 59330, 406-377-4755

Great Falls, Great Falls Primary Care Clinic, 1417 9th Street S., Suite 200, Great Falls, MT, 59405, 406-791-3200

Kalispell, Kalispell Primary Care Clinic, 31 Three Mile Drive, Kalispell, MT, 59901, 406-758-2700

Lewistown, 629 NE Main Street, Lewistown, MT, 59457, 406-535-4790

Miles City, VA Montana HCS VAMC Miles City MT Div, 210 South Winchester, Miles City, MT, 59301, 406-874-5600

Missoula, Missoula Primary Clinic Clinic, 2687 Palmer Street, Suite C, Missoula, MT, 59808, 406-829-5400

Regional Office:
Fort Harrison 59636-0188 (3633 Veterans Dr., PO Box 188, 1-800-827-1000)

Vet Centers:
Billings Vet Center, 2795 Enterprise Avenue, Suite 1, Billings, MT, 59102, 406-657-6071

Great Falls Vet Center, 615 2nd Avenue North, Great Falls, MT, 59401, 406-452-9048

Kalispell Vet Center, 690 N. Meridian Road, Suite 101, Kalispell, MT, 59903, 406-257-7308

Missoula Vet Center, 500 N. Higgins Ave., Suite 202, Missoula, MT, 59802, 406-721-4918

NEBRASKA

VA Medical Centers:
Grand Island, VA NWI HCS Grand Island Division, 2201 N. Broadwell Avenue, Grand Island, NE, 68803, 308-382-3660

Omaha, VA NWI HCS Omaha Division, 4101 Woolworth Avenue, Omaha, NE, 68105, 402-346-8800

Clinics:
Bellevue, 2501 Capehart Road, Bellevue, NE, 68113, 402-591-4500

Gordon, Gordon VA Outpatient Clinic, 300 E. 8th Street, Gordon, NE, 69343, 308-282-1442

Holdrege, VA Community Based Outpatient Clinic, 1118 Burlington Street, Holdrege, NE, 68949, 308-995-3760

Lincoln, VA NWI HCS Lincoln Division, 600 South 70th Street, Lincoln, NE, 68510, 402-489-3802
Norfolk NE, 710 S 13th Street, Suite 1200, Norfolk, NE, 68701, 402-370-4570
North Platte, VA North Platte Primary Care Clinic, 600 East Francis, Suite 3, North Platte, NE, 69101, 308-532-6906
Scottsbluff, 1720 East Portal Place, Scottsbluff, NE, 69361, 308-220-3930
Sidney, Sidney VA CBOC, 1116 10th Avenue, Sidney, NE, 69162, 308-254-6085

Regional Office:
Lincoln 68501 (3800 Village Drive, PO Box 85816 5631 S. 48th St.statewide 1-800-827-1000)

Vet Centers:
Lincoln Vet Center, 3119 O Street, Suite A, Lincoln, NE, 68510, 402-476-9736
Omaha Vet Center, 3047 South 72nd Street, Omaha, NE, 68124, 402-346-6735

National Cemetery:
Fort McPherson 69151-1031 (12004 S. Spur 56A, Maxwell, 888-737-2800)

NEVADA

VA Medical Centers:
VA Sierra Nevada HCS, 975 Kirman Ave, Reno, NV, 89502, 775-786-7200
Southern Nevada Health care System, 6900 North Pecos Road, North Las Vegas, NV, 89086, 702-791-9000

Clinics:
Carson Valley, VA Carson Valley Outpatient Clinic, 1330 Waterloo Lane, Gardnerville, NV, 89460, 775-782-5265
Ely, Ely Outpatient Clinic, William B. Ririe Hospital, 6 Steptoe Circle, Ely, NV, 89301, 775-289-2788
Lahontan Valley, VA Lahontan Valley CBOC, 345 West A Street, Fallon, NV, 89406, 775-428-6161
Pahrump, 2100 E. Calvada Blvd., Pahrump, NV, 89048, 775-727-7535
PCC Northeast, VA Northeast Primary Care, 4461 E Charleston Blvd., Las Vegas, NV, 89104, 702-791-9050
PCC Northwest, VA Northwest Primary Care, 3968 N Rancho Drive, Las Vegas, NV, 89130, 702-791-9020
PCC Southeast, VA Southeast Primary Care, 1020 S. Boulder Highway, Henderson, NV, 89015, 702-791-9030
PCC Southwest, VA Southwest Primary Care, 7235 S. Buffalo Drive, Las Vegas, NV, 89113, 702-791-9040

Regional Office:
Reno 89511 (5460 Reno Corporate Dr., statewide 1-800-827-1000)

Benefits Office:
North Las Vegas 89086 (4800 Alpine Pl., Suite 12, 1-800-827-1000)

Vet Centers:
Henderson Vet Center, 400 Stephanie Street, Suite 180, Henderson, NV, 89014, 702-791-9100
Las Vegas Vet Center, 1919 S. Jones Blvd., Suite A, Las Vegas, NV, 89146, 702-251-7873
Reno Vet Center, 5580 Mill Street, Suite 600, Reno, NV, 89502, 775-323-1294

NEW HAMPSHIRE
VA Medical Center:
Manchester, VA Medical Center, 718 Smyth Road, Manchester, NH, 3104, 603-624-4366

Clinics:
Conway, 71 Hobbs Street, Conway, NH, 3818, 800-892-8384 x3199
Portsmouth, VA Portsmouth Clinic, 302 Newmarket Street, Portsmouth, NH, 3803, 603-624-4366 x3199
Somersworth, 200 Route 108 N., Suite #2, Somersworth, NH, 3878, 603-624-4366 x3199
Tilton, Tilton CBOC, 630 West Main Street, Suite 400, Tilton, NH, 3276, 603-624-4366 x3199
VICC - St. Johnsbury - Littleton, 685 Meadow Street, Suite 4, Littleton, NH, 3561, 603-444-1323

Regional Office:
Manchester 03101 (Norris Cotton Federal Bldg., 275 Chestnut St., 1-800-827-1000)

Vet Center:
Berlin Vet Center, 515 Main Street, Gorham, NH, 3581, 603-752-2571
Manchester Vet Center, 1461 Hooksett Road, Suite 6, Hooksett, NH, 3106, 603-668-7060

NEW JERSEY
VA Medical Centers:
VA New Jersey HCS Lyons Campus, 151 Knollcroft Road, Lyons, NJ, 07939, 908-647-0180
VA New Jersey HCS E Orange Campus, 385 Tremont Avenue, East Orange, NJ, 07018, 973-676-1000
+
Clinics:
Atlantic County, Atlantic County VA Clinic, 1909 New Road, Northfield, NJ, 08225, 302-994-2511 x2800
Brick, James J. Howard Outpatient Clinic, 970 Rt 70, Brick, NJ, 08724, 732-206-8900

Cape May County, U.S. Coast Guard Trng. Ctr., 1 Munro Avenue, TRACEN Dispensary, Cape May, NJ, 08204, 302-994-2511 x2850
Camden (300 Broadway, Suite 103 Camden, NJ 08104) Phone: 877-232-5240Fax: 215-823-4514
Cumberland County, VA Health Clinic, 1051 W Sherman Avenue, Bldg 3 Unit B, Vineland, NJ, 08360, 302-994-2511 x6500
Elizabeth, 654 East Jersey St., 2nd Floor, Elizabeth, NJ, 07206, 908-994-0120
Fort Dix Outpatient Clinic at Marshall Hall, Fort Dix Outpatient Clinic at Marshall Hall, 8th and Alabama Streets, Joint Base McGuire-Dix, Building 5437, Lakehurst, NJ, 08640, 609-562-2999
Gloucester County, Veterans Health Clinic at Gloucester County, 211 County House Road, Sewell, NJ, 08080, 877-823-5230 Or 877-823-5230
Hackensack/Bergen County, Hackensack Health Practice, 385 Prospect Avenue, Hackensack, NJ, 07601, 201-487-1390
Hamilton, University Office Plaza 1, 3635 Quakerbridge Road, Hamilton, NJ, 08619, 609-570-6600
Jersey City, Jersey City Health Practice, 115 Christopher Columbus Drive, Suite 200, Jersey City, NJ, 07302, 201-435-3055
Morristown, 340 W. Hanover Avenue, Morristown, NJ, 7960, 973-539-9794
Paterson, Paterson CBOC, 275 Getty Avenue, Paterson, NJ, 07503, 973-247-1666
Piscataway, 14 Wills Way, Piscataway, NJ, 08854, 732-981-8193 x5481
Tinton Falls, The Atrium Building 4, 55 Gilbert Street, First Floor Suite 4101, Tinton Falls, NJ, 07701, 732-842-4751

Regional Office:
Newark 07102 (20 Washington Pl., statewide 1-800-827-1000) (Philadelphia, PA Regional Office serves counties of Atlantic, Burlington, Camden, Cape May, Cumberland, Gloucester, Salem)

Vet Centers:
Bloomfield Vet Center, 2 Broad Street, Suite 703, Bloomfield, NJ, 07003, 973-748-0980
Lakewood Vet Center, Parkway Seventy Plaza, 1255 Route 70, Unit 22N, Lakewood, NJ, 08701, 908-607-6364
Secaucus Vet Center, 110A Meadowlands Parkway, Suite 102, Secaucus, NJ, 07094, 201-223-7787
Trenton Vet Center, 934 Parkway Ave., Suite 201, Ewing, NJ, 08618, 609-882-5744
Ventnor Vet Center Ventnor Building, 6601 Ventnor Ave., Suite 105, Ventnor, NJ, 08406, 609-487-8387

National Cemeteries:
Beverly 08010 (916 Bridgeboro Rd., 215-504-5610)
Finn's Point 08079 (Box 542, R.F.D. 3, Fort Mott Rd., Salem, 215-504-5610)

NEW MEXICO

VA Medical Center:
New Mexico HCS, VA Medical Center, 1501 San Pedro Drive SE, Albuquerque, NM, 87108, 505-265-1711

Clinics:
Alamogordo CCBOC, 3199 N White Sands Blvd, Suite D10, Alamogordo, NM,88310, 575-437-9195
Artesia CBOC, 2410 W. Main St., Artesia, NM 88210-3712, 575-746-3531
Durango CCBOC, 1970 East Third Avenue, Suite 102, Durango, CO 81301, 970-247-2214
Espanola CCBOC, 105 S. Coronado Avenue, Espanola, NM, 87701, 505-367-4213
Farmington CBOC, 3605 English Road, Farmington, NM, 87402, 505-326-4383
Gallup CBOC, 520 State Hwy 564, Gallup, NM, 87301, 505-722-7234
Las Vegas CCBOC, 624 University Ave., Suite 300, Las Vegas, NM, 87701, 505-425-1910
Northwest Metro CBOC, Northwest Metro CBOC, 1760 Grande Blvd SE, Rio Rancho, NM, 87124, 505-896-7200
Raton CBOC, 1493 Whittier Street, Raton, NM 87440, 575-445-2393
Santa Fe CBOC, 2213 Brothers Road, Suite 600, Sante Fe, NM, 87505, 505-986-8645
Silver City CBOC, 2950 Leslie Road, Silver City, NM, 88061, 575-538-2921
Taos CCBOC, 1353 Paseo Del Pueblo Sur, Taos, NM 87571, 575-751-0328 or 575-751-0328
Truth or Consequences CCBOC, 1960 N Date Street, Truth or Consequences,NM, 87901, 575-894-7662

Regional Office:
Albuquerque 87102 (Dennis Chavez Federal Bldg., 500 Gold Ave., S.W., statewide 1-800-827-1000)

Vet Centers:
Albuquerque Vet Center, 1600 Mountain Road NW, Albuquerque, NM, 87104, 505-346-6562
Farmington Vet Center, 4251 E. Main, Suite A, Farmington, NM, 87402, 505-327-9684
Las Cruces Vet Center, 230 S. Water Street, Las Cruces, NM, 88001, 575-523-9826
Sante Fe Vet Center, 2209 Brothers Road, Suite 110, Sante Fe, NM, 87505, 505-988-6562

National Cemeteries:
Fort Bayard 88036 (P.O. Box 189, 915-564-0201)
Santa Fe 87501 (501 N. Guadalupe St., 505-988-6400 or toll-free 877-353-6295)

NEW YORK
VA Medical Centers:
Albany, VA Medical Center, 113 Holland Avenue, Albany, NY, 12208, 518-626-5000
Bath, VA Medical Center, 76 Veterans Avenue, Bath, NY, 14810, 607-664-4000
Bronx, Bronx VA Medical Center, 130 West Kingsbridge Road, Bronx, NY, 10468, 718-584-9000
Canandaigua, VA Medical Center, 400 Fort Hill Avenue, Canandaigua, NY, 14424, 585-394-2000
Castle Point Division-Hudson Valley HCS, Route 9-D, Castle Point, NY, 12511, 845-831-2000
Hudson Valley HCS VAMC Montrose NY Division, 2094 Albany Post Road, Montrose, NY, 10548, 914-737-4400 Castle Point Campus, 41 Castle Point Road, Wappingers Falls, NY 12590. 845-831-2000
New York Harbor HCS - NY Div., VA Medical Center, 423 East 23rd Street, New York, NY, 10010, 212-686-7500
New York Harbor HCS-Brooklyn-Poly Pl. Campus, VA Medical Center, 800 POLY PL, Brooklyn, NY, 11209, 718-836-6600
New York Harbor HCS-St. Albans Campus, St. Albans Extended Care Center, 17901 Linden Blvd, Jamaica, NY, 11434, 718-526-1000
Northport, VA Medical Center, 79 Middleville Road, Bldg 200, Northport, NY, 11768, 631-261-4400
Syracuse, VA Medical Center, 800 Irving Avenue, Syracuse, NY, 13210, 315-425-4400
VA Western New York HCS VAMC Buffalo NY Div., 3495 Bailey Avenue, Buffalo, NY, 14215, 716-834-9200
VA Western New York HCS VAMC Batavia NY Div, 222 Richmond Avenue, Batavia, NY, 14020, 585-297-1000

Clinics:
Auburn, Auburn Memorial Hospital, 17 Lansing Street, Auburn, NY, 13021, 315-255-7002
Bainbridge, 109 North Main Street, Bainbridge, NY, 13733, 607-967-8590
Bay Shore, Bay Shore CBOC, 132 East Main Street, Bay Shore, NY, 11706, 631-328-9092
Binghamton, Gavin Building, 425 Robinson Street, Binghamton, NY, 13901, 607-772-9100
Carmel (Putnam County), 1875 Route 6, Carmel, NY, 10512, 845-228-5291
Catskill, Greene Medical Arts Bldg, 159 Jefferson Heights, Suite 102, Catskill, NY, 12414, 518-943-7515
Chapel St, Chapel OPC, 40 Flatbush Avenue Extension, Brooklyn, NY, 11201, 718-439-4300
Clifton Park, 1673 Route 9, Clifton Park, NY, 12065, 518-626-5205
Cortland, 1451 Dryden Road, Freeville, NY, 13068, 607-347-4101
Dunkirk, 166 East 4th Street, Dunkirk, NY, 14048, 800-310-5001
East Meadow, East Meadow Clinic, 2201 Hempstead Turnpike, Building Q, East Meadow, NY, 11554, 631-754-7978

Elmira, Health Services Bldg Suite 2E, 200 Madison Ave, Elmira, NY, 14901, 1-877-845-3247 ext 44640

Fonda, Camp Mohawk Plaza, 2623 State Highway 30A, Fonda, NY, 12068, 518-853-1247

Glens Falls, 84 Broad Street, Glens Falls, NY, 12801, 518-798-6066

Goshen, (Orange County) NY, 30 Hatfield Lane, Suite 204, Goshen, NY, 10924, 845-294-6927

Harlem, VA Harlem Care Center, 55 West 125th Street, New York, NY, 10027, 646-273-8125

Harris (Monticello), 55 Sturgis Road, Monticello, NY, 12701, 845-791-4936

Jamestown, 608 West 3rd Street, Jamestown, NY, 14701, 716-338-1511

Kingston, 63 Hurley St., Kingston, NY, 12401, 845-331-8322

Lackawanna, OLV Family Care Center, 227 Ridge Road, Lackawanna, NY, 14218, 716-822-5944

Lackawanna-Springville, 27 Franklin Street, Springville, NY, 14141, 716-592-7400

Lockport, 5883 Snyder Dr., Lockport, NY, 14094, 716-438-3890

Malone, 3372 State Route 11 Main Street, Malone, NY, 12953, 518-483-1529

Massena, 1 Hospital Drive, Massena, NY, 13662, 315-769-4253

New City (Rockland County), 345 North Main Street, New City, NY, 10956, 845-634-8942

Niagara Falls, 2201 Pine Avenue, Niagara Falls, NY, 14301, 716-862-8580

Olean, 465 North Union Street, Olean, NY, 14760, 716-373-7709

Oswego, 437 State Route 104E, Oswego, NY, 13126, 315-207-0120

Patchogue, Clinic, 24 Phyllis Drive, Patchogue, NY 11772

Pine Plain, 2881 Church Street, Route 199, Pine Plains, NY, 12567, 518-398-9240

Plattsburgh, 80 Sharron Avenue, Suite 4, Plattsburgh, NY, 12901, 518-561-6247

Port Jervis, 150 Pike Street, Port Jervis, NY, 12771, 845-856-5396

Poughkeepsie, 488 Freedom Plains Road, Suite 120, Poughkeepsie, NY, 12603, 845-452-5151

Queens, Thomas P. Noonan Jr., Clinic, 47-01 Queens Blvd., Sunnyside, NY 11104

Riverhead, Riverhead Clinic, 300 Centre Drive, Riverhead, NY, 11901, 631-754-7978

Rochester, 465 Westfall Road, Rochester, NY, 14620, 585-463-2600

Rochester-Clinton Crossing, 919 Westfall Road, Rochester, NY, 14618, 585-463-2600

Rochester-Mt. Hope, 1867 Mt. Hope Avenue, Rochester, NY, 14620, 585-463-2600

Rome, VA Outpatient Clinic Rome, 125 Brookley Road, Building 510, Rome, NY, 13441, 315-334-7100

Saranac Lake, 33 Depot Street, Saranac Lake, NY, 12983, 518-626-5237

Schenectady, Sheridan Plaza, 1322 Gerling Street, Sheridan Plaza, Schenectady, NY, 12308, 518-346-3334

Staten Island, Staten Island Health Care center, 21 Water Street, Staten Is-

land, NY, 10304, 718-761-2973
Troy, 295 River Street, Troy, NY, 12180, 518-274-7707
Valley Stream, Valley Stream CBOC, 99 South Central Avenue, Valley Stream, NY, 11580, 631-754-7978
Watertown, 19472 US Route 11, Washington Street, Suite 102, Watertown, NY, 13601, 315-221-7026
Wellsville, 3458 Riverside Drive, Rt 19, Wellsville, NY, 14895, 607-664-4660
Westport, 7426 NYS Route 9N, Westport, NY, 12993, 518-626-5236
White Plains, White Plains VHA Clinic, 23 South Broadway, White Plains, NY, 10601, 914-421-1951
Yonkers, Yonkers VHA Clinic, 124 New Main Street, Yonkers, NY, 10701, 914-375-8055 x4400

Regional Offices:
Buffalo 14202 (Niagara Center, 130 S. Elmwood Ave., 1-800-827-1000)
    (Serves counties not served by New York City VA Regional Office.)
New York City 10014 (245 W. Houston St., statewide 1-800-827-1000)
    (Serves counties of Albany, Bronx, Clinton, Columbia, Delaware, Dutchess, Essex, Franklin, Fulton, Greene, Hamilton, Kings, Montgomery, Nassau, New York,
Orange, Otsego, Putnam, Queens, Rensselaer, Richmond, Rockland, Saratoga,
Schenectady, Schoharie, Suffolk, Sullivan, Ulster, Warren, Washington, Westchester.)

Benefits Offices:
Albany 12208 (113 Holland Ave., 1-800-827-1000)
Rochester 14620 (465 Westfall Rd., 1-800-827-1000)
Syracuse 13202 (344 W. Genesee St., 1-800-827-1000)

Vet Centers:
Albany Vet Center, 17 Computer Drive West, Albany, NY, 12205, 518-626-5130
Babylon Vet Center, 116 West Main St., Babylon, NY, 11702, 631-661-3930
Binghamton Vet Center, Binghamton Vet Center, 53 Chenango Street, Binghamton, NY, 13901, 607-722-2393
Bronx Vet Center, 2471 Morris Avenue, Suite 1A, Bronx, NY, 10468, 718-367-3500
Brooklyn Vet Center, 25 Chapel Street, Suite 604, Brooklyn, NY, 11201, 718-624-2765
Buffalo Vet Center, 2372 Sweet Home Road, Suite 1, Buffalo, NY, 14228, 716-862-7350
Harlem Vet Center, 2279 3rd Avenue, 2nd Floor, New York, NY, 10035, 212-426-2200
Manhattan Vet Center, 32 Broadway, 2nd Floor, Suite 200, New York, NY, 10004, 212-742-9591
Mieton Vet Center, 726 East Main Street, Suite 203, Mietown, NY, 10940, 845-342-9917

Nassau Vet Center, 970 South Broadway, Hicksville, NY, 11801, 516-348-0088
Queens Vet Center, 75-10B 91 Ave., Woodhaven, NY, 11421, 718-296-2871
Rochester Vet Center, 2000 S. Winton Road, Building 5, Suite 201, Rochester, NY, 14618, 585-232-5040
Staten Island Vet Center, 60 Bay Street, Staten Island, NY, 10301, 718-816-4499
Syracuse Vet Center, 109 Pine Street, Suite 101, Syracuse, NY, 13210, 315-478-7127
Watertown Vet Center, 210 Court Street, Suite 20, Watertown, NY, 13601, 315-782-5479
White Plains Vet Center, 300 Hamilton Ave., Suite C, White Plains, NY, 10601, 914-682-6250

National Cemeteries:
Bath 14810 (76 Veterans Ave., San Juan Ave., 607-664-4853/4806)
Calverton 11933-1031 (210 Princeton Blvd., 631-727-5410/5770)
Cypress Hills 11208 (625 Jamaica Ave., Brooklyn, 631-454-4949)
Long Island 11735-1211 (2040 Wellwood Ave., Farmingdale, 631-454-4949)
Saratoga 12871-1721 (200 Duell Rd., Schuylerville, 518-581-9128)
Woodlawn 14901 (1825 Davis St., Elmira, 607-732-5411)

NORTH CAROLINA
VA Medical Centers:
Asheville, VA Medical Center, 1100 Tunnel Road, Asheville, NC, 28805, 828-298-7911
Durham, VA Medical Center, 508 Fulton Street, Durham, NC, 27705, 919-286-0411
Fayetteville NC, VA Medical Center, 2300 Ramsey Street, Fayetteville, NC, 28301, 910-488-2120
W.G. (Bill) Hefner Salisbury VAMC, VA Medical Center, 1601 Brenner Avenue, Salisbury, NC, 28144, 704-638-9000

Clinics:
Albermale Primary Outpatient Clinic, 1845 West City Drive, Elizabeth City, NC, 27909, 252-331-2191
Charlotte Community Based Outpatient Clinic, 8601 University East Drive, Charlotte, NC, 28213, 704-597-3500
Charlotte Mental Health OPC, 601 East 5th Street, Suite 450, Charlotte, NC, 28202, 704-332-7471
Franklin, 647 Wayah Street, Franklin, NC, 28734, 828-369-1781
Goldsboro CBOC, 2610 Hospital Road, Goldsboro, NC, 27534, 919-731-9766
Greenville, 401 Moye Blvd., Greenville, NC, 27834, 252-830-2149
Hamlet, 100 Jefferson Street, Hamlet, NC, 28345, 910-582-3536
Hickory, Hickory CBOC, 2440 Century Place SE, Hickory, NC, 28602, 828-431-5600
Jacksonville, 241 Freedom Way, Suite 1, Midway Park, NC, 28544, 910-353-6406

Morehead City, 5240 Highway 70 West, Morehead City, NC, 28557, 252-240-2349

Raleigh, 3305 Sungate Blvd., Raleigh, NC, 27610, 919-212-0129

Robeson County (Lumberton), 139 Three Hunts Drive, Pembroke, NC, 28372, 910-272-3220

Rutherford County (Rutherfordton), 374 Charlotte Road, Rutherford, NC, 28139, 828-288-2780

Wilmington, Wilmington VA Health Care Center, 1705 Gardner Road, Wilmington, NC, 28405, 910-343-5300

Winston-Salem (Annex), Winston-Salem Annex, 2102 Peters Creek Parkway, Suite 200, Winston-Salem, NC, 27127, 336-761-5300

Winston-Salem (Main), 190 Kimel Park Drive, Winston-Salem, NC, 27103, 336-761-5300

Regional Office:
Winston-Salem 27155 (Federal Bldg., 251 N. Main St., statewide 1-800-827-1000,

Benefits Delivery at Discharge Office Winston-Salem 27101 (Attn: BDD, 100 N. Main St., Ste 1700)

Quick Start Office Winston-Salem 27101 (Attn: Quick Start, Federal Bldg, 100 N. Main Street. Suite 1900

Nationwide Loan Guaranty Certificate of Eligibility Center 1-888-244-6711

Vet Centers:
Charlotte Vet Center, 2114 Ben Craig Drive, Suite 300, Charlotte, NC, 28262, 704-549-8025

Fayetteville Vet Center, 4140 Ramsey St., Suite 110, Fayetteville, NC, 28311, 910-488-6252

Greensboro Vet Center, 3515 W. Market Street, Suite 120, Greensboro, NC, 27403, 336-333-5366

Greenville Vet Center, 1021 WH Smith Blvd, Suite 100, Greenville, NC, 27834, 252-355-7920

Jacksonville Vet Center, 110A Branchwood Dr.,, Jacksonville, NC, 28540, 910-703-0699

Raleigh Vet Center, 1649 Old Louisburg Road, Raleigh, NC, 27604, 919-856-4616

National Cemeteries:
New Bern 28560 (1711 National Ave., 252-637-2912)

Raleigh 27610-3335 (501 Rock Quarry Rd., 252-637-2912)

Salisbury 28144 (501 Statesville Blvd., 704-636-2661/4621)

Wilmington 28403 (2011 Market St., 252-637-2912)

NORTH DAKOTA

VA Medical Center:
Fargo VA HCS, VA Medical Center, 2101 Elm Street, Fargo, ND, 58102, 701-232-3241

Clinics:
Bemidji, 705 5th St., Bemidji, MN, 56601, 218-755-6360
Bismarck ND, 2700 State Street, Suite 5, Bismarck, ND, 58503, 701-221-9152
Devils Lake, 1031 7th St. NE, Devils Lake, ND, 58301
Dickinson, 528 21st St. W., Suite F, Dickinson, ND, 58601, 701-483-1850
Fergus Falls, 1839 North Park St., 56537, 218-739-1400
Grafton VA Clinic ND State Development Ctr., 700 West 6th Street, Grafton, ND, 58237, 701-352-4059
Grand Forks VA Outpatient Clinic, 3221 32nd Ave South, Suite 700, Grand Forks, ND, 58201, 701-335-4380
Jamestown, 2422 20th St. SW, Jamestown, ND, 58401, 701-952-4787
Minot, VA Outpatient Clinic 5th MedGroup, 10 Missile Avenue, Minot, ND, 58705, 701-727-9800
Williston CBOC, 205 Main Street, Williston, ND, 58801, 701-572-2470

Regional Office:
Fargo 58102 (2101 Elm St., statewide 1-800-827-1000)

Vet Centers:
Bismarck Vet Center, 619 Riverwood Drive, Suite 105, Bismarck, ND, 58501, 701-224-9751
Fargo Vet Center, 3310 Fiechtner Drive, Suite 100, Fargo, ND, 58103, 701-237-0942
Minot Vet Center, 1400 20th Ave SW, Suite 2, Minot, ND, 58701, 701-852-0177

OHIO
VA Medical Centers:
Chillicothe, VA Medical Center, 17273 State Route 104, Chillicothe, OH, 45601, 740-773-1141
Cincinnati, VA Medical Center, 3200 Vine Street, Cincinnati, OH, 45220, 513-861-3100
Dayton, VA Medical Center, 4100 West Third Street, Dayton, OH, 45428, 937-268-6511
Louis Stokes Cleveland, Louis Stokes Cleveland VAMC, 10701 East Blvd, Cleveland, OH, 44106, 216-791-3800

Clinics:
Akron, VA Community Based Outpatient Clinic, 55 W. Waterloo, Akron, OH, 44319, 330-724-7715
Ashtabula County , Ashtabula County Primary Care Clinic, 1230 Lake Avenue, Ashtabula, OH, 44004, 866-463-0912
Athens, VA Community Based Outpatient Clinic, 510 West Union Street, Athens, OH, 45701, 740-593-7314
Belmont, St. Clairsville VA Clinic, 103 Plaza Drive, Suite A, St. Clairsville, OH, 43950, 740-695-9321
Cambridge, Cambridge CBOC, 2146 Southgate Parkway, Cambridge, OH, 43725, 740-432-1963

Canton, VA Community Based Outpatient Clinic, 733 Market Avenue South, Canton, OH, 44702, 330-489-4600

Clermont County, Clermont County CBOC, 4600 Beechwood Road, Cincinnati, OH, 45244, 513-943-3680

East Liverpool, VA Community Based Outpatient Clinic, 15655 State Route 170, Suite A, Calcutta, OH, 43920, 330-386-4303

Gallipolis VA Clinic 323 A Upper River Road Gallipolis, OH 45631, 740-446-3934

Georgetown, VA Community Based Outpatient Clinic, 4903 State Route 125, Georgetown, OH, 45121, 937-378-3413

Grove City (Franklin County), VA Community Based Outpatient Clinic, 1955 Ohio Drive, Grove City, OH, 43123, 614-257-5800

Hamilton, VA Health care Associates of Butler County, 1750 South Erie Highway, Hamilton, OH, 45011, 513-870-9444

Lancaster, 1703 N. Memorial Drive, Lancaster, OH, 43130, 740-653-6145

Lima, VA Community Based Outpatient Clinic, 1303 Bellefontaine Ave., Lima, OH, 45804, 419-222-5788

Lorain, VA Community Based Outpatient Clinic, 205 West 20th Street, Lorain, OH, 44052, 440-244-3833

Mansfield, VA Community Based Outpatient Clinic, 1456 Park Avenue, Suite N, Mansfield, OH, 44906, 419-529-4602

Marietta, VA Community Based Outpatient Clinic, 418 Colgate Drive, Marietta, OH, 45750, 740-568-0412

Marion, VA Community Based Outpatient Clinic, 1203 Delaware Ave., Marion, OH, 43302, 740-223-8809

McCafferty, VA Community Based Outpatient Clinic, 4242 Lorain Avenue, Cleveland, OH, 44113, 216-939-0699

Middletown, VA Community Based Outpatient Clinic, 4337 N. Union Road, Middletown, OH, 45005, 513-423-8387

New Philadelphia, VA Community Based Outpatient Clinic, 1260 Monroe Avenue, #15, New Philadelphia, OH, 44663, 330-602-5339

Newark, VA Community Based Outpatient Clinic, 1855 W Main Street, Newark, OH, 43055, 740-788-8329

Painesville, 54 South State St., Suite 204, Painesville, OH, 44077, 440-357-6740

Painesville, VA Community Based Outpatient Clinic, 7 West Jackson Street, Painesville, OH, 44077, 440-357-6740

Parma, VA Community Based Outpatient Clinic, 8787 Brookpark Road, Parma, OH, 44129, 216-739-7000

Portsmouth, VA Community Based Outpatient Clinic, 840 Gallia Street, Portsmouth, OH, 45662, 740-353-3236

Ravenna, VA Community Based Outpatient Clinic, 6751 North Chestnut Street, Ravenna, OH, 44266, 330-296-3641

Sandusky, VA Community Based Outpatient Clinic, 3416 Columbus Avenue, Sandusky, OH, 44870, 419-625-7350

Springfield, VA Community Based Outpatient Clinic, 512 South Burnett, Springfield, OH, 45505, 937-328-3385

Toledo, Toledo VA Outpatient Clinic, 1200 S. Detroit Avenue, Toledo, OH, 43614, 419-259-2000
Warren, VA Community Based Outpatient Clinic, 1460 Tod Ave NW, Warren, OH, 44485, 330-392-0311
Wilmington (448 West Main Street, Wilmington, Ohio 45177) 937-382-3949
Youngstown, VA Community Based Outpatient Clinic, 2031 Belmont Avenue, Youngstown, OH, 44505, 330-740-9200
Zanesville, VA Community Based Outpatient Clinic, 2800 Maple Avenue, Zanesville, OH, 43701, 740-453-7725

Regional Office:
Cleveland 44199 (Anthony J. Celebrezze Fed. Bldg., 1240 E. 9th St., 1-800-827-1000)

Benefits Offices:
Cincinnati 45202 (36 E. Seventh St., Suite 210, 1-800-827-1000)
Columbus 43219 (420 N. James Road, 1-800-827-1000)

Vet Centers:
Cincinnati Vet Center, 801B W. 8th Street, Suite 126, Cincinnati, OH, 45203, 513-763-3500
Cleveland Vet Center, 5310 1/2 Warrensville Center Road, Maple Heights, OH, 44137, 216-707-7901
Columbus Vet Center, 30 Spruce Street, Columbus, OH, 43215, 614-257-5550
Dayton Vet Center, East Medical Plaza, 627 S Edwin Moses Blvd., 6th Floor, Dayton, OH, 45408, 937-461-9150
Parma Vet Center, 5700 Pearl Road, Suite 102, Parma, OH, 44129, 440-845-5023
Stark County Vet Center, 610 Cleveland Avenue N, Suite C, Canton, OH, 44702, 330-454-3120
Toledo Vet Center, 1565 S. Byrne Road, Suite 104, Toledo, OH, 43614, 419-213-7533

National Cemeteries:
Dayton 45428-1088 (4100 W. Third St., 937-262-2115)
Ohio Western Reserve 44270 (10175 Rawiga Rd. PO Box 8 Rittman, 330-335-3069)

OKLAHOMA

VA Medical Centers:
Muskogee, VA Medical Center, 1011 Honor Heights Drive, Muskogee, OK, 74401, 918-577-3000
Oklahoma City, VA Medical Center, 921 NE 13th Street, Oklahoma City, OK, 73104, 405-456-1000

Clinics:
Ada Adult Medicine Clinic, 301 N Monte Vista, Ada, OK, 74820, 580-436-2262

Altus, 201 S. Park Lane, Altus, OK, 73521, 580-482-9020
Ardmore, 2002 12th Ave. NW, Suite E, Ardmore, OK, 73401, 580-223-5311
Blackwell Family Medicine, 1009 W Ferguson Ave., Blackwell, OK, 74631, 580-363-0052
Enid, 915 E. Garriott, Suite H and G, Enid, OK, 73701, 580-242-5100
Hartshorne CBOC, 1429 E. Pennsylvania Ave., Hartshorne, OK, 74547, 888-578-1595
Jay VA Outpatient Clinic, 1569 North Main Street, Jay, OK, 74346, 888-424-8387
Lawton CBOC, 4303 Pitman & Thomas, Ft. Sill, OK, 73503, 580-585-5600
Stillwater, 320 N Perkins Road, Stillwater, OK, 74075, 405-624-0334
Tulsa, CBOC, Ernest Childers Outpatient Clinic, 9322 E 41st Street, Tulsa, OK, 74145, 918-628-2500
Tulsa-Behavioral Medicine, Tulsa Behavioral Medicine Service, 10159 E 11th Street, Tulsa, OK, 74128, 918-628-2100
Vinita CBOC, 269 S. 7th Street, Vinita, OK, 74301, 918-713-5400

Regional Office:
Muskogee 74401 (Federal Bldg., 125 S. Main St., Compensation & Pension: 1-800-827-1000, Education National Call Center: 1-888-442-4551, National Direct Deposit: 1-877-838-2778)

Benefits Office:
Oklahoma City 73102 (Federal Campus, 301 NW 6th St., Suite 113, 1-800-827-1000)
Tulsa 74145 (Ernest Childers Outpatient Clinic, 9322 East 41 St, Room 220, 1-800-827-1000)

Vet Centers:
Jack C. Montgomery East, 2414 E Shawnee Bypass, Muskogee, OK 74403, 918-577-3699
Lawton Vet Center, 1016 SW C Avenue, Suite B, Lawton, OK, 73501, 580-585-5880
Oklahoma City Vet Center, 1024 NW 47th Street, Suite B, Oklahoma City, OK, 73118, 405-456-5184
Tulsa Vet Center, 14002 E. 21st Street, Suite 200, Tulsa, OK, 74134, 918-628-2760

National Cemeteries:
Fort Gibson 74434 (1423 Cemetery Rd., 918-478-2334)
Fort Sill 73538 (2648 NE Jake Dunn Rd., 580-492-3200)

OREGON
VA Medical Centers:
Portland, 3710 SW US Veterans Hospital Rd., Portland, OR, 97239, 503-721-1498
Roseburg HCS, VA Roseburg Health Care System, 913 NW Garden Valley

Blvd., Roseburg, OR, 97471, 541-440-1000
Southern Oregon Rehabilitation Ctr & Clinics, VA SORCC, 8495 Crater Lake
Hwy., White City, OR, 97503, 541-826-2111

Clinics:
Bend, Bend CBOC, 2650 NE Courtney Drive, Bend, OR, 97701, 541-647-5200
Brookings CBOC, 555 - 5th Street, Brookings, OR, 97415, 541-440-1000
Burns, Oregon – Burns Outreach Clinic. 271 N. Egan Ave. Burns, OR 97720
(541) 573-3339
East Metro Portland, East Metro Portland CBOC, 10535 NE Glisan Street,
Suite 200, Portland, OR, 97220, 503-273-5142
Eugene CBOC, 100 E. River Avenue, Eugene, OR, 97404, 541-607-0897
Eugene-Annex, 2400 River Road, Eugene, OR, 97402, 541-607-0897
Grants Pass, 520 SW Ramsey Avenue, Suite 102, Grants Pass, OR, 97527,
541-955-5551
Klamath Falls, Klamath Falls CBOC, 2225 North Eldorado Blvd., Klamath
Falls, OR, 97601, 541-273-6206
La Grande CBOC, 202 12th Street, La Grande, OR, 97850, 541-963-0627
Morrow County PCTOC, 2 Marine Drive, Suite 103, P.O. Box 1859, Boardman,
OR 97818, 541-481-2255
North Bend CBOC, 2191 Marion Street, North Bend, OR, 97459, 541-440-
1000
North Coast CBOC-Camp Rilea Military Reservation, 91400 Neocoxie Street,
Bldg. 7315, Warrenton, OR, 97146, 503-220-8262 x52593
Salem CBOC, 1660 Oak Street SE, Suite 100, Salem, OR, 97301, 503-721-
1499
Wallowa County PCTOC, 401 NE 1st Street, Enterprise, OR, 97828, 541-426-
0219
West Linn, 1750 SW Blankenship Road, Suite 300, West Linn, OR, 97068,
503-210-4900
West Metro Portland, Hillsboro Community Outpatient Clinic, 1925 NW Amber-
glen Parkway, Suite #300, Hillsboro, OR, 97006, 503-906-5000

Regional Office:
Portland 97204 (100 SW Main St. FL2., 1-800-827-1000)

Vet Centers:
Central Oregon Vet Center, 1645 NE Forbes Road, Suite 105, Bend, OR,
97701, 541-749-2112
Eugene Vet Center, 190 East 11th Avenue, Suite 200, Eugene, OR, 97401,
541-465-6918
Grants Pass Vet Center, 211 SE 10th Street, Grants Pass, OR, 97526, 541-
479-6912
Portland Vet Center, 1505 NE 122nd Ave, Suite 110, Portland, OR, 97230,
503-688-5361
Salem Vet Center, 2645 Portland Road, Suite 250, Salem, OR, 97301, 503-
362-9911

National Cemeteries:
Eagle Point 97524 (2763 Riley Rd., 541-826-2511)
Roseburg 97470 (1770 Harvard Blvd, 541-826-2511)
Willamette 97266-6937 (11800 S.E. Mt. Scott Blvd., Portland, 503-273-5250)

PENNSYLVANIA
VA Medical Centers:
Butler, VA Medical Center, 325 New Castle Road, Butler, PA, 16001, 724-287-4781
Coatesville, VA Medical Center, 1400 Black Horse Hill Road, Coatesville, PA, 19320, 610-384-7711
Erie, VA Medical Center, 135 East 38th Street, Erie, PA, 16504, 814-868-8661
Heinz Division HCS, Pittsburgh HCS VAMC Aspinwall PA Div, 1010 Delafield Road, Pittsburgh, PA, 15215, 412-360-6000
James E. Van Zandt VA (Altoona), VA Medical Center, 2907 Pleasant Valley Boulevard, Altoona, PA, 16602, 814-943-8164
Lebanon, VA Medical Center, 1700 South Lincoln Avenue, Lebanon, PA, 17042, 717-272-6621
Philadelphia, VA Medical Center, 3900 Woodland Avenue, Philadelphia, PA, 19104, 215-823-5800
Pittsburgh HCS-University Drive, University Drive C, Pittsburgh, PA, 15240, 412-360-6000
VADOM Philadelphia, 1425-1429 Snyder Avenue, Philadelphia, PA, 19145, 267-292-9300
Wilkes Barre, VA Medical Center, 1111 East End Boulevard, Wilkes-Barre, PA, 18711, 570-824-3521

Clinics:
Allentown, Allentown Outpatient Clinic, 3110 Hamilton Boulevard, Allentown, PA, 18103, 610-776-4304
Armstrong County, 313 Ford Street, Suite 2B, Ford City, PA, 16226, 724-763-4090
Beaver CBOC, 90 Wagner Road, Monaca, PA, 15061, 724-709-6005
Belmont CBOC, 103 Plaza Dr., Suite A, St. Clairsville, OH 43950, ph. 740-695-9321
Berwick , Alley Medical Center, 301 West Third Street, Berwick, PA, 18603, 570-759-0351
Camp Hill , The Greater Harrisburg Outpatient Clinic, 25 N 32nd Street, Camp Hill, PA, 17011, 717-730-9782
Clarion County, 855 Route 58, Suite 1, Parker, PA, 16036, 724-287-4781
Coudersport, Coudersport Veterans Primary Care Center, 24 Maple View Lane, Suite 2, Coudersport, PA, 16915, 814-260-9342
Cranberry Township, 1183 Freedom Road, Suite A101, Cranberry Township, PA, 16066, 724-741-3131
Crawford County , Crawford County Primary Care Clinic, 16954 Conneaut Lake Road, Meadville, PA, 16335, 866-962-3210

DuBois, 5690 Shaffer Road, DuBois, PA, 15801, 814-375-6817

Elmira - Mansfield, Mansfield Veterans Primary Care Center, 63 Third Street, Suite 104, Mansfield, PA, 16933, 570-662-0507

Fayette County, CBOC 635 Pittsburgh Road, Suite 520, Uniontown, PA, 15401, 724-439-4990

Johnstown, James E Van Zandt VA Outpatient Clinic, 1425 Scalp Avenue, Suite 29, Johnstown, PA, 15904, 814-266-8696

Lancaster, Lancaster VA OC Greenfield Corp. Ctr., 1861 Charter Lane, Suite 121, Lancaster, PA, 17604, 717-290-6900

Lawrence County, Ridgewood Professional Center, 1750 New Butler Road, New Castle, PA, 16101, 724-598-6080

McKean County , McKean County CBOC, 23 Kennedy Street, Bradford, PA, 16701, 814-368-3019

Michael A. Marzano VA Outpatient Clinic, 295 N. Kerrwood Drive, Suite 110, Hermitage, PA, 16148, 724-346-1569

Northampton County, Phoebe Nursing & Rehab Ctr, 701 Slate Belt Boulevard, Bangor, PA, 18013, 610-599-0127

Philadelphia, 214 North 4th Street, Second Floor, Philadelphia, PA, 19106, 215-923-1163

Pottsville, Schuylkill Medical Center E, 700 Schulykill Manor Road, 2nd Floor Suite 6, Pottsville, PA, 17901, 570-621-4115

Pottsville-Frackville, Good Samaritan-Frackville, 10 East Spruce Street, Frackville, PA, 17931, 570-874-4289

Reading, 145 N. 6th Street, 3rd Floor, Reading, PA, 19601, 610-208-4717

Sayre, Sayre Outpatient Clinic, 1537 N. Elmira Street, Sayre, PA, 18840, 570-888-6803

Spring City Outpatient Clinic, 11 Independence Dr, Spring City, PA, 19475, 610-9384-7711

Springfield, Media Outpatient Clinic, 194 W Sproul Rd, Suite 105 Crozer Keystone Healthplex, Springfield, PA, 19064, 610-9384-7711

State College, 3048 Enterprise Drive, Ferguson Square Bldg #1, State College, PA, 16801, 814-867-5415

Tobyhanna, Tobyhanna Outpatient Clinic, Tobyhanna Army Depot Bldg 220, Tobyhanna, PA, 18466, 570-615-8341

Venango County, Venango County VA Clinic, 464 Allegheny Blvd., Franklin, PA, 16323, 866-962-3260

Victor J. Saracini VA Outpatient Clinic, 433 Caredean Drive, Horsham, PA, 19044, 215-823-6050

Warren County, Farm Colony Professional Building, 3 Farm Colony Drive, Warren, PA, 16365, 866-682-3250

Washington County CBOC, 1500 West Chestnut St., Washington, PA 15301, ph. 724-250-7790

Westmoreland CBOC, 5274 Route 30, Suite10, Greensburg, PA, 15601, 724-216-0317

Williamsport, Williamsport Outpatient Clinic, 1705 Warren Ave., Suite 304, Williamsport, PA, 17701, 570-322-4791

York County, 2251 Eastern Blvd., York, PA, 17402, 717-840-2730

Benefits Office:
Wilkes-Barre 18702 (1123 East End Blvd., Bldg. 35, Suite 11, 1-800-827-1000)

Regional Office:
Philadelphia 19101 (P.O. Box 8079, 5000 Wissahickon Avenue, statewide
1-800-827-1000) - Serves counties in Pennsylvania: Adams, Berks, Bradford,
Bucks, Cameron, Carbon, Centre, Chester, Clinton, Columbia, Dauphin,
Delaware, Franklin, Juniata, Lackawanna, Lancaster, Lebanon, Lehigh,
Luzerne, Lycoming, Mifflin, Monroe, Montgomery, Montour, Northampton,
Northumberland, Perry, Philadelphia, Pike, Potter, Schuylkill, Snyder,
Sullivan, Susquehanna, Tioga, Union, Wayne, Wyoming, York. Serves
counties in New Jersey: Atlantic, Burlington, Camden, Cape May,
Cumberland, Gloucester, Salem).
Pittsburgh 15222 (William S. Moorehead Federal Building, 1000 Liberty Ave.
stateside 1-800-827-1000) - Serves counties in Pennsylvania: Allegheny,
Armstrong, Beaver, Bedford, Blair, Butler, Cambria, Clarion, Clearfield, Craw-
ford, Elk, Erie, Fayette, Forest, Fulton, Greene, Huntington, Indiana, Jefferson,
Lawrence, McKean, Mercer, Somerset, Venango, Warren, Washington, and
Westmoreland. Serves counties in West Virginia: Brooke, Hancock. Marshall,
and Ohio)

Vet Centers:
Bucks County Vet Center, Bucks County Vet Center, 2 Canels End Road, Suite
201B, Bristol, PA, 19007, 215-823-4590
DuBois Vet Center, DuBois Vet Center, 100 Meadow Lane, Suite 8, DuBois,
PA, 15801, 814-372-2095
Erie Vet Center, Erie Vet Center, 240 West 11th Street, Suite 105, Erie, PA,
16501, 814-453-7955
Harrisburg Vet Center, 1500 N. Second Street, Suite 2, Harrisburg, PA, 17102,
717-782-3954
Lancaster County Vet Center, Lancaster County Vet Center, 1817 Olde Home-
stead Lane, Suite 207, Lancaster, PA, 17601, 717-283-0735
McKeesport Veterans Resource Center, McKeesport Veterans Resource Cen-
ter, 2001 Lincoln Way, Suite 21, McKeesport, PA, 15131, 412-678-7704
Montgomery County Vet Center, Montgomery County Vet Center, 314 E John-
son Hwy, Suite 201, Norristown, PA, 19401, 215-823-5245
Philadelphia Vet Center, Philadelphia Vet Center, 101 E. Olney Ave., Suite C-7,
Philadelphia, PA, 19120, 215-924-4670
Philadelphia Vet Center, Philadelphia Vet Center, 801 Arch Street, Suite 502,
Philadelphia, PA, 19107, 215-627-0238
Pittsburgh Vet Center, 2500 Baldwick Road, Suite 15, Pittsburgh, PA, 15205,
412-920-1765
Scranton Vet Center, 1002 Pittston Ave., Scranton, PA, 18505, 570-344-2676
Williamsport Vet Center, 49 E Fourth Street, Suite 104, Williamsport, PA,
17701, 570-327-5281

National Cemeteries:
Indiantown Gap 17003-9618 (R.R. 2, P.O. Box 484, Indiantown Gap Rd., An-nville, 717-865-5254/5)
Nat. Cem. of the Alleghenies 15017 (1158 Morgan Rd., Bridgeville, 724-746-4363)
Philadelphia 19138 (Haines St. & Limekiln Pike, 215-504-5610)
Washington Crossing 18940 (830 Highland Rd., Newtown, 215-504-5610)

PHILIPPINES
Clinics:
1302 Pasay City (1501 Roxas Boulevard, 011-632-318-8387, International Mailing Address: DPO
AP 96515)

Regional Office:
1302 Pasay City (1501 Roxas Boulevard, 011-632-550-3888, International Mailing Address: DPO
AP 96515)

PUERTO RICO
Medical Center:
San Juan, VA Caribbean Health care System, 10 Calle Casia, San Juan, PR, 921, 787-641-7582

Clinics:
Arecibo CBOC - Hospital Metropolitano, Barrio Victor Rojas 2, Zona Industrial Carr. 9, Arecibo, PR, 616, 787-816-1818
Ceiba CBOC, Building Lot #3 PR3 Km 54.9, Pueblo Ward, Ceiba, PR, 735, 787-522-2662
Guayama, FISA Building First Floor, Calle Arnaldo Bristol #850, Suite 1, Guayama, PR, 784, 787-866-8750
Mayaguez, VA Clinic, Avenida Hostos #345, Mayaguez, PR, 680, 787-834-6900
Ponce, VA Clinic, Paseo Del Veterano #1010, Ponce, PR, 716, 787-812-3030

Regional Office:
San Juan 00968-8024 (50 Carretera 165 Adjacent to El Nuevo Dia Building), Guaynabo. Serving all Puerto Rico and the Virgin Islands, 1-800-827-1000)

Benefits Offices:
Mayaguez 00680-1507 (Ave. Hostos 345, Carretera 2, Frente al Centro Medico, 1-800-827-1000)
Ponce 00731 (Paseo del Veterano #1010, 1-800-827-1000)
Arecibo 00612 (Victor Rojas II/ Zona Industrial Carr. 129, 1-800-827-1000)

Vet Centers:
Arecibo Vet Center, 50 Gonzalo Marin St., Arecibo, PR, 612, 787-879-4510
Ponce Vet Center, 35 Mayor Street, Suite 1, Ponce, PR, 730, 787-841-3260
San Juan Vet Center, Condominio Medical Center Plaza, 21 La Riviera, Suites 8-9 and 11, Rio Piedras, PR, 921, 787-749-4409

RHODE ISLAND

VA Medical Center:
Providence, VA Medical Center, 830 Chalkstone Avenue, Providence, RI, 2908, 401-273-7100

Clinic:
Middletown, One Corporate Place, Middletown, RI, 2842, 401-847-6239

Regional Office:
Providence 02903 (380 Westminster St.; statewide, 1-800-827-1000)

Vet Center:
Providence Vet Center, 2038 Warwick Ave., Warwick, RI, 2889, 401-739-0167

SOUTH CAROLINA

VA Medical Centers:
Charleston, Ralph H. Johnson VA Medical Center, 109 Bee Street, Charleston, SC, 29401, 843-577-5011
William Jennings Bryan Dorn , W.J.B. Dorn VA Medical Center, 6439 Garners Ferry Road, Columbia, SC, 29209, 803-776-4000

Clinics:
Aiken CBOC, 951 Millbrook Avenue, Aiken, SC, 29803, 706-733-0188
Anderson County, 1702 E. Greenville Street, Anderson, SC, 29621, 864-224-5450
Beaufort, 1 Pinckney Blvd., Beaufort, SC, 29902, 803-366-4848
Florence SC, Florence CBOC, 1822 Sally Hill Farms Road, Florence, SC, 29501, 843-292-8383
Goose Creek SC, 2418 NNPTC Circle, Goose Creek, SC, 29445, 843-577-0177
Greenville SC, 3510 Augusta Road, Greenville, SC, 29605, 803-776-4000
Myrtle Beach, 3381 Phillis Blvd., Myrtle Beach, SC, 29577, 843-477-0177
Orangeburg County, 1767 Villiagepark Drive, Orangeburg, SC, 29118, 803-533-1335
Rock Hill, 205 Piedmont Blvd, Rock Hill, SC, 29732, 803-776-4000
Spartanburg, North Grove Medical Park, 279 North Grove Medical Park Drive, Spartanburg, SC, 29303, 803-776-4000
Sumter County, 407 North Salem Ave., Sumter, SC, 29150, 803-776-4000

Regional Office:
Columbia 29209 (6437 Garners Ferry Rd 1-800-827-1000)

Vet Centers:
Charleston Vet Center, 5603-A Rivers Ave., N. Charleston, SC, 29406, 843-789-7000
Columbia Vet Center, 1710 Richland Street, Suite A, Columbia, SC, 29201, 803-765-9944
Greenville Vet Center, 3 Caledon Court, Suite B, Greenville, SC, 29615, 864-271-2711
Myrtle Beach Vet Center, 2024 Corporate Center Drive, Suite 103, Myrtle Beach, SC, 29577, 843-232-2441

National Cemeteries:
Beaufort 29902-3947 (1601 Boundary St., 843-524-3925)
Florence 29501 (803 E. National Cemetery Rd., 843-669-8783)
Fort Jackson 29229 (4170 Percival Rd., Columbia, 803-699-2246)

SOUTH DAKOTA
VA Medical Centers:
Black Hills HCS - Fort Meade, 113 Comanche Road, Fort Meade, SD, 57741, 605-347-2511
Black Hills HCS - Hot Springs, 500 North Fifth Street, Hot Springs, SD, 57747, 605-745-2000
Sioux Falls VA HCS, 2501 West 22nd Street, Sioux Falls, SD, 57117, 605-336-3230

Clinics:
Aberdeen Aberdeen VA Clinic, 2301 8th Ave NE, Suite 225, Aberdeen, SD, 57401, 605-229-3500
Eagle Butte SD, Eagle Butte Center, 8000 Highway 212, Eagle Butte, SD, 57625, 605-964-8000
Eagle Butte-Faith, Faith Community Health, 112 N. 2nd Ave. W., Faith, SD, 57626, 605-967-2644
Eagle Butte-Isabel, Prairie Community Health, 118 North Main Street, Isabel, SD, 57633, 605-466-2120
Kyle, Kyle Health Center, P.O. Box 540, Kyle, SD, 57752,
McLaughlin, Veterans Industries, P.O. Box 519, McLaughlin, SD, 57642, 605-823-4574
Mission, Rosebud CBOC-Mission Medical Center, 153 S. Main Street, Mission, SD, 57555, 605-856-2295
Pierre, Linn Medical Clinic, 1601 N. Harrison, Suite 6, Pierre, SD, 57501, 605-945-1710
Pierre-Wessington Springs, 602 1st Street NE, Wessington Springs, SD, 57382, 605-945-1710
Pine Ridge, VA PTSD Building, Hospital Road-Pine Ridge Indian Reservation, Pine Ridge, SD, 57770, 605-867-2393
Rapid City SD, Rapid City VA Clinic, 3625 5th Street, Rapid City, SD, 57701, 605-718-1095
Wagner, , 400 W Highway 46, Wagner, SD, 57380, 605-384-2340

Watertown, 917 29th Street SE, Watertown, SD, 57201, 605-884-2420
Winner, Avera Winner Medical Clinic-Winner CBOC, 1436 E. 10th Street, Winner, SD, 57580, 605-842-2443

Regional Office:
Sioux Falls (2501 W. 22nd St., 57105 statewide 1-800-827-1000)

Vet Centers:
Rapid City Vet Center, 621 6th Street, Suite 101, Rapid City, SD, 57701, 605-348-0077
Sioux Falls Vet Center, 3200 W 49th Street., Sioux Falls, SD, 57104, 605-330-4552

National Cemeteries:
Black Hills 57785 (20901 Pleasant Valley Dr., Sturgis, 605-347-3830)
Fort Meade 57785 (P.O. Box 640, Old Stone Rd., Sturgis, 605-347-3830)
Hot Springs 57747 (500 N 5th St., 605-347-3830)

TENNESSEE
VA Medical Centers:
Memphis, VA Medical Center, 1030 Jefferson Avenue, Memphis, TN, 38104, 901-523-8900
Middle Tennessee HCS, VA Medical Center, 1310 24th Avenue South, Nashville, TN, 37212, 615-327-4751
Middle Tennessee HCS-Alvin C. York Division, 3400 Lebanon Pike, Murfreesboro, TN, 37129, 615-867-6000
Mountain Home, James H. Quillen VA Medical Center, Sidney & Lamont Streets, Mountain Home, TN, 37684, 423-926-1171

Clinics:
Bolivar, 107 Tennessee Street, Bolivar, TN, 38008, 731-658-6395
Chattanooga VA Outpatient Clinic, 150 Debra Road, 6200 Building Suite 5200, Chattanooga, TN, 37411, 423-893-6500
Clarksville, Gateway Medical Ctr-Physicians Office, 1832 Memorial Street, Suite 110, Clarksville, TN, 37043, 800-876-7093 x64000
Cookeville Veterans Primary Care Clinic, 851 S Willow Ave., Suite 108, Cookeville, TN, 38501, 931-284-4060
Covington CBOC, 3461 Austin Peay Highway, Memphis, TN, 38128, 901-261-4500
Dover, 1021 Spring Street, Dover, TN, 37058, 931-232-5329
Dyersburg, 433 East Parkview Street, Dyersburg, TN, 38024, 731-287-7289
Jackson TN, 180 Old Hickory Blvd., Suite A, Jackson, TN, 38305, 731-661-2750
Knoxville, William C. Tallent Outpatient Clinic, 8033 Ray Mears Blvd., Knoxville, TN, 37919, 865-545-4592

Maury County, 833 Nashville Highway, Columbia, TN, 38401, 931-981-6930
McMinnville CBOC, 1014 S. Chancery Street, McMinnville, TN, 37110, 931-474-7700
Memphis-South Clinic, 1056 E. Raines Road, Memphis, TN, 38116, 901-271-4900
Morristown, 925 East Morris Boulevard, Morristown, TN, 37813, 423-586-9100
Roane County, 450 South Chamberlain Ave, Rockwood, TN, 37854, 865-354-7668
Rogersville, 401 Scenic Drive, Suite 201, Rogersville, TN, 37857, 423-235-1471
Savannah (Hardin County), 765 Florence Road, Savannah, TN, 38372, 731-925-2300
Sevierville Clinic, 1124 Blanton Drive, Suite 100, Sevierville, TN, 37862, 865-286-6950
Tullahoma VA Outpatient Clinic, 225 1st Street, Arnold AFB, TN, 37389, 931-454-6134

Regional Office:
Nashville 37203 (110 9th Ave., South, statewide 1-800-827-1000)

Vet Centers:
Chattanooga Vet Center, 951 Eastgate Loop Road, Building 5700, Suite 300, Chattanooga, TN, 37411, 423-855-6570
Johnson City Vet Center, 2203 McKinley Road, Suite 254, Johnson City, TN, 37604, 423-928-8387
Knoxville Vet Center, 2817 E. Magnolia Ave., Knoxville, TN, 37914, 865-545-4680
Memphis Vet Center, 1407 Union Ave., Suite 410, Memphis, TN, 38104, 901-544-0173
Nashville Vet Center, 1420 Donelson Pike, Suite A-5, Nashville, TN, 37217, 615-366-1220

National Cemeteries:
Chattanooga 37404 (1200 Bailey Ave., 423-855-6590)
Knoxville 37917 (939 Tyson St., N.W., 423-855-6590)
Memphis 38122 (3568 Townes Ave., 901-386-8311)
Mountain Home 37684 (P.O. Box 8, VAMC, Bldg. 117, 423-979-3535)
Nashville 37115-4619 (1420 Gallatin Rd. S., Madison, 615-860-0086)

TEXAS
VA Medical Centers:
Amarillo HCS, VA Medical Center, 6010 Amarillo Blvd. West, Amarillo, TX, 79106, 806-355-9703
Bonham VAMC, Bonham VA Medical Center, 1201 E. 9th Street, Bonham, TX, 75418, 903-583-2111
Dallas VAMC, Dallas VA Medical Center, 4500 S. Lancaster Road, Dallas, TX, 75216, 214-742-8387

El Paso HCS, 5001 North Piedras, El Paso, TX, 79930, 915-564-6100.
Domiciliary Care for Homeless Veterans Program, 7329 Fannin Street, Houston, TX, 77030, 713-794-7848
Houston, VA Medical Center, 2002 Holcombe Blvd., Houston, TX, 77030, 713-791-1414
Kerrville VAMC, Kerrville VA Medical Center, 3600 Memorial Blvd., Kerrville, TX, 78028, 830-896-2020
San Antonio VAMC, San Antonio VA Medical Center, 7400 Merton Minter Blvd., San Antonio, TX, 78229, 210-617-5300
Temple VAMC, Olin E. Teague Veterans' Medical Center, 1901 Veterans Memorial Drive, Temple, TX, 76504, 254-778-4811
Waco VAMC, Waco VA Medical Center, 4800 Memorial Drive, Waco, TX, 76711, 254-752-6581
West Texas Health Care System, VA Medical Center, 300 Veterans Blvd., Big Spring, TX, 79720, 432-263-7361

Clinics:
Abilene, Abilene CBOC, 3850 Ridgemont Drive, Abilene, TX, 79606, 325-695-3252
Austin CBOC, 7901 Metropolis Drive, Austin, TX, 78744, 512-389-1010
Beaumont, CBOC, 3420 Veterans Circle, Beaumont, TX, 77707, 409-981-8550
Beeville, Beeville Family Practice Clinic, 302 S. Hillside Drive, Beeville, TX, 78102, 361-358-9912
Bonham Area Primary Care Network, Paris Clinic, 635 Stone Avenue, Paris, TX, 75460, 903-785-9900
Brownwood, CBOC, 2600 Memorial Drive, Brownwood, TX, 76801, 325-641-0568
Cedar Park CBOC, 701 E. Whitestone Blvd., Cedar Park, TX, 78613, 512-260-1368
Charles Wilson VA OPC, Charles Wilson VA Outpatient Clinic, 2206 N John Redditt Dr., Lufkin, TX, 75904, 936-671-4300
Childress, Childress CBOC, 1001 Highway 38 North, Childress, TX, 79201, 940-937-8528
Cleburne Area PCN, Waxahacie Clinic, 207 Ferris Avenue, Waxahachie, TX, 75165, 817-238-1807
College Station (Bryan), CBOC, 1651 Rock Prairie Road, Suite 100, College Station, TX, 77845, 979-680-0361
Conroe, 800 Riverwood Court, Suite 100, Conroe, TX, 77304, 936-522-4000
Corpus Christi Satellite Outpatient Clinic, 5283 Old Brownsville Rd, Corpus Christi, TX, 78405, 361-806-5600
Dalhart, Dalhart CBOC, 325 Denver Avenue, Dalhart, TX, 79022, (806) 249-0673
Dallas County Primary Care Network, Southeast Dallas Health Center, 9202 Elam Road, Dallas, TX, 75217, 214-590-0104
Decatur Area Primary Care Network, 806 Woodrow Wilson Ray Circle, Bridgeport, TX, 76426, 940-683-2538
Del Rio, 612 Bedell, Del Rio, TX, 78840, 830-775-1166
Denton Area Primary Care Network, 2223 Colorado Blvd., Denton, TX, 76205,

940-891-6350

East El Paso (El Paso County), 2400 Trawood Drive, El Paso, TX, 79936, 915-217-2428

Eastland Area Primary Care Network, Action Clinic, 601 Fall Creek HWY, Granbury, TX, 76049, 817-326-3902

Fort Stockton, Ft. Stockton VA Outreach Clinic, 1735 North Main, Fort Stockton, TX 79735, 432-336-0700

Fort Worth Satellite, Fort Worth VA Outpatient Clinic, 2201 Southeast Loop 820, Fort Worth, TX, 76119, 817-335-2202

Frank M. Tejeda Satellite, Frank Tejeda Satellite Outpatient Clinic, 5788 Eckert Road, San Antonio, TX, 78240, 210-699-2100

Galveston County, Galveston County CBOC (Island), 3828 Avenue N, Galveston, TX, 77550, 409-761-3200

Galveston County-Texas City, 9300 Emmet F. Lowery, Suite 206, Texas City, TX, 77591, 409-986-2900

Greenville Area PCN, Community Health Center, 4006 Wellington Road, Greenville, TX, 75401, 903-450-4788

Harlingen , 2106 Treasure Hills Blvd, Harlingen, TX, 78550, 956-366-4500

Hobbs, Hobbs CBOC, 1601 N. Turner (4th Floor), Hobbs, NM 88340, 575-391-0354

Katy, Katy CBOC, Westgreen Professional Building, 750 Westgreen Blvd., Katy, TX, 77450, 713-791-1414

La Grange Rural Outreach Clinic, 890 E. Travis St., La Grange, TX 78945, 979-968-5878

Lake Jackson, 208 S. Oak Drive, Suite 700, Lake Jackson, TX, 77566, 979-230-4852

Laredo, Laredo CBOC, 4602 N. Bartlett Avenue, Laredo, TX, 78041, 956-523-7850

Longview, Longview Community Based Outpatient Clinic, 1005 N Eastman Road, Longview, TX, 75601, 903-247-8262

Lubbock TX, Lubbock CBOC, 6104 Avenue Q South Drive, Lubbock, TX, 79412, 806-472-3400

McAllen Satellite, McAllen Satellite Outpatient Clinic, 2101 S. Colonel Rowe Blvd., McAllen, TX, 78503, 956-618-7145

New Braunfels (Comal County), 189 East Austin Street, Suite 106, New Braunfels, TX, 78130, 830-643-0717

Odessa, Permian Basin CBOC, 8050 E. Highway 191, Odessa, TX 79762, 432-685-2110

Permian Basin CBOC, 8050 E. Hwy. 191, Odessa, TX 79762 432-685-2110

Palestine, Palestine Community Based Outpatient Clinic, 2000 S. Loop 256, Suite 124, Palestine, TX, 75801, 903-723-9006

Richmond, 22001 SW Frwy, Suite 200, Richmond, TX, 77469, 832-595-7700

San Angelo, San Angelo CBOC, 2018 Pulliam, San Angelo, TX 76905, 325-658-6138

San Antonio Area PCN, 4318 Woodcock Drive, Suite 120, San Antonio, TX, 78228, 210-731-0285

San Antonio TX, North Central Federal Clinic, 17440 Henderson Pass, San

Antonio, TX, 78232, 210-483-2900
San Antonio-Northeast 410, 2391 NE Loop 410, Suite 101, San Antonio, TX, 78217, 210-590-0247
San Antonio-Northwest 410, 4318 Woodcock Drive, Suite 120, San Antonio, TX, 78228, 210-736-4051
San Antonio-Pecan Valley, Pecan Valley, 4243 E Southcross, Suite 206, San Antonio, TX, 78222, 210-337-4316
San Antonio-Southwest Military, 1714 SW Military Drive, Suite 101, San Antonio, TX, 78221, 210-923-0777
Seguin (Guadalupe County), 526 East Court Street, Seguin, TX, 78155, 830-643-0717
Sherman, 3811 US 75 North, Sherman, TX, 75090, 903-487-0477
South Bexar County, South Bexar County CBOC, 4610 East Southcross Blvd., San Antonio, TX, 78222, 210-648-1491
Stamford, Stamford VA Outreach Clinic, 1601 N. Columbia, Stamford, TX 79553, 325-773-5733
Texas Valley Coastal Bend - Harlingen HCS, Harlingen CBOC, 2601 Veterans Drive, Harlingen, TX, 78550, 956-291-9000
Tomball, Tomball CBOC, 1200 W. Main Street, Tomball, TX, 77375, 713-791-1414
Tyler, Tyler VA Primary Care Clinic, 3414 Golden Road, Tyler, TX, 75708, 903-590-3050
Victoria, Victoria CBOC, 1908 N. Laurent Street, Suite 150, Victoria, TX, 77901, 361-582-7700
Wichita Falls, Veterans Clinic of North Texas, 1800 7th Street, Wichita Falls, TX, 76301, 940-723-2373

Regional Offices:
Houston 77030 (6900 Almeda Rd., statewide, 713-383-1999 or 1-800-827-1000. Serves counties of Angelina, Aransas, Atacosa, Austin, Bandera, Bee, Bexar, Blanco, Brazoria, Brewster, Brooks, Caldwell, Calhoun, Cameron, Chambers, Colorado, Comal, Crockett, DeWitt, Dimitt, Duval, Edwards, Fort Bend, Frio, Galveston, Gillespie, Goliad, Gonzales, Grimes, Guadeloupe, Hardin, Harris, Hays, Hidalgo, Houston, Jackson, Jasper, Jefferson, Jim Hogg, Jim Wells, Karnes, Kendall, Kennedy, Kerr, Kimble, Kinney, Kleberg, LaSalle, Lavaca, Liberty, Live Oak, McCulloch, McMullen, Mason, Matagorda, Maverlck, Medina, Menard, Montgomery, Nacogdoches, Newton, Nueces, Orange, Pecos, Polk, Real, Refugio, Sabine, San Aug. ine, San Jacinto, San Patricio, Schleicher, Shelby, Starr, Sutton, Terrell, Trinity, Tyler, Uvalde, Val Verde, Victoria, Walker, Waller, Washington, Webb, Wharton, Willacy, Wilson, Zapata, Zavala)
   Waco 76799 (One Veterans Plaza, 701 Clay Ave; statewide, 1-800-827-1000; serves the rest of the state. In Bowie County, the City of Texarkana is served by Little Rock, AR, VA Regional Office, 1-800-827-1000.)

Benefits Offices:
Abilene 79602 (Taylor County Plaza Bldg., Suite 103, 400 Oak St., 1-800-827-1000)
Amarillo 79106 (6010 Amarillo Blvd. W., 1-800-827-1000)
Austin 78741 (2901 Montopolis Dr., Room 108, 1-800-827-1000)
Camp Mabry in Austin 78763 (Bldg. 10, Room 217, 1-800-827-1000)
Corpus Christi 78405 (4646 Corona Dr., Suite 150, 1-800-827-1000)
Dallas 75216 (4500 S. Lancaster Rd., 1-800-827-1000)
El Paso 79930 (5001 Piedras Dr., 1-800-827-1000)
Fort Hood 76544 (Bldg. 18010, Room A-308, 1-800-827-1000)
Ft. Worth 76119 (2201 SE Loop 820., 1-800-827-1000)
Lubbock 79410 (6104 Ave. Q S Drive, Rm. 132, 1-800-827-1000)
McAllen 78503 (109 Toronto Ave., 1-800-827-1000)
San Antonio 78240 (5788 Eckert Rd., 1-800-827-1000)
Temple 76504 (Sub-office located at the Olin E. Teague Veteran's Medical Center, 1901 Veterans Memorial Dr., Temple, Texas, Bldg. 208), 1-800-827-1000) (W-F 9 a.m.-12 p.m.)
Tyler 75701 (1700 SSE Loop 323, Suite 310, 1-800-827-1000)

Vet Centers:
Amarillo Vet Center, 3414 Olsen Blvd., Suite E, Amarillo, TX, 79109, 806-354-9779
Austin Vet Center, Austin Vet Center, Southcliff Bldg, 2015 S IH 35, Suite 101, Austin, TX, 78741, 512-416-1314
Corpus Christi Vet Center, 4646 Corona, Suite 250, Corpus Christi, TX, 78411, 361-854-9961
Dallas County Vet Center, Dallas County Vet Center, 502 West Kearney, Suite 300, Mesquite, TX, 75149, 972-288-8030
Dallas Vet Center, Dallas Vet Center, 10501 N Central Expy, Suite 213, Dallas, TX, 75231, 214-361-5896
El Paso Vet Center, 1155 Westmoreland, Suite 121, El Paso, TX, 79925, 915-772-0013
Fort Worth Vet Center, 6620 Westworth Blvd, Westworth Village, TX, 76114
Harris County Vet Center, 14300 Corner Stone Villiage Drive, Suite 110, Houston, TX, 77014, 713-578-4002
Houston Vet Center, 2990 Richmond, Suite 325, Houston, TX, 77098, 713-523-0884
Houston Vet Resource Center, 701 N. Post Oak Road, Suite 102, Houston, TX, 77024, 713-682-2288
Jefferson County Vet Center, Brighton Professional Building, 990 IH 10 North, Suite 180, Beaumont, TX, 77702, 409-347-0124
Killeen Heights Vet Center, Killeen Heights Vet Center, 302 Millers Crossing, Suite #4, Harker Heights, TX, 76548, 254-953-7100
Laredo Vet Center, Laredo Vet Center, 6999 McPherson Road, Suite 102, Laredo, TX, 78041, 956-723-4680
Lubbock Vet Center, Lubbock Vet Center, 3106 50th Street, Suite 400, Lubbock, TX, 79413, 806-792-9782

McAllen Vet Center, McAllen Vet Center, 2108 S. M Street, MedPoint IV, Unit 2, McAllen, TX, 78503, 956-631-2147
Midland Vet Center, 2817 W Loop 250 North, Suite E, Midland, TX, 79705, 432-697-8222
San Antonio NW Vet Center, San Antonio NW Vet Center, 9910 W Loop 1604 N, Suite 126, San Antonio, TX, 78254, 210-688-0606
San Antonio Vet Center, San Antonio Vet Center, 9504 IH 35 N, Suites 214 and 219, San Antonio, TX, 78233, 210-650-0422
Tarrant County Vet Center, 3337 W Pioneer Pkwy, Northlake Center, Pantego, TX, 76013, 817-274-0981
Taylor County Vet Center, Taylor County Vet Center, 3564 N 6th Street, Abilene, TX, 79603, (phone) 325-232-7925

National Cemeteries:
Dallas-Fort Worth 75211 (2000 Mountain Creek Parkway, 214-467-3374)
Fort Bliss 79906 (Box 6342, 5200 Fred Wilson Rd., 915-564-0201)
Fort Sam Houston 78209 (1520 Harry Wurzbach Rd., San Antonio, 210-820-3891/3894)
Houston 77038 (10410 Veterans Memorial Dr., 281-447-8686)
Kerrville 78028 (VAMC, 3600 Memorial Blvd., 210-820-3891/3894)
San Antonio 78202 (517 Paso Hondo St., 210-820-3891/3894)

UTAH
VA Medical Centers:
Salt Lake City HCS - George E. Wahlen VAMC, VA Medical Center, 500 Foothill Blvd., Salt Lake City, UT, 84148, 801-582-1565

Clinics:
Nephi Memorial Clinic, 48 WEST 1500 NORTH, NEPHI, UT, 84648, 435-623-3129
Nephi-Fountain Green, Fountain Green Clinic, 48 West 1500 North, Nephi, UT, 84648,
Ogden VA Outpatient Clinic, 982 Chambers Street, South Ogden, UT, 84403, 801-479-4105
Orem VA Outpatient Clinic, 1443 West 800 North, Suite 302, Orem, UT, 84057, 801-235-0953
Price Community Outbased Patient Clinic 189 South 600 West, Suite B Price, UT 84501 435-613-0342
Roosevelt Outpatient Clinic, 245 West 200 North, Roosevelt, UT, 84066, 435-725-1050
St. George Outpatient Clinic, 1067 E. Tabernacle, Suite 7, St. George, UT, 84770, 435-634-7608
Western Salt Lake, WSL CBOC, 2750 South 5600 West, Suite B, West Valley City, UT, 84120, 801-417-5734
Regional Office:
Salt Lake City 84158 (P.O. Box 581900, 550 Foothill Dr., statewide 1-800-827-

1000)

Vet Centers:
Provo Vet Center, 1807 North 1120 West, Provo, UT, 84604, 801-377-1117
Salt Lake Vet Center, 1354 East 3300 South, Salt Lake, UT, 84106, 801-584-1294
Washington County Vet Center, 1664 S. Dixie Drive, Suite C-102, Saint George, UT, 84770, 435-673-4494

VERMONT
VA Medical Center:
White River Junction, VAMC, 215 N. Main St., White River Junction, VT, 5009, 802-295-9363

Clinics:
Bennington, VA Bennington Clinic, 186 North Street, Bennington, VT, 5201, 802-447-6913
Brattleboro, 71 GSP Drive, Brattleboro, VT, 5301, 802-251-2200
Burlington Lakeside, Innovation Center, 128 Lakeside Avenue, Suite 260, Burlington, VT, 5401, 802-657-7000
Rutland, 232 West Street, Rutland, VT, 5701, 802-772-2300
VICC - Littleton, 141 Railroad Street, St. Johnsbury, VT, 5819, 603-444-1323

Regional Office:
White River Junction 05009 (215 N. Main St., 1-800-827-1000)

Vet Centers:
So. Burlington Vet Center, 359 Dorset St., South Burlington, VT, 5403, 802-862-1806
White River Junction Vet Center, Gilman Office Center Bldg. 2, 222 Holiday Inn Drive, White River Junction, VT, 5001, 802-295-2908

VIRGINIA
VA Medical Centers:
Hampton, VA Medical Center, 100 Emancipation Drive, Hampton, VA, 23667, 757-722-9961
Richmond, VA Medical Center, 1201 Broad Rock Boulevard, Richmond, VA, 23249, 804-675-5000
Salem, VA Medical Center, 1970 Roanoke Boulevard, Salem, VA, 24153, 540-982-2463

Clinics:
Albemarle Primary Outpatient Clinic 1845 W. City Drive Elizabeth City, North Carolina 27909 252-331-2191
Bristol, Preston Square, 2426 Lee Highway, Suite 200, Bristol, VA, 24202, 276-645-4520

Charlottesville, Charlottesville CBOC, 650 Peter Jefferson Parkway, Suite 160, Charlottesville, VA, 22911, 434-293-3890
Danville, 705 Piney Forest Road, Danville, VA, 24540, 434-710-4210
Emporia, 1746 East Atlantic Street, Emporia, VA, 23847, 434-348-1055
Fort Belvoir, Fort Belvoir Community Based Outpatient Clinic, 9300 Dewitt Loop, Fort Belvoir, VA, 22060, 571-231-2408
Fredericksburg, 130 Executive Center Parkway, Fredericksburg, VA, 22401, 540-370-4468
Harrisonburg, 1755 South High Street, Harrisonburg, VA, 22801, 540-442-1773
Lynchburg, 1600 Lakeside Drive, Lynchburg, VA, 24501, 434-316-5000
Norfolk-Virginia Beach, 244 Clearfield Blvd., Suite 401, Virginia Beach, VA, 23462, 757-722-9961 x1900
Norton, 654 Hwy 58 East, Norton, VA, 24273, 276-679-8010
Staunton, 102 Business Way, Staunton, VA, 24401, 540-886-5777
Stephens City, Stephens City CBOC, 170 Prosperity Drive, Kernstown, VA, 22602, 540-869-0600
Tazewell, Tazewell Family Physicians, 123 Ben Bolt Avenue, Tazewell, VA, 24651, 276-988-2526
Wytheville, 165 Peppers Ferry Road, Wytheville, VA, 24382, 276-223-5400

Regional Office:
Roanoke 24016-1928 (116 North Jefferson Street, statewide 1-800-827-1000)

Benefits Offices:
Hampton 23605 (5200 West Mercury Blvd., Suite 295)
Norfolk 23513 (2551 Eltham Avenue, Suite E)

Vet Centers:
Alexandria Vet Center, 6940 South Kings Highway #204, Suites D & E, Alexandria, VA, 22310, 703-360-8633
Norfolk Vet Center, 1711 Church Street, Suite A and B, Norfolk, VA, 23504, 757-623-7584
Richmond Vet Center, 4902 Fitzhugh Ave., Richmond, VA, 23230, 804-353-8958
Roanoke Vet Center, 350 Albemarle Ave., SW, Roanoke, VA, 24016, 540-342-9726
Virginia Beach County Vet Center, 324 Southport Circle, Suite 102, Virginia Beach, VA, 23452, 757-248-3665

National Cemeteries:
Alexandria 22314 (1450 Wilkes St., 703-221-2183/2184)
Balls Bluff 22075 (Rte. 7, Leesburg, 540-825-0027)
City Point 23860 (10th Ave. & Davis St., Hopewell, 804-795-2031)
Cold Harbor 23111 (6038 Cold Harbor Rd., Mechanicsville, 804-795-2031)
Culpeper 22701 (305 U.S. Ave., 540-825-0027)
Danville 24541 (721 Lee St., 704-636-2661)
Fort Harrison 23231 (8620 Varina Rd., Richmond, 804-795-2031)

Glendale 23231 (8301 Willis Church Rd., Richmond, 804-795-2031)
Hampton 23667 (Cemetery Rd. at Marshall Ave., 757-723-7104)
Hampton 23669 (VAMC, Emancipation Dr., 757-723-7104)
Quantico 22172 (P.O. Box 10, 18424 Joplin Rd. (Rte. 619), Triangle 703-221-2183/2184)
Richmond 23231 (1701 Williamsburg Rd., 804-795-2031)
Seven Pines 23150 (400 E. Williamsburg Rd., Sandston, 804-795 2031/2278)
Staunton, 24401 (901 Richmond Ave., 540-825-0027)
Winchester 22601 (401 National Ave., 540-825-0027)

VIRGIN ISLANDS

Clinics:
St Croix, The Village Mall #113, RR2 Box 10553, Kingshill, St. Croix, VI, 850, 340-778-5553
St Thomas CBOC VI Med Foundation, 50 Estate Thomas, Suite 101, St. Thomas, VI, 802, 340-774-6674

Benefits:
Served by San Juan, Puerto Rico, VA Regional Office, 1-800-827-1000

WASHINGTON

VA Medical Centers:
American Lake, VA Puget Sound HCS-American Lake Div., 9600 Veterans Drive, Tacoma, WA, 98493, 253-582-8440
Seattle, VA Puget Sound HCS-Seattle Division, 1660 S. Columbian Way, Seattle, WA, 98108, 800-329-8387 x71234
Spokane, VA Medical Center, 4815 N. Assembly Street, Spokane, WA, 99205, 509-434-7000
Vancouver, Vancouver CBOC, 1601 E 4th Plain Blvd, Vancouver, WA, 98661, 360-759-1901
Walla Walla, VA Medical Center, 77 Wainwright Drive, Walla Walla, WA, 99362, 509-525-5200

Clinics:
Bellevue CBOC (Valor Healthcare) Delate: King County, 13033 Bel-Red Road, Suite 210, Bellevue, WA, 98005, 425-214-1055
Bremerton (Kitsap County), 925 Adele Avenue, Bremerton, WA, 98312, 360-782-0129
King County, 13033 Bel-Red Road, Suite 210, Bellevue, WA, 98005, 425-214-1055
King County-Federal Way, 32020 32nd Avenue South, Suite 110, Federal Way, WA, 98001, 877-927-8387
King County (Valor Healthcare) 34617 11th Place South, Suite 301, Federal Way, WA 98003Mount Vernon, 307 S. 13th Street, Suite 200, Mount Vernon, WA, 98274, 360-848-8500
North Olympic Peninsula CBOC, 1114 Georgiana St., Port Angeles, WA 98362, 360-565-7420

NW Central Washington CBOC, 2530 Chester Kimm Road, Wenatchee, WA, 98801, 509-663-7615
Richland CBOC, 825 Jadwin Ave., Suite 250 (Federal Bldg.), Richland, WA, 99352, 509-946-1020South Sound, Lewis County Mall, 151 NE Hampe Way, Suite B2-6, Chehalis, WA, 98532, 360-748-3049
South Sound (Sterling Medical), Lewis County Mall, 151 NE Hampe Way, Suite B2-6, Chehalis, WA, 98532, 360-748-3049

Yakima CBOC, 717 Fruitvale Blvd., Yakima, WA, 98902, 509-966-0199

Regional Office:
Seattle 98174 (Fed. Bldg., 915 2nd Ave., statewide 1-800-827-1000)
Benefits Offices:
Fort Lewis 98433 (Waller Hall Rm. 700, P.O. Box 331153, 253-967-7106)
Bremerton 98337 (W. Sound Pre-Separation Center, 262 Burwell St., 360-782-9900)

Benefits Offices:
Joint Base Lewis McChord 98433 (Waller Hall Bldg 2140 Rm. 700 Mail Stop 62, P.O. Box 339500, 253-967-7106)
Bremerton 98337 (W. Sound Pre-Separation Center, 264 Burwell St., 360-782-9900)

Vet Centers:
Bellingham Vet Center, 3800 Byron, Suite 124, Bellingham, WA, 98229, 360-733-9226
Everett Vet Center, 3311 Wetmore Ave., Everett, WA, 98201, 425-252-9701
Seattle Vet Center, 4735 E. Marginal Way South, Room 2401, Seattle, WA, 98134, 206-553-2706
South King County Vet Center, 32020 32nd Ave. South, Suite 110, Federal Way, WA, 98032, 253-838-3090
Spokane Vet Center, 13109 E. Mirabeau Parkway, Spokane Valley, WA, 99216, 509-444-8387
Tacoma Vet Center, 4916 Center St., Suite E, Tacoma, WA, 98409, 253-565-7038
Walla Walla Vet Center, 1104 West Poplar Street, Walla Walla, WA, 99362, 509-526-8387
Yakima Valley Vet Center, 2119 W Lincoln Ave, Yakima, WA, 98902, 509-457-2736

WEST VIRGINIA
VA Medical Centers:
Beckley, VA Medical Center, 200 Veterans Avenue, Beckley, WV, 25801, 304-255-2121
Clarksburg, Louis A. Johnson VA Medical Center, 1 Medical Center Drive, Clarksburg, WV, 26301, 304-623-3461
Huntington, VA Medical Center, 1540 Spring Valley Drive, Huntington, WV,

25704, 304-429-6741
Martinsburg, VA Medical Center Martinsburg, 510 Butler Avenue, Martinsburg, WV, 25405, 304-263-0811

Clinics:
Braxton County CBOC, 93 Skidmore Lane, Sutton, WV, 26601, 304-765-3480
Charleston, Charleston Primary Care Clinic, 104 Alex Lane, Charleston, WV, 25304, 304-926-6001
Franklin, 314 Pine Street, Franklin, WV, 26807, 304-358-2355
Greenbrier County, Greenbrier County CBOC, 804 Industrial Park Road, Lenore VA Rural Health Care Clinic 2867 Route 65 Lenore, WV 25676 304-475-3000
Maxwelton, WV, 24957, 304-497-3900
Monongalia, 40 Commerce Drive, Suite 101, Westover, WV, 26501, 304-292-7535
Petersburg, 15 Grant St., Petersburg, WV, 26847, 304-257-9535
Tucker County Veterans Center, 206 Senior Lane, Parsons, WV, 26287, 304-478-2219
Wood County CBOC, 2311 Ohio Avenue, Suite A, Parkersburg, WV, 26101, 304-422-5114

Regional Office:
Huntington 25701 (640 Fourth Ave., statewide 1-800-827-1000; counties of Brooke, Hancock, Marshall, Ohio, served by Pittsburgh, Pa., VA Regional Office)

Vet Centers:
Beckley Vet Center, 1000 Johnstown Road, Beckley, WV, 25801, 304-252-8220
Charleston Vet Center, 521 Central Avenue, Charleston, WV, 25302, 304-343-3825
Huntington Vet Center, 3135 16th Street Road, Suite 11, Huntington, WV, 25701, 304-523-8387
Martinsburg Vet Center, 300 Foxcroft Avenue, Suite 100, Martinsburg, WV, 25401, 304-263-6776
Morgantown Vet Center, 34 Commerce Drive, Suite 101, Morgantown, WV, 26501, 304-291-4303
Princeton Vet Center, 905 Mercer Street, Princeton, WV, 24740, 304-425-5653
Wheeling Vet Center, 1054 E. Bethlehem Blvd., Wheeling, WV, 26003, 304-232-0587

National Cemeteries:
Grafton 26354 (431 Walnut St., 304-265-2044)
West Virginia 26354 (42 Veterans Memorial Ln, Grafton, 304-265-2044)

WISCONSIN

VA Medical Centers:
Madison WI, William S. Middleton-Memorial VH, 2500 Overlook Terrace, Madison, WI, 53705, 608-256-1901
Milwaukee, Clement J. Zablocki VA Medical Center, 5000 W. National Avenue, Milwaukee, WI, 53295, 414-384-2000
Tomah, VA Medical Center, 500 East Veterans Street, Tomah, WI, 54660, 608-372-3971

Clinics:
Appleton VA CBOC, 10 Tri-Park Way, Appleton, WI, 54914, 920-831-0070
Baraboo VA Clinic, 1670 South Blvd., Baraboo, WI, 53913, 608-356-9318
Beaver Dam VA Clinic, 215 Corporate Drive, Plaza II, Beaver Dam, WI, 53916, 920-356-9415
Chippewa Valley Clinic, 2503 County Road I, Chippewa Falls, WI, 54729, 715-720-3780
Clark County VA Outpatient Clinic, 8 Johnson Street, Owen, WI, 54460, 715-229-4701
Cleveland VA CBOC, 1205 North Avenue, Cleveland, WI, 53015, 920-693-5600
Hayward VA Outpatient Clinic, 15954 River's Edge Drive, Suite 103, Hayward, WI, 54843, 715-934-5454
Janesville CBOC, 2419 Morse St., Janesville, WI, 53545, 608-758-9300
Kenosha CBOC, 8207 22nd Avenue, Kenosha, WI, 53143, 262-653-9286
La Crosse, River Valley Clinic, 2600 State Road, La Crosse, WI, 54601, 608-784-3886
Milo C. Huempfner VA Outpatient Clinic (Green Bay), 2851 University Avenue, Green Bay, WI, 54311, 920-431-2500
Rhinelander CBOC, 639 West Kemp Street, Rhinelander, WI, 54501, 715-362-4080
Twin Ports VA Outpatient Clinic, 3520 Tower Ave., Superior, WI, 54880, 715-392-9711
Union Grove CBOC, 21425 Spring Street, Wallace Hall, Union Grove, WI, 53182, 262-878-7001
Wausau CBOC, 515 S. 32 Avenue, Wausau, WI, 54401, 715-842-2834
Wisconsin Rapids Clinic, 555 West Grand Avenue, Wisconsin Rapids, WI, 54495, 715-424-4682

Regional Office:
Milwaukee 53214 (5400 W. National Ave., statewide 1-800-827-1000)

Vet Centers:
Green Bay Vet Center, 1600 S Ashland Ave., Green Bay, WI, 54304, 920-435-5650
Lacrosse Vet Center, 20 Copeland Avenue, La Crosse, WI, 54601, 608-782-4403
Madison Vet Center, 706 Williamson Street, Suite 4, Madison, WI, 53703, 608-

264-5342
Milwaukee Vet Center, 7910 N. 76th Street, Suite 100, Milwaukee, WI, 53223, 414-434-1311

National Cemetery:
Wood 53295-4000 (5000 W. National Ave., Bldg. 1301, Milwaukee, 414-382-5300)

WYOMING

VA Medical Centers:
Cheyenne, VA Medical Center, 2360 E. Pershing Blvd., Cheyenne, WY, 82001, 307-778-7550
Sheridan VA Health care System, VA Medical Center, 1898 Fort Road, Sheridan, WY, 82801, 307-672-3473

Clinics:
Casper Clinic, 4140 S. Poplar Street, Casper, WY, 82601, 866-338-5168
Evanston VA Primary Care TeleHealth Outreach Clinic 1565 South Highway 150 #E, Evanston, WY 82930
Fort Collins MSOC 2509 Research Blvd. Fort Collins, CO 80526-8108 970-224-1550
Gillette VA Clinic, 604 Express Drive, Gillette, WY, 82718, 866-621-1887
Greeley MSOC 2001 70th Ave Suite# 200 Greeley, CO 80631-4621 970-313-0027
Laramie Mobile Telehealth Clinic 112 South 5th Street Laramie, WY 82702 888-483-9127 X 3816
Newcastle, Weston County Health Services Bldg, 1124 Washington Blvd., Newcastle, WY, 82701, 307-746-4491
Powell VA Clinic, 777 Avenue H, Powell, WY, 82435, 888-284-9308
Rawlins Primary Care Telehealth Outpatient Clinic (PCTOC) 1809 East Daley Street 82301 307-324-5578
Riverton CBOC, 2300 Rose Lane, Riverton, WY, 82501, 866-338-2609
Rock Springs VA Clinic, 1401 Gateway Blvd, Suite #1, Rock Springs, WY, 82901, 866-381-2830
Sidney Multi-Specialty Outpatient Clinic (MSOC)   1116 10th Ave Sidney, NE 69162 308-254-6085
Sterling Mobile Telehealth Clinic 100 College Dr.   Sterling, CO 80751 888-483-9127 X 3816

877-733-6128
Wheatland Mobile Clinic 759 East Cole Street Wheatland, WY 82201 888-483-9127 X 3816
Worland Primary Care TeleHealth Outreach Clinic 510 South 15th Suite D, Worland WY 82401 877-483-0370

Benefits Office:
Cheyenne 82001 (2360 E. Pershing Blvd., statewide 1-800-827-1000)
Vet Centers:
Casper Vet Center, 1030 North Poplar, Suite B, Casper, WY, 82601, 307-261-5355
Cheyenne Vet Center, 3219 E Pershing Blvd, Cheyenne, WY, 82001, 307-778-7370
Fort Collins 702 W Drake Building C. Fort Collins CO 80526 970-221-5176

FEDERAL BENEFITS FOR VETERANS, DEPENDENTS AND SURVIVORS 2014
Publication Order Form

Order Processing Code 3603	**Toll Free:** 866 512–1800 **Phone:** 202 512–1800 **Fax:** 202 512–2104	**Mail:** US Government Printing Office P.O. Box 979050 St. Louis, MO 63197–9000

☐ **YES!** please send me_____copies of *Federal Benefits for Veterans, Dependents and Survivors 2014* S/N 051–000–00247–4, ISBN 978-0-16-092508-5, single copies only. $5.00 per single copy.

☐ **YES!** please send me_____copies of *"Beneficios Federales para los Veteranos, sus Dependientes y Sobrevivientes" 2014*. S/N 051-000-00250-4 ISBN 978-0-16-092530-6 single copies only. $5.00 per single copy.

The total cost of my order is $_____. Price includes regular postage and handling and price is subject to change. International customer please add 40%. Price subject to change without notice.

Personal name   (Please type or print)

Company name

Street address

City, State, Zip code

Daytime phone including area code

Charge your order, It's easy!

VISA   MasterCard   DISCOVER NOVUS   AMERICAN EXPRESS

☐ Check payable to *Superintendent of Documents*

☐ **SOD Deposit Account** ☐☐☐☐☐☐☐

☐ VISA ☐ MasterCard ☐ Discover/NOVUS ☐ American Express

☐☐☐☐☐☐☐☐☐☐☐☐☐☐☐☐☐☐☐☐

☐☐☐☐ (expiration date)

Thank you for your order!

GPO

Authorizing signature